ROMANS AND THE POWER
OF THE BELIEVER

SEMEIA STUDIES

Jacqueline M. Hidalgo, General Editor

Editorial Board:
Eric D. Barreto
Jin Young Choi
L. Juliana M. Claassens
Gregory Cuéllar
Rhiannon Graybill
Emmanuel Nathan
Shively T. J. Smith

Number 99

ROMANS AND THE POWER OF THE BELIEVER

Richard J. Britton

PRESS

Atlanta

Copyright © 2022 by Richard J. Britton

All rights reserved. No part of this work may be reproduced or transmitted in any form or by any means, electronic or mechanical, including photocopying and recording, or by means of any information storage or retrieval system, except as may be expressly permitted by the 1976 Copyright Act or in writing from the publisher. Requests for permission should be addressed in writing to the Rights and Permissions Office, SBL Press, 825 Houston Mill Road, Atlanta, GA 30329 USA.

Library of Congress Control Number: 2022951417

*This book is dedicated to the memory of my close friend Simon Mapp
and is also for Olivia, Ruby, and Chloe*

CONTENTS

Foreword by Peter Oakes..ix
Foreword by Kimberley A. Fowler...xi
Preface...xiii
Abbreviations... xvii

Introduction 1

1. Belief 21

2. Grace 67

3. Graft 115

In Conclusion..171

Bibliography..177
Primary Sources Index 187
Modern Authors Index..191
Subject Index...193

FOREWORD

Getting a word in edgeways was often a challenge. A gradually rotating cast, particularly David, Stephen, Elif, Andy, Soon Yi, and Richard himself (although not the unperceived, yet real, Pyung-Soo, who was elsewhere doing things such as actually writing his dissertation), crammed into the office in the basement of the west wing. The students in my first substantial PhD group modeled the kind of vigorous, deeply inclusive, academic engagement now seen in Richard's marvelous book.

Richard's book gives great attention in three directions: radical theory, surprising detail, and big questions. On theory, Richard carries out Derridean deconstruction within a framework that is substantively creative. He also manages the rare feat of expressing such theoretical approaches very lucidly. You will come away from this book with a better appreciation of Derrida as well as of Romans. The use of theory is complemented by an eye for unusual, fascinating detail, both in the text of Romans and in a set of other ancient texts that you are unlikely to have encountered before. Both the theory and the detail then build towards the largest of questions. For Richard, the power of the believer not only is the power to interpret, as one would rightly expect from Richard's theoretical stance, but a power that radically reenvisions the relations of agency between the divine and the human. It has been a great pleasure to be involved in Richard's research, and it is a great pleasure to commend his book to you.

Peter Oakes
Rylands Professor of Biblical Criticism and Exegesis
University of Manchester, UK

FOREWORD

This challenging but accessible analysis of Paul's Letter to the Romans is as much a study of the *interpreter* as it is the text to be interpreted. The onus is placed on the reader of the biblical text (be they ancient or modern) as an active agent in their own relationship with the divine. Resisting a wholly one-way, top-down model of God's influence, the believing reader of Romans is viewed as fully participating and determining the evolving contours of the divine plan. Long-debated issues are creatively upended by bringing into conversation Roman writers and lesser-known individuals mentioned in documentary papyri with poststructuralists (most significantly Derrida) and cognitive linguists, among others. The result is an appreciation of a deeper complexity of meaning both in Romans and near-contemporary comparative sources than traditionally acknowledged, both for their readers and users in antiquity and today.

There is a rich tapestry of ideas here for those with interest in a range of related disciplines and critical approaches that this book weaves together, including sociocultural exegesis, theology, philosophy, semiotics, and linguistics. Yet, even when the hermeneutical benefits of deconstruction theory and the almost boundless possibilities of metaphorical language in Romans are put aside, the framing of this study in relation to the real-world implications of interpreting religious literature is powerful. Both for individuals and communities, the metanarrative confronts the dangers of assumed passivity to a pure and unalterable truth among Christian readers of biblical texts (and by extension adherents of other textually focused religions or philosophies). The concluding words of this book explicitly invite believers and citizens—active participants in religious and/or nonreligious life—to recognize and embrace the power of their own individual agency and impact upon the meanings and values of these spheres. If this challenge rightly appeals, then I recommend *Romans and the Power of the Believer* as an excellent place to begin the necessary critical reflection.

Kimberley A. Fowler
University of Glasgow, UK

PREFACE

I will never forget those halcyon days at the University of Manchester between 2009 and 2014. I had taken voluntary redundancy from a busy and challenging career in college lecturing to pursue my master's degree and then my doctorate in Religions and Theology, which I had an urge to do. Through the inspirational teaching of Peter Oakes, I became enthralled by the poetics of the New Testament, especially the Pauline corpus. I have the fondest memories of our peer group tutorial in the basement of the Samuel Alexander Building West Wing, with David, Stephen, Andy, Elif, and others, such as Soon Ye and Isaac, in which Peter would give us that added value of academic career advice, moral support, and exciting discussion. I remember the dark corridors and the serpentine bannisters.

Thursday was always our departmental day where we might audit some lectures and tutorials first, have our group supervision late morning, and then enjoy a lunch together and grab a coffee (and snack) before the inspiring—if sometimes intimidating—Ehrhardt Seminar, in which we ran an unofficial bingo on whether Cynics or Stoics might be mentioned. Kimberley Fowler and Francesca Frazer, from other supervision groups, would also be there. For lunch we might go to the Vegetarian Cafe with its inquisitive dog or to the Simon Building for a build-your-own-stir-fry, which was coordinated by a passionate chef. I now realize that these are the experiences you can never reconstruct—once they end, once people move away, graduate, or move home, they are gone, but the memories are treasures that are a privilege to retain.

First and foremost, I would like to thank Peter Oakes. His wisdom, kindness and faith, at all stages, knew no bounds.

On the same level, I thank my husband Paul Williams, who lived day-to-day with both my doctoral study and then the process of writing this book. I am immensely grateful for all of his encouragement, love, and faith, which you will be able to read in the spirit of this book.

I thank my mother Rosemary Gillian Britton and my father Stephen John Britton for their high expectations of me from a young age and the unwavering support they gave to my academic ambitions, both materially and spiritually. I also thank my maternal grandfather Andrew Thomson and my paternal grandmother Ethne Britton for all of the time they spent with me encouraging me to write and learn. As the dedication shows, I am eternally grateful for the support of my close friend Simon Mapp. I thank Katie and Ellie for their love and support.

I thank Jeremy Tambling, who mixed humor with occasional sharpness to help me get to grips with the quantum mechanics that is Derridean critical theory.

I thank my sister Jemma Britton, who, through her struggles and bravery, taught me about the wonderful spirituality of Alcoholics Anonymous, and my brother Chris Britton, who shares my taste for movies, music, and comedy.

I thank Lynn Trillo for all her practical and emotional support throughout my studies.

I thank Jacqueline Hidalgo, Steed Davidson, and Gerald West for having faith in this book and for all their intensive support and feedback. I thank Nicole L. Tilford for her work editing this manuscript.

I am truly grateful to Gordon Stewart FRCO, Jane and David Forshaw, Jane Kear, Val and Phil Dangerfield, Penny Noon, Sheena Cartledge, Elizabeth and Michael Brueck, Anne Shields, Viv and Phil Knott, Reverend Alison Termie, and many others at my second home of Providence United Reformed Church in New Mills, who have lived with me through the process of getting this done, with love.

I am grateful to Ward Blanton and Michael Hoelzl for offering me suggestions on this book.

I thank David Harvey, Kimberley Fowler, Stephen MacBay, Andy Boakye, Elif Karaman, Charlotte Naylor, and Francesca Frazer for all their advice and academic fellowship.

I thank the following who have given me emotional and practical support: Daniel Lamont, Joan Jones, my parents-in-law Mary and Graham Williams, Karen and Graham Broderick, my late uncle Leonard Hansford, my late aunt Jennifer Weiss, my aunt Linda Thomson and uncle Jasper, my aunt Claire and uncle Vincent Hooper, my uncle Clive and my aunt Jan Britton, my aunt Lorraine Britton, my uncle Tim and my aunt Jane Thomson, my cousins Michael Johnson and Ben Ellis, my cousin Daniel Britton, my cousins Kieran and Ryan Hooper, my nieces Olivia and Ruby Britton and Chloe Broderick, my sister-in-law Sam Britton, our good friends Elizabeth and Jason Nagle and Marja Ilo and Teemu Pihlatie, Elaine Jones, Simon Catterall, Sara Hartley, Paul Protheroe, Sara Grumble, Matthew Ryder, Ian Southon, Ursula Southon, Derek Trillo, Pam Baker, Geraldine Mapp, Janet Oakes, Reverend Mark Townsend, Fiona Chisnall, Jeremy Davis, Elizabeth Robins, Calia Swain, and David Gilbert. Lastly, I thank all of my other family members, friends, and work colleagues, who have offered me so much love and support.

After studying for my master's degree and achieving it with a high level of distinction, I won a departmental scholarship. As such, I am grateful to the University of Manchester for this financial support. While studying, I also applied for and was awarded the Widening Participations Fellowship, in which I spent time publicizing classics and theology to school children visiting the university on open days, as well as designing and delivering interactive activities.

Richard Britton
New Mills, United Kingdom
April 2022

ABBREVIATIONS

Ab urbe cond.	Livy, *Ab urbe condita*
A.J.	Josephus, *Antiquitates judaicae*
ANT	Actor Network Theory
Amat.	Plutarch, *Amatorius*
Arch.	Vitruvius, *De architectura*
Ben.	Seneca, *De beneficiis*
BibInt	Biblical Interpretation
Caus. plant.	Theophrastus, *De causis plantarum*
Cher.	Philo, *De cherubim*
CTU	Dietrich, Manfreid, Oswald Loretz, and Joaquín Sanmartín, eds. *The Cuneiform Alphabetic Texts from Ugarit, Ras Ibn Hani and Other Places*. Münster: Ugarit-Verlag, 1997.
CurTM	*Currents in Theology and Mission*
Ep.	Seneca, *Epistulae morales*
Georg.	Vergil, *Georgica*
Hist. Plant.	Theophrastus, *Historia Plantarum*
HTR	*Harvard Theological Review*
JSNT	*Journal for the Study of the New Testament*
LSJ	Liddell, Henry George, Robert Scott, Henry Stuart Jones. *A Greek-English Lexicon*. With revised supplement. Oxford: Clarendon, 1968.
Kil.	Kil'ayim
m	mishnah
Nat.	Pliny, *Naturalis historia*
NTS	*New Testament Studies*
Op. agr.	Palladius, *Opus agriculturae*
Orac.	Astrampsychus, *Oraculum*

P.Flor.	Vitelli, Girolamo. *Papiri greco-egizii, Papiri Fiorentini.* Supplementi Filologico-Storici ai Monumenti Antichi. Milan: Hoepli, 1960.
P.Mert. 12	Bell, Harold Idris, and Colin H. Roberts, eds. *A Descriptive Catalogue of the Greek Papyri in the Collection of Wilfred Merton.* London: Emery Walker Limited, 1948.
P.Mich. 8	Youtie, Herbert C., and John G. Winter, eds. *Papyri and Ostraca from Karanis.* Vol. 8 of *Michigan Papyri.* Ann Arbor: University of Michigan Press, 1951.
P.Oxy. 3	Grenfell, Bernard P., and Arthur S. Hunt, eds. *The Oxyrhynchus Papyri.* Part 3. London: Egypt Exploration Society, 1903.
P.Oxy. 7	Hunt, Arthur S., ed. *The Oxyrhynchus Papyri.* Part 7. London: Egypt Exploration Society, 1910.
P.Oxy. 12	Grenfell, Bernard P., and Arthur S. Hunt, eds. *The Oxyrhynchus Papyri.* Part 12. London: The Egypt Exploration Fund, 1916.
P.Oxy. 42	Peter J. Parsons, ed. *The Oxyrhynchus Papyri.* Part 42. London: The Egypt Exploration Society, 1974.
P.Rein. 18	Reinach, Théodore, Wilhelm Spiegelberg, and Seymour de Ricci. *Papyrus Grecs Et Demotiques Recueillis en Égypte et Publiés.* Milan: Cisalpino-Goliardica, 1972.
P.Tebt. 1	Grenfell, Bernard P., Arthur S. Hunt, and J. Gilbert Smyly, eds. *Tebtunis Papyri.* London: Oxford University Press, 1902.
Plant.	Aristotle, *De plantis*
Pro Phorm.	Demosthenes, *Pro Phormian*
P.W.	Thucydides, *Peloponnesian War*
Quaest. conv.	Plutarch, *Quaestionum convivialum libri IX*
Rust.	Columella, *De Re Rustica*; Varro, *De re rustica*
SemeiaSt	Semeia Studies
TWNT	Kittel, Gerhard, and Gerhard Friedrich, eds. *Theologische Wörterbuch zum Neuen Testament.* 10 vols. Stuttgart: Kohlhammer, 1932–1979.
WBC	Word Biblical Commentary

INTRODUCTION

Can the eternal justice pleased receive
The prayers of those, who ignorant, believe?
—Thomas Chatterton, "The Defence"

A metaphor is a glorious thing,
A diamond ring,
The first day of summer.
A metaphor is a breath of fresh air,
A turn-on,
An aphrodisiac.
—Sparks, "Metaphor"

In this book I argue through Rom 4 and 11 that the believer is not a passive recipient of grace and righteousness from God, one who blindly and ignorantly accepts divine truths and shows this with attentive worship and prayer. Instead, the believer is an interpreter, a reader, and a decision maker who is actively involved in both reciprocal exchange and enhancement of God's eschatological and soteriological project. At the same time, the believer becomes able to negotiate meaning through their own interaction with texts and traditions in combination with their own personal relationship with the divine and the world. Dispensing with the notion of absolute meaning, the believer becomes empowered to resist the autocracy of those who try to dominate them and mediate on their behalf.

The believer is an *active agent*, meaning that, even though there are forces and authorities outside of their control, they can influence their own destiny and creatively shape their world through their prerogative to interpret and understand. To make this argument, I focus on key texts from Rom 4 and 11 that employ financial, gift, and olive tree metaphors. I examine these in the light of other near-contemporary intertexts—papyri and horticultural manuals—historicizing the deconstruction theory of Jacques Derrida, Friedrich Nietzsche, Georges Canguilhem, Giorgio

Agamben, and others. My method does not focus on the *poseur* of literary, political, and philosophical intertexts, such as Seneca, Epictetus, Josephus, Philo, and others, although it does add them into context. Instead, I focus more intensely on the seemingly mundane and neglected texts that have unexplored literary, philosophical, and theological ramifications, such as mortgage deeds, loan agreements, letters between family and friends, and horticultural manuals and notebooks. Such texts are the missives of ordinary people going about their daily business and those writing down practical instructions for increasing production of fruits.

There are real world theological problems of one-directional theology, and to address these we need to indicate the benefits alternative readings can bring. In this book, I hope to show that, in Romans, the believer has power and onus in a relationship with God that is not one-way, but mutual, reciprocal, and creative. At the end of each chapter, I indicate the implications of my deconstruction readings of these Romans passages in conversation with ancient intertexts.

Background

Passive blind faith expectations in worship and faith communities can lead to problems such as intolerance and exclusion and even hate crimes, extremism, and terror. It is at the sites of such issues where biblical studies and theology have an important civic role to play, without becoming subsumed into expectations to justify its own worth in society. Extremism is found within our own churches, mosques, synagogues, temples, our media, online, and even in our own homes. It is found in our wider culture, society, and faith. Violation of the individual's right to understand on their own terms is the most foundational violence that occurs before physical harm is possible. Violating violence is disavowed to the point that we are convinced it does not exist (see Derrida 1978a; 2001a, 148). For instance, if a church assembly begins their service with the assumption that all babies are born in sin or that Christianity is the only truth, then it violates the freedom of the people congregating. It is a silent blow. The most violating aspect of a regime is the repression of freedom to have opinions or to criticize or to form one's own conscience and opinions.

From the perspective of the violation of the individual, I have been thinking more about how biblical studies and theology can impact our lives—both for good and ill—and have been mindful of its potential. We oppress people by how we understand our religion and our religious texts.

In all cases of religious extremism and fundamentalism, the right of the individual to negotiate and determine their beliefs and views are subjugated to ideological preferences that are often lacking in theological dexterity. This narrative of theopolitical oppression is not new but runs from ancient times to the present.

While the Roman multicultural arena offered an impromptu diversity and even formative multiculturalism, it was punctuated by ideological ordering that forcefully separated threatening religions and philosophies from those that conformed. Roman violence distinguished between Jews and Christians (Blanton 2014, 35), although it did so through law first, with the *threat of violence* that permitted and enforced violations in people's freedoms. Without opening a debate on institutionalized violence, it is sufficient to say that just as we see the violence of institutional order in Paul's day, we see the same in the twenty-first century, albeit in different manifestations. Many of the mores, laws, and values we live by include presuppositions that exclude and oppress, and our governments, courts, media, social bodies, and churches are permitted by consensus to enforce these. It is rare in today's Western society that we acknowledge the seeds of fundamentalism, underpinned by veiled threats of violence—not necessarily of the physical kind—that are present. For example, we are trained to identify extremism as being Other and in another place, within an inferior society in the grip of a belated dark age that has yet to reach maturity of enlightenment. In spheres of progressivism, such as the academy and public services, we are expected to set our consciences on autopilot routes of political correctness, which leave little room for the individual to critique. Such disingenuity is comforting and helps us feel superior, but it is unhealthy and leads to harm. The seeds of murder can be found in the oppression of others, no matter how small scale or benign they seem, through the violation of integrity (Derrida 2001b, 112–13). If we, in our church assembly, reject someone because of their homosexuality or others because of their opposition to it, then we have oppressed them by our extremism—as also we do the so-called immoral person to whom we decline a religious marriage, the woman to whom we refuse incardination, or the baby we consider to be full of sin when they died unbaptized.

The idea that the believer is a passive recipient of pure and perfect grace from God and has no meaningful or effective influence is, I think, not only preposterously paradoxical but more significantly a cause, or, at least, a symptom of many deep-rooted problems in religion and society at large. I suggest that extremism, hate, and terror in all faiths result from this presupposition. However, prescriptive belief does not only negatively affect society at a criminogenic level; it pervades many forms of mainstream worship too: the gay teenager told he is not loved by God, the parents of the epileptic infant told they did not have enough faith, the widow told she did not pray hard enough to cure her husband's cancer, the people who are warned of hell if they do not accept Christ as their savior or Allah as their only god. These are just some examples of the poisonous effects that can be traced back to prescriptive belief—examples that can be seen in contexts of worship that many of us would never think of as extremist.

One major reason these people have been treated this way is because of the way in which we understand religion and religious texts. As a criminal justice practitioner in my day job, I know that extremism results not necessarily from an alien cult that seeks to infest but from the so-called respectable and moral society—our own respectable and moral society—that seeks to control what people think and believe according to a vision of absolute truth. This is what I will call prescriptive belief.

As a literary theologian of sacred texts, I consider that we can trace these problems back to the page and, more widely, how we communicate our faith. When I was an undergraduate, I studied English literature, and one of the first assignments we were given was practical criticism, which is a beautifully useful yet oversimplified form of analysis. This involves taking a text, usually a short poem, and ignoring anything *a priori*, analyzing it based only on what sense it contains—what you observe empirically there and then. This Leavisite approach is radical and distinct from biblical (or other) exegesis because it ignores historical context and, more importantly, evades biographical context, yet like exegesis it involves a dissection of the text—helpful because we are not limited by the perceived author and are focusing on the text. However, a disadvantage of such an approach is that it presupposes a bounty in the text that needs to be extracted, like treasure from a tropical island or ore from a rich mine. The medical paradigm of both practical criticism and exegesis objectify an outcome akin to diagnosis, cure extraction.

Biblical exegesis in one sense is much more diverse than practical criticism because it expects the interpreter to frame the text historically, biographically, linguistically, theologically, and culturally. These aspects are useful for a holistic reading of the text. However, where practical criticism hinges on the present reader's independent view, exegesis denies their vantage point and expects them to approach the text with a set of theological and semiotic presuppositions—mainstream traditional biblical studies. *Exegesis* in Greek has a meaning prior to that of biblical analysis, of soldiers being led, triumphantly, out of a city, probably with spoils of a concluded war. Thus, emphasis is placed on the leading, with a sense that there is something to be led and taken out and a specified amount and constituency of it (see Dinkler 2019, 74). It may seem problematic that one of our original Western concepts of interpretation includes an analogy of military violence, and some may wish for this to be replaced or altered for better ethical direction. However, as Derrida (2001a, 116) revealed, the distinction between discourse and violence is impossible, and to see language as having an originary innocence infected by a disease or subject to a fall through disruption of interaction is to condemn it with another violence that oppresses dissent through morality conforming to elite powers (see Derrida 1976, 106).

In this metaphor, there is a problem with endless readers making meaning compared with soldiers led out: soldiers can only be led out again once unless they reenter—the text is not empty to one person if someone before reads it. Exegesis implies only one occasion that meaning can be made and be right, and that the reader merely traces this back to its origin. By challenging this view, we can try to see exegesis as an exercise by which we order the soldiers of meaning back into the city, letting them scatter and inhabit places they were not before, then to lead them out in lots of different ways. This would be an exegesis where the reader is an active agent, not a passive one (Dinkler 2019, 77). Despite this, authoritative exegesis continues to exist (Dinkler 2019, 77), and this is often romanticized as nontheoretical and nonideological, making an expectation of analytical purity that is itself ideological (see Philips 1990, 12).

There is much to gain from the traditional practice of exegesis, in which it is expected that any academic writing an essay, minister planning a sermon, or even an individual using the Bible for guidance goes back to the drawing board every time. Just as an anatomy student never takes it for granted the liver looks a certain way, the exegete follows a process of looking at the text as if it were brand new every time and making sense of it on that occasion, rather than only deferring to the interpretations of others. My own analysis in this book borrows from this tradition of exegetic inquiry, as does the planning of my sermons and my own private biblical study. Having said that, there is still, within the concept of traditional exegesis, an expectation of absolute truth to be found and recovered, with each occasion offering the possibility for this bounty or more of it. At the same time, exegesis *always-already* contains within itself its own deconstruction—what truth is in the text to be brought out is subjective, and the individual situations of the voyeurs of the text fragments any possibility of one absolute truth. It is this approach to truth that I bring into my text-level analysis of the Romans excerpts in this book.

There is no such thing as pure objectivism—or a pure outside view—so we deal with the subjective in any enquiry. This book affirms the role of the believer as an assessor, so the activity, rather than passivity, of faith is presupposed. The activity and power of the believer is located in interpretation. This means that the plasticity of language figures predominantly in our study. So too does the relevance of ambiguity over the idealism of clarity. In these conditions, the role of the believer in negotiating meaning becomes prominent, because there is no such thing as correct wisdom. The act of faith thus establishes the legitimacy of imagination within analysis.

The Approach

There are four dimensions to this study, each of which flows into the other: first, the choice of text; second, the emphasis on faith; third, the use of critical theory; and fourth, the focus on metaphor and language. I therefore begin by explaining why Romans and indeed these texts in chapters 4 and 11 form the basis for our study.

(1) In terms of texts: Paul's letter to the Romans is one of the grand texts of foundational Christian theology on what it means to be a believer, among other important themes. Without this text, there would be no Christian or Christianity with a capital C. Romans is wheeled out, like a reliable family matriarch or as a dutiful bride to the gospels, to be the guarantor of a coherent Christian theology when such coherence is questioned. We assume that any enigmas it may contain can be cracked and that once this happens a stable theology can be drawn from it, like a freshwater well in a desert. Stephen Moore (2019, 119–20) exposes the paradox whereby scholars assume their articles accurately capture the meaning of texts, yet writing an article presupposes the text's insufficiency. Of course, this descends from scholarship's presumption that the texts need to be mediated, although this is further contradicted by the need for continued scholarship, showing the text was not explained well enough in the first exposition.

Whoever masters the text, some assume, can have authority over what it means to understand Christian theology, and this often results in the justification of blind faith—why do you need to understand something when your superior can do so on your behalf? Ward Blanton (2014, 124) identifies Rom 7, for example, as a "machine" through which one can think out a problem, and I wonder, in the same spirit, if Romans as a whole, indeed every text, is an algorithm through which ideas and experiences can be processed, in which the reader, as much as the author and prior interpreting authorities, intertexts, cotexts, and contexts, provide input, with the output determined by this combination of influences, not the text or author alone in the name of the authority.

Intertexts are also contrasted with Romans, including financial papyri when examining *pistis* and economics in chapter 1, papyri on gift giving in chapter 2's analysis of gift in Rom 4, and practical agricultural texts in terms of the olive tree allegory in Rom 11, the subject of chapter 3. The reason I choose papyri and horticultural manuals is because I aim to take the Romans texts to *ground level*—looking at the everyday realisms of the time (an approach spearheaded by Peter Oakes in his book *Reading Romans in Pompeii: Paul's Letter At Ground Level*, 2009). Whereas Oakes focuses on sociological data available through the excavations at Pompeii, I will use literary analysis of realistic everyday texts to contextualize Romans. By bringing texts to ground using ordinary texts, we can reempower the believer in Paul's time and then translate this into the power of the believer today.

(2) In terms of faith: In this book, I aim to redirect readers away from traditional ideas of faith and belief toward a faith in which the believer is empowered in their relationship to God through their ability to inquire and create. Faith is situated between the freedoms of interpretation and imagination. Faith is not about blindly accepting a prescribed truth or being passive recipients of meaning. The believing individual is not a vessel in which truth is filled but an ever-flowing cup in which truths are poured in but also spill out plentifully in different forms—the *kenotic* potential of the believer. In order to show this, I focus on *pistis* alongside other financially charged words in Rom 4 in my first chapter, and then I move on to link faith to the expected altruism in Rom 4 in my second chapter. In my third chapter, I widen this to the allegory of the olive tree, which has further ramifications on faith.

(3) In terms of theory: In this study, deconstruction theory is drawn upon strongly, including that of Derrida, Agamben, Canguilhem, and others. Gary Philips (1990, 12) says that "non-theoretical, non-ideological exegesis has never existed, except as a romantic construct, itself an ideological imposition." Biblical studies is "fighting to retain what the text

'really means" so it is important to counter the "closures" of writing or where writing is contained (Strømmen 2019, 94, 96). In the interpretation of Romans in this work, certain aspects of the senses of words are seen to be retained and others elided. However, such elision or erosion does not finalize meaning in a text. The idea that words only lose meaning over etymological erosion ignores the role the unconscious plays. Words might lose certain specific aspects of a perceived former sense, but such loss creates a debt of meaning, resulting in an accruing interest if you like, which exerts influence at an unconscious level.

Derrida (1982, 210) explains how *usure* certainly involves "erasure by rubbing, exhaustion, crumbling away," but it also involves "supplementary product of a capital, the exchange which far from losing the original investment would fructify its initial wealth, would increase its return in the form of revenue, additional interest, linguistic surplus value." Furthermore, the withdrawal of certain senses of words, or indeed the withdrawal of their metaphoricity through certain intended use, can lead to "an indiscreet and overflowing insistence" and an "over-abundant remanence" elsewhere (Derrida 1978b, 8)—*retrait*. The expected profit of the conceptual and metaphorical detours is arguably the perceived authorial intention or the authorized interpretations that relate to the authorial intention. However, the unexpected surplus, or accrued interest, is not under authorial control and may affect the reader or hearer individually at an unconscious level. It is like a popular fairground game whack-a-mole, where you use a mallet to hit a figure only for another to pop-up elsewhere. This effect, which I call *usure-retrait*, dictates that when certain aspects of a word's apparent prior senses are elided or held back, they only emerge and increase in another form, unexpectedly, unconsciously, yet in a way in which is significant and conspicuous when it is interpreted using this method.

The elision or erosion of certain senses of words leads to an overspill or springing up elsewhere in different forms. We find suppression of meaning in the way financial words are understood in Rom 4 in chapter 1, the idealism of the gift in chapter 2, and the olive tree allegory in chapter 3. By reading our texts of study alongside ground-level realistic documents rather than elite philosophical or political tracts and using deconstruction techniques, we have a method to appreciate the suppressed aspects of our text. I call this the *usure-retrait method*. My method has formed the basis of my initial exegesis before integration into the analysis in this book.

The notion of *usure* and *retrait* of senses of meaning can be seen through Derrida's analysis of George Canguilhem's *La connaissance de la vie* (1969), which contains the story of how the biological term *cell* first became coined by the English natural philosopher Robert Hooke (1665) when he saw a plant cell under the microscope. Hooke named it cell after the compartment of a beehive that it resembled. Canguilhem poses this question as to whether Hooke's text, in deriving the term cell from the honeycomb chambers, imports other aspects and notions from the context from which it derives:

> who knows, whether, in consciously borrowing from the beehive the term cell in order to designate the element of the living organism, the human mind has not also borrowed from the hive, almost unconsciously, the notion of the co-operative work which the honeycomb is the product? (Canguilhem 1969, 49)

Derrida is using Canguilhem's query to open the possibility for the unconscious effects that the metaphoricity of the language have on the reader of Hooke's *Micrographia*. Bees are, according to Derrida (1982, 261), "individuals entirely absorbed by the republic." The suggestion is that the perceived politics and sociology of insects may be carried over into plant biology, the hermeneutical prognosis of which could be ideological and political socialism and communism in future readings.

As Bernard Harrison (1999, 508) summarizes, Derrida is committed that "language trumps intention," in that metaphor, which is language in its entirety, is not controllable by the conscious will of reader or writer and "a speaker cannot, by putting his signature to a text, establish any right to rule out as inadmissible, as inconsonant with his intentions, all but a chosen subset of possible readings; in the end how we understand what we read depends not on the private intentions of the writer but on the potentialities inherent in the public language in which he has chosen to write." As such, metaphor is a feature of the unconscious force of language, and meaning can be generated in texts that the author or speaker did not consciously intend. As Leitch (1983, 254) summarizes, the author is only a guest in his text, and Derrida's work (along with Barthe 1967), "not only de-centers the text, but defers the conclusion" because "a text cannot be located or stopped at the author," whose conclusions on the text "rank in potential value with any other reader's." Any attempt to look only at the conscious use of metaphor (for example, the author meant this to be metaphor but not this) by an author fails to examine the metaphoricity of the language properly and thus fails to understand the meaning properly.

Consequently, in our present study I examine in each chapter how aspects of certain words have unintentional import. So, for instance, the economic sense of *pistis* as financial trust impacts on the dynamics of Rom 4.

(4) In terms of language and specifically metaphor: The area of language where we can see vulnerability when it comes to interpretation is metaphor, so it makes sense to begin our study of belief by concentrating on some texts in Romans accepted to be figurative and others that are not yet have significant metaphorical implications. More importantly, however, from George Lakoff and Mark Johnson (1980) to Derrida, we see that metaphor is not just metaphor, but so fundamental to our collective consciousness that it moves our thinking and behaviors. Deconstruction, with its focus on the unconscious, shows that metaphor in the very core of language has implications beyond the obvious and conscious. Metaphors are not trick vaudeville ponies; they do not do philosophy's[1] or theology's will, to make something complicated more conveniently clear, only to be put away when serious discourse occurs. They are not detachable from the philosophical text in that, if they were not present, then meaning through formal concepts would be retained. Instead, metaphors are fundamental to the philosophical text as much as the literary or poetic text. So when the unconscious is evoked, metaphors work outside of conscious intention. Metaphors are transcendent in a collective unconscious. While intention can be affirmed at any point, the significance of metaphors goes beyond that of an author or interpreting authority, such as the church, government, or elites. The metaphorical dimension of language invites the individual to interpret and imagine. So the individual believer is given the power and onus to be faithful by examining metaphor, which exists in the space between the rational and the creative, the intellectual and the emotional.

Faith as Supplement

The metaphysics of presence in objectivity is unraveled and the subjectivity of the individual rehabilitated in philosophy by deconstruction and other paradigm shifting approaches. If faith is by default subjective, then this makes it supplement. It is at once necessary and at the same time sur-

---

1. *Philosophy* in this sentence refers to the elite academic Western project of insisting upon the separateness between formal discourse and literature.

plus. Economics, which is the focus of two sections of this book, is similarly reliant on the tension between surplus and necessity through finance and currency. For instance, if a person catches twenty fish in a day, which is arbitrary, they will be unable to eat them and may not need so many; however, they may need something else or, more importantly, may need something else in the future. They could sell the fish they are not eating tonight for cash to a restaurant and keep that cash to purchase something else they need. Or they could barter the fish for other items they need. It is their choice of what they do, and the values are based on their own determination and the market. Similarly, faith involves an economic twist in which the believer is in arbitrary reception of signs, and they take them to market, meaning they negotiate as to what these signs are equivalent to. Depending on their life situation, they may exchange the surplus for things relevant to their current situation or negotiate meaning like someone in a bazaar. Such acts involve imagination and a process of valuation in which the sovereignty of capital returns to the people. Truly liberal capital allows the individual to think about how they use and develop their wealth, making way for imagination within limits. Similarly, the protestant spirit of capital in interpretation allows the believer to adhere to the conditions and contexts of interpretation but with the license for imagining.

The economic sense of *pistis* and *fides* has been highlighted for a while and more prominently in recent literature (see Oakes 2018; Morgan 2015). Economics shows itself not to meet the standards of objectivity that many materialists insist on in the physical sciences. Both the abstract as well as the concrete motivate the economic turn, just as with language. Economics asks for the subject to assess; this is never straightforward and definitive but requires intuition, imagination, and insight. The claim for science that there are absolute truths to be ascertained through experimentation, however untrue, is convincing for physical sciences but not for economics or language. For instance, if we use experimentation to determine the properties of carbon, there is a level of consistency of outcome for whoever performs this, wherever they are, in whatever context. However, a loaf of bread may be of more value to an average person in a country with debased currency such as Zimbabwe than gold is to a millionaire in Monaco. It is even more specific than this: if someone really wants to see a rock star at a concert, they may pay huge amounts over the ticket price, whereas someone who does not like that artist might need to be paid to go! The concrete and abstract are not distinguishable in the economy either; using money or items, we can exchange for ideas, rights, secrets, experiences, esteem, and pleasure. Economy therefore is itself surplus. So is language, and so is belief! The assessment in the economic sense of *pistis* and belief I propose in this work is therefore not clinical or legalistic but wide and open to the imaginative interpretation of the individual believer. Faith is therefore somewhere between interpretation and imagination.

Faith and Intepretation

Scholarship shows that there is no stable translation between *pistis* in the Greek and *fides* in the Latin and any English words such as faith, belief, or trust. Instead, there is a plurality of links between them and therefore a plasticity in the resulting concepts. There are several authors addressing these questions in recent works in innovative ways, but for the purposes of our study, I think it is sufficient and necessary for clarity to focus on *pistis* in our New Testament text as faith interchangeable to some extent with belief but with an emphasis on trust and empowerment of the person giving trust. This is not to dismiss the other manifestations of words translated from Greek or Latin but to showcase one aspect of them in a plethora of such discourse.

At the beginning of 1 Corinthians, Paul sets faith against wisdom in a binary. Paul describes how Jews demand signs and Greeks desire wisdom (1Cor 1:22) and condemns wisdom by stating that "God's foolishness is wiser than human wisdom" (1 Cor 1:25). He claims that Jesus came so that "your faith might rest not on human wisdom but on the power of God" (1 Cor 2:5). He also warns that wisdom of the present age is in fact foolishness and then recites the catena "He catches the wise in their craftiness" and "The Lord knows the thoughts of the wise, that they are futile." It would be deceptive to try and read against Paul's attitude that wisdom, as an understanding gained from human efforts within a context of mystery, is afflicted by pride and grasping. For Paul, it is the accumulation of knowledge (so you are independent of a need for something external) and the superiority of possessing crafts that together provide the ability to deceive powers and evade divine justice. Nevertheless, here wisdom is not synonymous with intellect or analysis but, in the Jewish and Greek context, with tradition, which (once again) could imply induction and reception rather than active participation. Philosophical thought since Plato tends to presume that an absolute truth is out there to be found, that people can discuss things along the Socratic route as much as they want as an exercise, but that when all is good and done, the truth is the truth and anything else becomes redundant eventually, like the shed skin of a snake.

Faith, on the other hand, is alive and active to Paul. It is not seen as a static corpus of wisdom tradition but as a dynamic and inexhaustible process. The human can only ever fully understand its human spirit, and only God can ever fully comprehend the Spirit of God (1 Cor 2:11). Yet now people have "received not the spirit of the world but the Spirit that is from God," with the purpose that we "understand the gifts bestowed on us by God" (1 Cor 2:12). Such understanding involves speaking in "words not taught by human wisdom but taught by the Spirit" in order for the "interpreting" of "spiritual things to those who are spiritual."

While the perpetual deferral of human ability to understand God establishes a limiting process of deference that traps the human in a position of reliance on God, it also retains the possibility to liberate human interpretation from the despotism of an absolute meaning and truth dictated by an authority on behalf of God. Belief is widened to an active interpretive process and exalts the believer to someone who can analyze and put into action the Spirit of God. The binary of text and cosmos breaks down, as does the boundary between them, and so the acts of interpreting and doing, of communication and action, become intertwined. There is consequently no longer any separation between text and material, so the belief of the believer has a determination and an effect somewhere at the point where thought and world, or mental and physical, meet. As Derrida (1976, 158) shows, the location of deconstruction is not outside the text but originates within it. Here we can see a primitive deconstruction movement in Paul's own use of binary, in which the role of the believer as interpreter emerges.

Paradox lies at the heart of traditional biblical scholarship's notion of the role of the believer and the eschatological tension. The already-not-yet status is presented as a solution but shows instability that reveals the believer's agency. N. T. Wright (1991), James Dunn (1988a; 1988b; 2006; 2009), and Andrew Lincoln (1981), for instance, on this matter presuppose the passivity of the believer but at the same time expect their agency. This is more prominent in Oscar Cullmann (1951), who perhaps emphasizes agency more keenly. Cosmic dimensions to the eschatological tension can be found that show such contingency, in which the apostles continue to "drive back the still constantly active power of conquered death" (Cullmann 1951, 237) and "triumph is not yet final" and believers participate in the "cosmic drama" and "heavenly direction" (Lincoln 1981, 187, 192).

Perhaps this view draws on the plasticity of Hellenistic religion, in which the power of Zeus has limits and agency lies with both gods and mortals (Albinus 2000, 64).

Such ambivalence runs throughout the theological establishment. For Cullmann, it is wrong for what he calls "primitive" Christianity, by which he means early Christianity, to consider the "interest for the individual man" [sic] as being "at the most, only on the margin" of redemptive history. Instead, the individual human is "built into" Christianity's historical structure, "actively sharing in the redemptive history" (Cullmann 1951, 217). There is no "general ethical rule" (230) for how the Jewish law is to be obeyed or applied, and Christ's message was that "fulfilment of the law" is "not literal" but requires "radical application" of it to "concrete situations" (226), thus necessitating the Christ-following believer to make "ethical judgements"—"the demand of the believer to recognise ever anew at each moment the commandment that the situation at each time presents" (225). The believer is thus positioned in a responsible and powerful role.

These margins of freedom are evidenced by the history of belief where fundamental tenets are always-already at stake, and "what the Christian believes today about God, life after death, the universe" and so on "is not what he believed a millennium ago—nor is the way he responds to ignorance, pain, and injustice the same as it was then" (Asad 1993, 46) For example, the early-modern valorization of pain as participating in Christ's suffering is at odds with the modern Catholic perception of "pain as an evil to be fought against and overcome as Christ the Healer did" (46).

Despite this changeability, Wright (1995) allegorizes biblical texts as architectures that protect the authority of God, using house metaphors. Derrida's *Truth in Painting* (1987) exposes such a tendency in metaphysics. Wright's house metaphor is an example of conservative biblical scholarship's need to organize, frame, and control interpretation of Paul. On the dissonance between structural certainty and frailty of authoritative Pauline meaning, Blanton (2007, 107) comments how Heidegger sometimes "participates with the most popular biblical critics in their use of specific techniques that promise to conjure the authentic Paul from the many ancient and modern dissimulators, misinterpreters, and traitors of the religious experience for which he has come to stand." However, "by the same token, and as we might have expected by now, Heidegger also contests the propriety, which is to say the property rights, of the biblical critics in relation to the Pauline heritage itself" (107). In other words, the house of meaning can be altered, extended, reduced, adapted, or refurbished. It can also be knocked down and rebuilt.

By challenging the exclusivity and authority over meaning, we can redistribute the rights to interpret the text back to the individual and the believer. The paradox is summarized effectively by Paul S. Fiddes (2000, 23): "there has to be a certainty about the overcoming of evil and the triumph of God's purposes, but the freedom of God and the freedom of human beings to contribute to God's project in creation also demands an openness in the future." Within this framework, belief is not about blind acceptance of theological regulations but an organic process of fresh interpretation in which the believer is tasked with forming meaning unregulated and unfettered by the metaphysical authorities that have formed within and outside the texts and traditions and that pass themselves off as natural (or even divine or true/truth). The individual believer has as many property rights over the text as the perceived author and the accepted regulators of their interpretation.

Power and Understanding

Powers in one form or another have always been preoccupied with securing public authority from the risk of the individual engaging in public expressions of personal belief. Clifford Geertz (1973, 109) explains that "religious belief always involves the prior acceptance of authority." Amidst the network of metaphysical myths of the West is the transference of truth from the ultimate sovereign that is God, to the believer, via the ordained political powers and principalities in the world, who control and delimit the misunderstanding of the message, which paradoxically is incorruptible yet must be protected from corruption. No challenges or complex expectations are made of the subjects apart from passive and simple reception and acceptance of this message. Margins and discrepancies are denied or mitigated. This process is enforced as being one-directional, an oppressively over-simplistic dictation from the sovereign to the subject, which is further conflated with pure grace and gift as part of its condescension, in which meaning is nonnegotiable and the believer is expected to accept blindly, never question, and then respond only on that limited basis.

Unequal binaries lie at the heart of these authority structures (see Derrida 1976), exposing how people are labelled, controlled, and excluded: white/black, male/female, rich/poor, heterosexual/homosexual, beautiful/ugly, good/evil, sacred/profane, spiritual/material, teacher/student, author/reader, priest/worshiper, among many others. The master binary is the metaphysics of presence—the exaltation of presence over absence, being over nonbeing, Being (existence) over non-Being (nonexistence) (see Culler 1983, 92). Further to this, in terms of interpretation we have *logocentrism*, in which philosophy prioritizes speech over writing due to the former's spontaneity and presence of the authorized speaker and the latter's apparent delay and absence of someone to control how it is understood (90). Generic active/passive binaries are significant because the privileged factor is active and the other is passive. The privileged actives retain the right to create, decide, instruct, design, and explain, and passives are invested with lesser roles—to follow, respond, and obey.

Another binary is literal/metaphorical, in which the former is real meaning and the latter a provisional one (Morris 2000, 227), suitable for elaboration of the serious but not a permanent substitution (Derrida 1982). It is as if metaphor is the protracted voyage of Ulysses, returning with argosies of real meaning (Harrison 1999, 513). Another metaphor of metaphor is currency—the coin is acceptable in transactions if necessary, but it must be honored with the wealth it represents (see Saussure 1959, 115; Derrida 1982, 218). Despite attempts to mitigate the discrepancies between proper and figurative meaning, it becomes apparent that philosophy's core concepts are themselves metaphorical—*theoria, eidos, logos* (Derrida 1982, 224). For instance, *theoria* has a literal meaning "to see." This means metaphor is inescapable, even in the scientific text, and so is ambiguity. The interpreter is therefore empowered to make meaning from the text. Stephen D. Moore (1994) shows this in his rereading of John 4:7–15, in which the boundaries between the literal and the metaphorical are challenged, and the Samaritan woman is positioned as an active interpreter who teaches Christ about the instability of a distinction between living and spiritual waters, with the theological outcome that no one person is the source and every believer has their own agency.

The idea that religions and their texts are to be interpreted, decoded, or translated has met with challenge by some, railing against the textualist attitude. Manuel Vasquez (2011, 228) argues that "the religion scholar caught in the textualist attitude acts as the authorised interpreter of texts and the endless discourses on them, or of the deepest feelings and beliefs of the faithful." He also describes how Geertz and others see religion as needing to be decoded prior to it being able to be "related to its structural conditions" (244). The interpretation of religion is vulnerable, through the decoding mindset, to being disproportionately influenced by whatever powers are dominant at a specific time and place. A takeaway from Vasquez's critique of text-centric interpretation is that tradition must be made far more prominent in our understanding of biblical texts. One of the approaches of this book is to avoid deferring to the elite literary and philosophical discourse and to look at ancient texts at ground level (as per Oakes), such as papyri and horticultural practical manuals. These texts reflect tradition that is wider than the literary-philosophical discourse but that also show the poetic in the mundane.

My Arguments and the Texts

1. Romans 4:4–6 and 4:23–25

In chapter 1, I focus on Rom 4:4–6 and 4:23–25 and argue that *pisteuō* and *pistis* (and indirectly *logizomai*, *dikaiosunē*, *dikaiō*, and *dikaiōsis*) in Rom 4:3–5 and 4:22–24 have for a long time been interpreted to confirm one-way direction of power and onus from God to the believer. I use ordinary papyri near contemporaneous to Romans to contextualize this.

In this chapter, I flag up certain problems of one-way directional readings. The believer has been placed as a passive recipient of God's grace who has no determination or power. I argue this leads not to righteousness, nor a benign erroneous devotion, but to problems such as extremism. Disingenuity of the division and delay in belief through the rejection of payment in the economic paradigm compounds into perpetual deferral to authority. *Pistis* as blind faith rather than trust is myopic and leads to fundamentalism and extremism. The rejection of agency in the economic paradigm denies the freedom of the individual believer and allows for a collective oppression. When transcendence of debt is presented as emancipating, it allows for perpetual obligation rather than liberation—owing and being owed permits accountability of all parties. One-directional views repress any questioning of authority by the believer and deny them their power and onus to affect change. At the end of the chapter, I signal some implications of my deconstruction readings and how they can enhance discourse, such as the affirmation of the active role of the individual to prevent extremism, the rejection of perpetual deferral to corrupt religious authorities that uphold the myth of perfection at the expense of the individual believer, the rejection of the blind-faith position of mainstream fundamentalism, the allowance of critique and agency of the individual to determine meaning, and the increase in accountability, which allows them to challenge authority.

To pursue these problems, in this chapter I review economic metaphor using deconstruction and the literary context of seemingly mundane financial papyri. I analyze this papyri to appreciate the equality of actors in financial transactions so that the role of the believer is reframed as active and the relationship between God and the believer is reciprocal. It is assumed in scholarship that in finance as in this Romans text, the one accounting holds the power and onus whereas the one believing, or trusting, lacks them. However, our papyri show roughly contemporary examples in financial scenarios where the one trusting can make decisions and has power.

2. Romans 4:4–6, Focusing on Gift and Grace

In chapter 2, I focus specifically on gift and grace in Rom 4:4–5. I challenge scholars' easy acceptance that ancient altruistic gift-giving in the form of Seneca affirms the grace of God, and I use ancient papyri texts to propose that such grace is an effect of material subjection rather than a theological or ethical absolute.

In this chapter, I identify some problems with the paradigm of altruistic gift as grace in Romans. I propose that the altruistic gift disavows a perpetual debt that is unresolvable and renders the recipient in perpetual debt to the giver while concurrently denying this obligation so it cannot be accounted for. I show that the presupposition of the forced gift denies self-empowerment of the individual that translates into prescribed theology. I show that altruism relies on austerity to foster a culture of dependence and dismissal of personal thrift, which represents the removal of agency of the individual believer to interpret. Furthermore, I propose that the framing of the economic essential as luxury through altruism denies the believer the right to determine what theological propositions are essential to them and prevents them from having freedom of interpretation and expression through the *jouissance* of supplement. At the end of the chapter, I signal some implications of my deconstruction readings and how they can enhance discourse in terms of the benefits of exchange between unequal parties of learning and faith, the empowerment of self-education and enlightenment over prescribed theology, and the reliance on self over others to interpret and create meaning.

To pursue these problems in this chapter, I demonstrate that affirming gift as grace transposes economic oppression into the theological field. I further argue that attempts to distinguish the material and spiritual in the gift as grace are undermined by the practical challenges of apostolic mission exemplified by Paul in Romans. Using ancient papyri again, I propose that an acceptance of the economic gift as grace enhances the gospel and empowers those commissioned to spread it. In P.Oxy. 12.1481, Theonas tries to convince his mother Tetheus that he is not ill nor in need. He acknowledges presents sent through her from others and hopes she is not obliged or burdened by this. In P.Oxy. 42.3057 Ammonius tried to underplay several gifts and the letter sent to him, yet at the same time infers obligation and inability to pay back such gifts. In P.Mert. 12, Chairas affirms the importance of friendship to ward off obligation, highlights his thrift, and indicates a need for resolution to attempted altruism. From this analysis, I show that pretending altruistic gift affirms God's grace collaborates with the oppression that denies the individual economic autonomy through perpetual, unresolvable debt. I explain that such analogues refuse the theological autonomy of the believer, with meaning deferred, but rather than being open, it is infinitely absolute and settled. I suggest that being realistic about gift as a delayed form of economy in opposition to the altruistic gift is indicative of the relationship between God and the believer, which is eternally deferred yet open and constantly changeable.

3. Olive Tree Grafting Allegory in Romans 11:17–23

In chapter 3, I focus on the grand olive-tree grafting allegory in Rom 11:17–23, using ancient horticultural texts to contextualize this. In this chapter, I identify some problems with one-way benefit in this grafting paradigm in Rom 11. The first issue is how the allegory has been used to justify the superiority of certain religious creeds and doctrines over others, especially converts into Messianic Judaism or Christianity. The second issue I raise is how the prominence of the tree has been used to affirm the need for a righteous corporate whole, with the graft used to show that an individual incorporated is inferior or merely representative of a superior source, rendering the individual as unimportant. The third is how the tree grafting allegory is used to justify exclusion and selective inclusion of individuals to an oppressive fascistic pattern. Any difference or variation introduced by the individual is rejected, resulting in a replication of ideas and belief that prevents creativity and development. At the end of the chapter, I indicate some implications of my deconstruction readings, how they can enhance discourse to promote equality, the role of the individual believer, and wider inclusivity.

I reject the prominent view that this text merely inverts Theophrastus of Eresius's instructions on grafting branches of cultivated olive trees onto wild ones—in that wild branches are instead grafted onto cultivated trees—to portray the gentile believers to be either wanting or in need of reproach. I also reject that this allegory portrays the gentile believers as morally rejuvenating Israel. Furthermore, I question the view that it is primarily based on practices explained in texts by Roman writers Columella and Palladius, in which shoots from wild olive trees are indeed grafted onto cultivated ones to revive and refresh the latter, thus advancing this argument for the gentile believers rejuvenating Israel. This chapter finds that the allegory and metaphor of the olive tree and the grafting process shows the wider dimensions of mutual exchange over hierarchical directive. The tree can encapsulate ideas of change and evolution, as well as difference and contestation; to show this, I use ancient horticultural intertexts of Theophrastus, Columella, and Palladius and even a prescient text from the Book of Mormon, alongside pieces of other ancient grafting texts and Derrida's (1969) own metaphor of the graft as writing, to emphasize mutuality. Implicit in these ancient texts is a sense of exchange, albeit asymmetric, rather than one-directional benefit from tree to graft or graft to tree. The graft is an artificial intervention into nature. However, at the same time, we can see that any intention of grafting is undermined by the intertext of the wider exchanges of nature. Equally, the purity of nature is undermined by the subject's glance, their attempt to interpret the world around them. The exchange between subject and object is ever evolving and fluid.

1
BELIEF

What then are we to say was gained by Abraham, our ancestor according to the flesh? For if Abraham was justified by works, he has something to boast about, but not before God. For what says the scripture? "Abraham trusted God, and it was accounted to him for righteousness." Now to the one working, the wages are not accounted according to gift, but according to debt-owed. But to the one not working, but believing on the one justifying the ungodly, his trust is accounted for righteousness. Now to the one who works, wages are not accounted as a gift but as something due. But to the one not-working, who trusts him who justifies the ungodly, such trust is accounted as righteousness.
—Romans 4:3–5

Now, "it was accounted to him" was not written for his sake alone but also for us, to whom it will be accounted to those of us who believe on the one having raised Jesus the Lord of us from the dead ones, who [Jesus] was handed over to death because of our trespasses and was raised for the purpose of our justification.
—Romans 4:23–25

That Pharaoh's wisdom o'er again is sooth of lose-and-win
For "up an' down an' round," said 'e, "goes all appointed things,
An' losses on the roundabouts means profits on the swings!"
—Patrick Chalmers, "Roundabouts and Swings"

Romans 4:3–5 and 23–25 is compared in this chapter with roughly contemporaneous economically oriented papyri under the guidance of deconstruction theory. In this chapter, I demonstrate how critical the economic associations of *pistis* are for understanding the exchange of faith in Rom 4. I also indicate the importance of *logizomai* and *diakiō* related words. I compare our Romans texts to near contemporary papyri texts that use *pistis* and related words. The first papyri text is P.Oxy. 3.486.7 from 131 CE, a petition from Dionysia to a prefect regarding a dispute with Sarapion, in which she asserts she purchased land rather than acquired it on mortgage. Second, P.Tebt. 1.14.9 from 114 CE, is a letter from Menches to Horus (both officials), concerning Heras being tried for murder and discussing his property being kept in trust. The third papyri is P.Rein. 18.10 from 108 BCE, concerning an arrangement whereby Dionysios and his mother have borrowed land from Admentos-Chestothes and in doing so promised their land in guarantee.

Ultimately, I show how the understanding of *pistis* in the context of trust and credit in the papyri moves us away from a metaphysical passivity on the part of believers in our Romans texts and into a greater sense of reciprocity in the relationship between believers and God.

Argument

My argument begins by positing that *pisteuō* and *pistis* (and indirectly *logizomai, dikaiosunē, dikaiō,* and *dikaiōsis*) in Rom 4:3–5 and 4:22–24 have been interpreted in mainstream biblical and theological scholarship to uphold a one-way direction of power and responsibility from God to the believer. I caution how such readings, whether intentional or not, place the believer as a passive recipient of authority and grace and thus has no influence or agency. I link such one-directional readings with various religious and geopolitical problems in the world, including autocracy, prejudice, and extremism. I offer the view that economic and financial metaphor has been interpreted through elitist and patriarchal capitalist approaches that limit meaning to authorized traditions. My approach then reinterprets the economic metaphor using deconstruction theory-as-method to appreciate the equality of individuals involved in transactions and emphasize the power of the junior partners in financial relationships. In doing so, I argue that the role of the believer—like any individual involved in a transaction—is reframed as active, that the relationship between God and the believer is not just one-way but instead is reciprocal. It is assumed in scholarship that in finance, as in this Romans text, the one accounting holds the power and onus whereas the one believing, or trusting, lacks them. I suggest that such views are supported by sleight of hand in exegesis which, in reference to financial texts, is highly selective, accepting certain features and ignoring others. Ancient papyri, I show, exhibit examples in financial scenarios where the one trusting, to some extent, wields some power over the one who seems to hold all the cards. Papyri may be inconvenient or dismissed by some; however, their implications are significant when we fully appreciate that these documents are testament to an insistent empowering use of *pisteuō* and *pistis* words around the time of Paul. Finally, my thesis suggests ways in which reciprocal readings can enhance our attitudes to religion and ideology in the world.

The Economics of *Pistis*

Studies of *pistis* so far rely on a linear etymological progression. However, semantic change is not as simple, and a matrix of connected meanings and semantic ranges is likely to be more illustrative of how words develop. Words are heavily dependent on specific contexts and the understanding of individuals as much as a shared agreement of meaning. The relational quality of *pistis* is affirmed in recent scholarship. For instance, Teresa Morgan (2015, 12) factors in Augustine of Hippo's division of faith between *fides quae* creditor and *fides qua* creditor—the faith that is believed and the faith by which it is believed. Both are intertwined, but an emphasis on *fides qua* indicates "a relationship of trust between the believer and God and Christ."

Pistis, along with *philia*, is one of the foundational building stones of Greek politics and society (Reden 1995). Encompassed within *pistis* are the bonds of family, kinship, neighborhood, and moral obligations. Economic and sociological studies emphasize *pistis* as the historical root of confidence and good faith that exists across the social, political, economic, and spiritual spheres. Such work relies on *pistis* words as having the semantic range in the New Testament texts of being steadfast to one's word or promises, being worthy enough to be believed, being trustworthy and having "dependable speech" (Chan and Lee 2009, 92). Whether these meanings were intended or not, this can be the possible effects dependent on the context of interpretation. What is intended by ancient writers, or privileged interpreters, should not determine a final meaning.

Parmenides and Aristotle, according to Morgner (2013, 512), show that *pistis* is important for prosocial integration into the polis. Morgner also defines the counterpart *apista* meaning a level of doubt in which moral principles and their philosophical roots are rejected. This rendering of *pistis* seems in opposition to the notion of an individual's right and power to engage in *pistis*, or trust. However, Morgner finds in *pistis* an overlap between trust within a system and the personal trust people affirm to each other (510–11, 528). Read alongside Pauline *pistis*, Morgner's position could help recenter the role of the individual believer. What is more important for Plato is *pistis* as a form of cognition that is in opposition to knowledge, one that involves being able to discern the physical world. The Stoics saw *pistis* as a "firmness of the mind" (512), which involved the ability to inform on the truth and provide advice and orientation to others. The Platonic and Stoic definitions, despite differing in their prioritizing of cognition and truth respectively, both see *pistis* as something quite different from the concept of faith as developed in the history of the church. *Pistis* is thus somewhere between "faith" and "assessing" semantically.

The *pistis/apista* binary emphasizes the role of the rational element of *pistis*, rather than the blind-faith connotations of the church. On relational *pistis*, Morgan (2015, 4) argues that "in its earliest years ... we should not expect the meaning of Christian *pistis* (or *fides*) language to be wholly *sui generis*. We should expect those who use it to understand it within a range of meanings which are at play in the world around them.... This means that we should not, for instance, [like Bultmann] dismiss the possibility that Christian pistis toward God has features in common with 'trust-in-God in general.'" *Pistis* is not a one-way and self-assured connection between God and the believer that does not rely on or relate to anything else. Furthermore, Morgan (2015, 6) discusses how *pistis* and *fides* "in some sense always involve reciprocity, because they always involve relationships" even if we concede that the "reciprocity is commonly asymmetrical"—for example, an army offering loyalty to its commander or a slave to his master. Oakes (2018) more explicitly acknowledges this relational value of *pistis*. A useful contemporary economic example would be that between a shopkeeper and a customer; the transaction may seem a one-sided relationship, in which the customer is the one to whom all deference and service is to be afforded, but, of course, the customer is obliged to pay and not commit theft, to keep to the terms of business, to not violate the shop premises or stock, to show respect to the shopkeeper, and to be truthful and not lie about the standard of service she has received. If someone writes an inaccurate or unfair review online of business, they could be subject to legal action. Similarly, a waged worker has rights and expectations of their employer, even in ancient times.

The Problem with the Believer as a Passive Agent

Passivity of the believer is not a sign of righteousness, nor is it even a benign indication of misplaced devotion; instead it leads to big problems.

Trickle down consequences follow from the attitude that the believer is a passive agent who exerts no power or influence. Some of these negative effects are religious, but many may be understood as secular too. Once we invest everything in the figure of an unquestionable sovereign God, we find the need for those in authority to regulate the meaning of what this sovereign says and create a Sovereign to represent him. Such a dynamic, rather than being a top down tyranny, includes resonances in which perceptions of God and powers mutually reinforce each other (Keller 2005). The role of the human believer as an agent and independent shaper of their own destiny is suppressed by other humans' perceptions of God's authority. The most obvious outcome is religious fundamentalism, in which the supposed will of God is prioritized above human rights and secular law. Evangelical nationalists who supported Donald Trump and Jair Bolsanaro, white supremacist Christians in the far-right groups of Europe and America, the Protestant denominations that collaborated with Hitler, the orthodox clerics who feed Russian nationalism, the medieval crusaders, Al Qaeda and ISIS, the Catholic Inquisition, the Taliban, Hindu supremacists in India, Buddhist extremists in Myanmar and Sri Lanka, Buddhist apologists for eastern far-left dictatorships, to name a few, all prioritize the authority of God, or an equivalent concept, as justification for the harm they cause to others in asserting authority on his/her/their/its behalf. However, as discussed in the introduction, such examples are merely the most easily identifiable forms of extremism. The presupposition of the passivity of the believer is what allows pockets of extremist ideology to pervade everyday parts of our faith and society. All the members of the underclass must remain as grateful recipients of the generosity of the rich and powerful who monopolize authority with money, influence, and nepotism. Authority structures then strip agency and power from the differing individual and suggest that certain people do not contribute or have anything worthwhile to offer.

Some Christian readings of Romans have fallen into this oppressive pattern. For instance, it is from Protestant readings of Lutheran expositions of Romans and Galatians that the justification by faith alone doctrines emerged, which prescribed right-belief and accused Judaism, Catholicism, and at times Islam[1] of being based around works. Such maneuvers

---

1. In some situations Islam has related well to Protestantism due to the rejection of icons, but the perception of some Protestant traditions that Islam does not prioritize faith has increased a sense that its requirements of worship—its pillars—are works.

hardened the dichotomy between economics and altruism, in which the former becomes entangled with works and the latter with faith. The new perspective on Paul as championed by Sanders and to some extent Dunn and Wright, albeit with varying approaches, has made important progress in countering this prejudice; however, this movement has not managed to undo the oppressive weight of faith priority and the accusation of works it carries. Justification by faith alone in its unrelenting form has been the theological engine of European antisemitism, ethnic racism, military nationalism, and the rise of Nazism. Through colonization and neocolonialism, this doctrine has transposed onto other religions and traditions; by this, I mean that when the West introduced Protestant Christianity into the colonies, the local religions adopted some of its missiology and its discipline of blind faith. Its transposition has helped to fuel oppression of Muslims by evangelical Buddhists in Myanmar and Sri Lanka and the rise in Hindu far-right nationalism, for example.

Consequently, hardened justification by faith alone readings of Romans have a lot to answer for in terms of extremism. However, they also transcend into the mainstream through fundamentalism and forms of evangelical religion. Romans, and readings of faith within it, has been a conduit for this problematic perspective of a one-way top-down reading of faith between God and the believer as a passive agent. I have identified five key pathologies.

1. The division and delay of economy is disavowed, and only infinite capitalist production is affirmed.

The first problem is how division and delay in economic and theological exchange is ignored and resolution is presumed to be absolute. There is a disavowal of how the economy cannot be escaped, that it involves inequalities and imbalances, divisions and separations. Resolution is made to appear spontaneous and absolute, yet at the same time, the altruistic defers resolution infinitely. Such a maneuver compounds a sense of faith being prescribed and absolute, rather than negotiated. Damnation of the economic prevents the believer from interacting and contributing through their power and onus, denying their own delay and deferral.

Delays and deferrals punctuate the cycles of power and resource, and it is the role of the individual to orient these and help determine fate. We must deal with and acknowledge these dynamics for fairness to occur. If we whitewash with charity or altruism, it becomes self-righteous and oppressive. Whatever is given leads to a return. Whatever payment is made needs a return, and, when someone pays, they do so because of a prior stimulus. Even God is subject to making payment, even if this is much greater than anything the believer can offer.

2. *Pistis* is accepted only as blind faith, and the semantics of mutual trust or good faith are ignored.

Pistis in the New Testament has been rendered, against the grain of contemporary economic and theological texts, as blind faith rather than assessing and imaginative trust. Many mainstream readings of the economic imagery in Rom 4 prefer blind faith over any sense of trusting in another party and having a stake. The recent work of Morgan and Oakes has recentered the importance of trust in faith, although mostly this aspect is avoided by other scholars. The economic reality of *pistis* as encompassing religious faith and economic good faith, and the interconnections between, is rarely configured into faith in Romans or other Pauline texts. Anything other than blind faith is disavowed, and this leads to significant depth and context being missed when these texts are coded into doctrine and authority.

Instead of an active trust that relies on the individual to question, assess, and affirm, a passive faith is often prioritized in which the believer merely accepts and surrenders to the views of religious authorities. Passivity emboldens fundamentalism and even extremism, because the power and onus of the believer is subjugated. At the same time, prejudice against certain views and traditions become mainstreamed.

3. The agency in economy is ignored, and the participant is reduced to a mere subject rather than a stakeholder.

The ability of the individual to exert agency in their financial dealings, as demonstrated in the papyri evidence, is ignored by many scholars. This facilitates a view of the believer and individual being denied in many readings of Romans, the ability to initiate and engage mutually, even if asymmetrically, with God. Prerogative and sovereignty of even the least powerful individual is denied to support a reading of Romans that is informed by an erroneous understanding of ancient economic reality. What is denied is that in any initiation of exchange in economy there is a prior mover and someone more powerful, and a reading is forced in which the believer is pathetic and powerless. This reading cancels out any sense that God responds to the believer in mutual exchange, allowing for a sense of autocracy. Such an approach elides the willingness and grace of God to interact with his people and use their individual strength and character to shape his kingdom. Religious authorities consequently repress the agency of the individual in relationship with God to uphold their own temporal authoritative regime.

4. People are denied the ability to have power through owing, as well as being owed.

Being in legal and ethical debt, as much as being owed, can be empowering because it presupposes expectations and demands of the lender according to terms. However, these demands have been ignored by some, who use the rhetorics of gift and charity to support infinite and unmeasurable gratitude and unquestioning loyalty. The position of power in a mutual exchange of both owing and being owed is denied. Being able to raise and clear a debt can be positive because it shows independence and sovereignty, whereas being a recipient of a gift can place one under perpetual thrall. Many readings of Romans ignore the empowerment of owing as much as that of being owed in their pursuit of altruistic gift as grace. Elided from the conversation is how every person is subject to debt or loyalty to another person or actor, no matter how powerful they are. Oversimplistic understanding of the intricacies of debt leads to a flawed reading of Romans, in which the power and the onus of the believer to interact with God through their own stakeholding and choice to accept the terms of such a relationship is prevented and the authorities of religion replace it. Resulting oppression keeps religion in aspic and damages the missiology and growth of God's eschatological project.

5. Economic inequalities are used to justify preventing the questioning of authority.

Throughout history we have tolerated religious and secular leaders as experts based only on their power. We also accept the views of celebrities based on their fame and status, often in place of those of experts. Yet, we exhibit top-down dismissal of our individualism and onus in not only our religious institutions but also our political institutions, however often this ignorance is based around religious fundamentalism. For instance, we have politicians such as Donald Trump publicly and mindfully ignoring the advice of experts in the field they hold portfolio in, based upon pseudoscience influenced by dodgy right-wing spirituality; there is a short distance between antivax ideology and antisemitism, for example. In religion, we have members of the Church of England and other Protestant churches voting against the advice of bishops to allow gay marriage. In some denominations of various religions, we have the views and opinions of professionals and experts ignored in terms of the use of contraception, blood transfusion, the validation of other sexualities and gender changes, the need to prevent sexual abuse, tackling misogyny and chauvinism, and many others. I propose that some of this top-down approach descends from a poor reading of economics in the paradigms of texts such as Rom 4.

Top-down readings of financial trust, reckoning, and justification of debt and wage ignore a mass of evidence that less-powerful parties still retain some power. Financial and material inequality is relied upon and normalized as a standard through which the believer's relationship with God is regulated through religious authority and even academic scholarship. From this, a theology in which the believer is viewed as being inadequate to interact with God is undergirded by an ulterior motive for authorities to subjugate the individual to their elite figures. Frankly dodgy readings of Rom 4 economic metaphor mean the believer is prevented from questioning the authority of powers that run religion. Faith becomes the preserve of powers that dictate what God means and says rather than a healthier spiritual protocol where the relationship and interaction between the believer and God is sacredly evolving and inclusive.

Economic Metaphor

As part of the unconscious drive to control meaning, biblical scholars are selective about what constitutes metaphor and what does not, often for their own ideological and confessional reasons. Selectivity is justified through cognitive linguistics (Lakoff and Johnson, 1980) and a perception that metaphors have been lexicalized into the new theological discourse of Romans and cut off from their intertexts (in line with Ricoeur 1975).[2] The

---

2. In *Metaphors We Live By*, Lakoff and Johnson make a pertinent case for metaphor being hardwired into our cognitive patterns but rely too heavily on the distinction between the metaphorical and the proper, neglecting when this binary collapses. On the other hand, lexicalization in Ricoeurian thought is when a word that is transferred to another discourse field becomes so familiarized there that it stops being

figure of the author is used to justify the thrift in the proliferation of meaning and to ensure a tight austerity (Strømmen 2019, 97).

In this book, I do not propose abolishing the author but rather using the metaphorical ramifications of *pistis* as trust to widen the overlap between author and hearer: God, via Paul, and the believer. Steed Davidson's (2015, 42) work on the effect of the island environment on faith perspective is illuminating for this present argument: just as islands are bounded, they are also open to immigration and emigration. They consist of small pieces of land in a vast sea; however, the sandy beaches and the tides allow different perspectives on where the boundary between land and sea is. Davidson's comparison is a good metaphor for metaphor in faith too. Any attempt to control the boundaries of the metaphorical and literal is as futile as marking the land end point on a sandy island's tidal beach. Similarly, in my article on alliteration and John Ruskin's faith, I explore how scientific discoveries about the impermanence of geological features causes him to reassess his evangelical certainty; like the peaks of Mont Blanc, his own faith changes through constantly moving metaphors (Britton 2017).

In Romans, traditional scholarship conceded that *logizomai* is metaphorical in the sense of "taking account" (see Dunn 2006, 377; Witherington and Hyatt, 2004, 121; Keck 2005, 121; Barth 1933, 121). However, it has disavowed that of *pisteuō* and *pistis*, which might be why it is neglected in commentaries of Rom 4. Only attributing an economic sense to *logizomai* and not appreciating the economic senses of *pisteuō* and *pistis* inscribes a one-way relationship between God and the believer, in which God is the only active and powerful party judging the rightness of the believer. Through these readings, the act of having faith becomes not about trust in the mutual sense but in a sense in which one is expected to presume the provider is so superior and capable that trust is a given and not doubted. Faith of the believer in the metaphysical sense is therefore like a child, who cannot question their parents, being sure they will be fed and cared for.

Through the appreciation of the thus-far neglected economic senses of these other words, the economic reality of *charis*, along with the impact of other words of economic import, such as *diakiō*, *misthos*, *opheiēlma*, reveal other readings that can be made of Rom 4. Away from such a metaphysical

---

metaphorical and becomes a definite concept: for instance, "let's shine some light on this" transfers the literal photonic light to the sphere of understanding. This view ignores the unconscious links between the two spheres of discourse.

standpoint, the faith of the believer is like a farmer who has the right and means to assess the ability of someone to whom he rents his land to pay the instalments on time. Or, it is like a bank deciding if they will give me a loan based on a credit check rather than merely considering me to be trustworthy due to my good reputation.

The metaphysical model of faith is not really faith but reliance or dependence. It leaves the believer as passive recipient, with no role in providing something for God, thus rendering them without any power or responsibility. However, by considering the mutuality of *pistis*, the relationship between God and the believer is two-way. This relationship consists of two related transferals that constitute an exchange that can be seen to elevate the believer to a status of higher determination than has been accorded to them previously in the works of some New Testament scholars (such as Cullmann 1951; Lincoln 1981; Wright 1991; and Dunn 1988a; 1988b; 2006; and 2009). These scholars' work is undermined, unconsciously, by traces of a more empowered and active believer. The relationship between God and the believer, while certainly not one of equality, is one of mutual reciprocity of power and influence. The believer has a degree of agency, power, and an onus to measure and judge God's own performance and trustworthiness as deity and his ability to deliver what he promises.

The triads of (1) *logizomai*, (2) *pisteuō* and *pistis*, and (3) *dikaiosunē*, *dikaiō*, and *dikaiōsis* in Romans 4:3–5 and 4:22–24

It is worth noting the rhetorical distribution of words fitting into three main semantic groups that have been described as key (Schliesser 2007, 335). In the first, forms of *logizomai*; in the second, forms of *pisteuō* and *pistis*; and in the third, forms of *dikaiosunē*, *dikaiō*, and *dikaiōsis*. Words from each of these three groups are used in triads and couplets throughout the text of Rom 4. The triads of these words complement the chiastic structure of this text in that we find this triad near the beginning of the text at 3:28 and near the end at 4:24–5. The beginning and end of this rhetorical structure can be seen as 3:26 and 5:1, respectively, which both contain the couplet of words from the second and third semantic group. Meanwhile, the lone uses of faith in 3:27 and 5:2 also widen this rhetorical structural boundary a little further. This shows how the rhetorical pattern of the triad in this text points us to some significant segments of the argument.

While the economic sense of forms of *logizomai* (as well as *charis*, *misthos*, *opheilēma*, and others) is widely accepted by scholars as exerting metaphorical effect on the text, the effectiveness of the economic senses of words from the group *pisteuō* and *pistis* are generally ignored or not recognized. For instance, Benamin Schliesser (2007, 335) explores the financial sense of *logizomai* but only the literalness of *pisteuō* (337). Some scholars, while likely being aware of the metaphoricity of *logizomai*, do not consider this an important matter to be discussed. However, there is the possibility for the economic sense of *logizomai* utilized in the author's alleged intentional financial metaphor, as well as *charis, misthos, opheilēma*, and *dikaiōsis*, to activate the financial sense of the words *pisteuō* and *pistis*, even if at only an unconscious level. In order to show this, we will first establish the financial metaphoricity of *logizomai*, but then, more importantly, prove how the financial senses of the words from the semantic group containing *pisteuō* and *pistis* could be present and current to the possible hearers of Romans.

Economic aspects of *pistis* cannot be rubbed away and elided, even in Rom 4. They will continue to persist due to the import of intertexts. There has been an assumption that *pistis* is merely a "trust in," forming the plenary keynote on faith of the Christian theology of a variety of denominations (Bultmann 1952, etc.). *Pistis* as "trust in" is the idea that faith in God is not dependent on, or related to, anything else. However, *pistis* in socioeconomic and political contexts is always dependent on other transactions, proofs, assurances, and relationships. Trust is always a risk and so coexists with its opposites—fear, doubt and skepticism (Kasperson 1992). We can be even more radical though, and say that trust and distrust "are better seen as a single bipolar construct, neither separable nor two extremes of a spectrum" (Lewicki, McAllister, and Bies 1998) and that distrust is useful because it ensures people do not become "gullible or complacent and that they defend their interests effectively" (Hardin 2002). *Pistis*, therefore, even in a Christian context, cannot escape the economy of trust. In the ancient world there was a reliance on the reciprocal operation of trust in commercial contexts in which we can "see the New Testament *pistis* as a similarly reciprocated relationship between human beings and God" (Schumacher 2009). We cannot understand *pistis* outside of this insisting, economic context. Economics is at the heart of every part of life, and to consider that it can be risen above is naïve or blinkered idealism.

Ancient Papyri and Deconstruction Theory

It is worth noting that only a tenth of the Oxyrhynchus papyri is literary. The vast majority are documents of a practical and personal administrative nature. Much of the corpus includes bills, accounts, sales, leases, mortgages, wills, legal documents, private letters, inventories, petitions, registers, contracts, and other financial economic items. Horoscopes are perhaps the most sublime elements; however, in this time they performed a much more practical role. The papyri contain a wealth of examples of how words have been used in economic and financial situations and in different power dynamics. The Oxyrhynchus manuscripts date from around the third century BCE to 640 CE; however, the three texts used in our present study are dated 108 BCE, 131 CE, and 114 CE. There are other texts in this corpus that can inform economic metaphor in New Testament texts more widely; however, for the purpose of this study we will focus on three strong examples. The practical essence of the papyri I draw upon informs our study in terms of how these texts from Rom 4 might have been understood at ground-level, because they do not idealize economics and finance. As the most real reference for these terms, they will have been at the forefront of the minds of the hearers of Romans rather than the more eloquent uses in philosophical and classical texts of the elite Greco-Romans.

Greek papyri that are roughly contemporaneous with Romans show uses of *logizomai* in terms of "reckoning" or "putting toward one's account." Most of the time this involves the accounting of money and agricultural produce. An example close to Paul in time is P.Oxy. 12.1434.8 (107–8 CE): "Here the sufficient money and grain are *reckoned*."[3] Examples that are a bit later, but nonetheless still significant, are in P.Flor. 2.123.7 (254 CE): "*reckoning* to him (the wine) at sixteen drachma [currency] per monochre [unit of measurement]" and also in P.Oxy. 7.1056.5 (360 CE): "One artaba [dry measurement of, in this case, chickpeas] *reckoned* in dinarii [value] at one hundred and eighty myriad [unit of measurement]."[4] The first example denotes something owed, and the second and third an accounting of how much something is worth. All three examples share an unresolved payment: what is due to be paid or what should be paid to satisfy the value of something. From a financial-economic perspective, therefore, *logizomai* is the suspending of payment or the intention to fulfil a payment that is as yet unfulfilled or merely at a propositional stage. The words *dikaiosunē*, *dikaiō*, and *dikaiōsis* have financial implications as well. *Dikaiosunē* is positioned as if it were a financial commodity, although this

---

3. *ta argurika kai seitika kath ēkonta (en)thade logizetai.*
4. P.Flor. 2.123.7: *logizomenou autō tou monochōrou drachmōn deka-hex.* P.Oxy. 7.1056.5: *tēs artabēs mias logizomenēs ek dēnariōn muriadōn ekaton ogdoēkonta.*

is due to it being identified as part of a financial-like exchange (this will be made clearer further on).[5]

The noun *pistis* occurs most frequently in Rom 4, and while it does not occur in all of the triadic combinations, its semantically related word *pisteuō* occurs where it is absent. This means that *pistis* can be said to have some significant bearing on occurrences of *pisteuō*. Nonliterary Greco-Roman Egyptian papyri contain uses of *pistis* in a purely financial-economic sense. These examples provide proof that uses of *pistis* in a financial-monetary context were not only current to Rom 4, but also could have exerted influence on the text, even if only at an unconscious level. There are also a few uses in literary texts to hand in LSJ that are in a financial sense too, particularly in terms of people having *pistis* "credit" for so much money available to them.[6] For our purposes, here is a short summary of the papyri.

The words in italics are the ones that are translated from *pistis*: the first papyri text is P.Oxy. 3.486.7 from CE 131, which is a petition from Dionysia to a prefect in which she claims she bought land with cash rather than gained it *on mortgage*. In this document Dionysia restates her case to a prefect in a dispute with someone called Sarapion. The dispute concerns the ownership of land that Dionysia asserted that she had purchased from Sarapion's father. Sarapion, however, claimed that Dionysia only held this land on mortgage, and he laid forth an accusation that Dionysia's mother had been involved in poisoning! The *epistrategos* (overseeing officer) Claudius Quintianus referred this case to the prefect, who demanded that both parties travel to Alexandria for a hearing. While Dionysia obeyed this ruling, Sarapion did not, and after procrastinating somewhat, Dionysia petitioned the prefect, who referred her back to the *epistrategus*, a role now held by a Julius Varianus. Dionysia then wrote to the new *epistrategus* restating her complaint. In this letter she writes how a dispute arose

---

5. A further study, outside of the reach of this present work, should explore the financial-economic import of this group of *dikaiosunē* words. The limits of this current study, however, require that I focus on *logizomai* and, more importantly, *pistis* words, although I do not ignore the significance of the role *dikaiosunē* words play in this conceptual-metaphorical triad.

6. LSJ, s.v. "πίστις." Described under the subheading "commercial sense, credit": *p. tosoutōn chrēmatōn essti tini par tisi*; Demosthenes, *Pro Phorm.* 36.57; *eis pistin didonai* [*titini*]; Demosthenes, *Pro Phorm.* 32.16; *ei hexō elpida pisteōs*; Astrampsychus, *Orac.* 68.P.6H.

between her and Sarapion, son of Mnesitheus, claims that she bought a vineyard and some corn-land from Mnesitheus as long ago as the eleventh year of Hadrianus Caesar, the lord, having paid to his father and a creditor the agreed price. Then she continues with the claim of Sarapion she is refuting: *kai lambousa kathēkonta tēs ōnēs dēmosi [on chrēma] tismon elegeu* **en pistei** *me echein auta*—"and having received the regular official contract of the sale, declared that I held this (the land) **on mortgage**."

Putting aside the possibility that Dionysia is telling the truth and that she did pay for the land, and proposing that she did merely have this land on mortgage, or credit, then some important observations can be made about her relationship with Sarapion and his father. First, Sarapion and his father are providing benefit to Dionysia, and she is in their debt. Second, these men wield a certain amount of power over Dionysia, and she is under obligation to them. If we align Sarapion with Abraham (or the believer) who provides God with *pistis* and Dionysia to God who has received *pistis*, this opens the possibility for thinking about the faith of Abraham and the believer in Rom 4 as being something provided under loan, with not only an obligation placed on God to return it but also placing God in a position of a debtor.

Our second papyri is P.Tebt. 1.14.9 from CE 114. Previously, a *basilicogrammateus* (royal scribe) named Horus has written to a certain *komogrammateus* (administrative official of an area) named Menches about someone called Heras, who is to be tried for murder. This letter is a response to the first letter; in it, Menches discusses this charge as well as the seizure of Heras's property. At the start of his letter, Menches acknowledges that Horus has asked him to give notice to Heras of his arraignment for murder and the need for Heras to appear in three days for trial. Until this trial reaches a conclusion, Menches is to make a list of his property and place it **in bond**, or more precisely, in trust: *anagrapsamenos autou ta huparchonta suntaxai theinai* **en pistei**. Menches continues by stating that he was also to make a report of the measurements, adjoining areas, and values of Heras's property in detail and, presumably having done so, states what land he owns and values it at one talent of copper.

Effectively, with him being under arraignment, Heras's ownership of his land has been suspended due to his trial for murder. The land is transferred from being legally owned to being under the protection of the authorities, in the person of the bureaucrat Menches. It is in a position that is between ownership and being in trust. This twilight zone of ownership is comparable to mortgage or credit, where the mortgagee or creditee enjoy many of the rights of ownership as long as they make payments but lose such rights if they fail to do so.

Furthermore, the owner Heras has has forfeited many of his rights to enjoy and dispense with the land as he sees fit. The authorities have acquired those rights, placing Heras in a position that might be compared to a debtor; he must be able to prove his innocence in order to regain the full rights of ownership just as a debtor or mortgagee must keep up with their agreed payments or settle their balance. Menches, who is the one providing the trust under which Heras's property is placed and thus providing the moral and financial credit to Heras, is in a position of power, whereas Heras, as a recipient of this justice, is subordinated. Equally, Menches is under a state-sanctified duty and moral responsibility to protect Heras's property while he is under arraignment, and Heras has a right and a legal expectation that these duties will be met with diligence and honesty. In this scenario, Menches, who is providing the means for *pistis*, could be aligned with Abraham or the believer, and Heras, as the recipient, could be aligned with God. The result of such a comparison could be to find that Abraham or the believer are able to provide this kind of *pistis* as a form of trust to God.

Our third papyri is P.Reinach 18.10 from BCE 108. This document concerns an arrangement whereby a certain Dionysios and his mother have borrowed land from Admentos-Chestothes and in doing so promised their land *in guarantee*.[7] In this letter to Asklepiades, the cousin of the king and *epistrategos*, Dionysios complains that Admetos has not honored his commitments to him, which has increased his own financial losses. The relevant part of the letter states that Dionysios has signed a contract in front of the *mnemoneion* (a memorial) to borrow 150 *artabes* (measurement based on yield) of corn-land from Admetos in a specified year. It continues: *ou monon d' alla kai* [sic.] ... *ethemēn autoi* **en pistei** *kath' ōn exō psilōn to[p] ōn suggraphēn upothēxēs* [sic.]— "I [Dionysios] have signed over to him **in guarantee** a mortgage contract on the cultivated lands I own." Putting aside for a moment the likely possibility that Dionysios is lying, and even if he was an example of the type of financial arrangement and situations in which this use of *pistis* is possible, we can say that Admetos is providing a type of guaranteed credit to Dionysios. This puts Admetos in a position of

---

7. With thanks to Pam Baker for translating the original French translations of the Greek, which provided me with a comparison for my own translation of the Greek.

moral and financial power over Dionysios, as well as holding responsibility toward him. Having said that, Dionysios could be seen to be purchasing this credit from Admetos as she has something to secure this loan with, giving her some secondary or lesser form of power in the relationship, as well as onus to meet her obligations. Another layer of complexity in this relationship is that Dionysios has in effect transferred a mortgage, another debt, to Admetos, not ownership. This means that both of these actors are in debt and have received credit from another agency, perhaps another, more wealthy, person or institution. If Admetos, the initial giver in this relationship, is aligned to Abraham and the believer through this use of *pistis*, then this places Abraham and the believer in a position of power and duty in terms of their relationship to God. God, aligned with Dionysios as the recipient of *pistis*, could be compared to a debtor and thus under obligation to pay back this faith to Abraham and the believer, but as a client of credit and thus in expectation of financial justice.

These papyri will be used to illuminate our study by showing the semantic plasticity of *pistis* and opening possibilities for interpretation of Rom 4. Deconstruction theory offers us a way of looking at metaphor that justifies our use of the papyri and approach to the reciprocity between God and the believer. The challenge is determining the significance of *pistis* in a financial context as compared to its use in a theological context, which is very different. Priority is given to the diachronic over the synchronic; that is, the focus is on how a word changes over time. (Derrida 1982, 215). As Derrida has shown, the life of a word involves "erasure by rubbing, exhaustion, crumbling away" in its meaning (210). However, it also involves "supplementary product of a capital, the exchange which far from losing the original investment would fructify its initial wealth, would increase its return in the form of revenue, additional interest, linguistic surplus value" (210) and "an indiscreet and overflowing insistence" and an "over-abundant remanence" elsewhere (Derrida 1978b, 8). While the word *pistis* in Romans may be seen by scholars as not having the sense of active assessing another's financial worthiness and economic empowerment, this sense emerges in the unconscious of the hearer and creates implications not in accordance with the possible intended theology. To question the proposed authority of God we must do the same with the authority of the author by looking beyond intended meaning to find a plurality of voices, including that of the hearer.

A reading of Rom 4:3–5 and 4:23–25 that integrates the papyri and approaches we have introduced shows the reciprocity and exchange in the relationship between God and Abraham and God and the believer. In the conventional scholarship we have surveyed, *logizomai* has many aspects of its financial sense retained in its use in Rom 4, such as the notion of counting, checking, measuring, and keeping track. This is because such scholarship aims to emphasize that God is the one in the position of power, measuring and judging the believer's faith. However, it also has certain aspects of its financial sense removed in order that the interpretation protects God's superiority, such as money, the notion of payment, the idea of being owed, and indeed the legal right to receive what you are owed. The idea of God being indebted or obligated to the believer is heretical and politically troublesome. Similarly, *pisteuō* and *pistis* retain the financial aspects of good faith and the giving of the benefit of the doubt to a financial partner you are engaging with. Removed, though, are aspects including assessing the ability to pay, credit check, and wield financial power. The idea that believers can assess God's trustworthiness or that he can owe them is unacceptable from a traditional perspective. However, as we see, the process of transaction between God and Abraham and the believer is not one-way but an exchange, even if it is an uneven one in which God still retains difference.

Division and Delay of the Economic Turn

The Letter to the Romans is riddled with economic language and metaphor that is divisional in the Derridean sense. By divisional, I mean that economy presupposes compartmentalization of resources or information, with a system to control the flow between sections; it also presupposes inequality of distribution, negotiation, power, and exchange between different domains. The economic division extends into the spiritual economy too, including in Romans. For instance, Paul may have a huge wealth of spiritual teachings to offer a missionary outpost, however; this can only be released through donations of money held by benefactors whose wealth is kept apart, in a private reserve, from the wealth of other individuals or the public coffers. Likewise, the collection for the saints may be in coinage or documents that are promissory, and documents that are promissory and require clearance from banking authorities before the materials and services may be released that facilitate missionary activity and allow the individual to subsequently realize the wealth of spiritual teaching. Economy is not driven by equilibrium or equity but by imbalance and the perpetual negotiation of equivalence and value. Economy is also a paradigm for interpretation and spirituality.

Economy is not mere metaphor but transcends the metaphorical and the proper. There is a matrix of economic and financial language within which Rom 4:3–5 and 4:23–25 is situated and thus the import of these texts cannot be written off as allegorical decoration. In 2:5 Paul uses economic metaphor, accusing people of "storing up" wrath—the word *thesaurizeis* means the storing of goods and valuables in a container. Rather than having riches to draw upon, however, the addressees here have wrath from God. In 5:5, on the other hand, God's love is a commodity poured into the container of people's hearts, a positive contrast to the previous metaphor.

These two examples show the physicality of economy and its limitations in that God's love and wrath are not omnipresent but have to be moved from one place to another and sufficiently held and enforced somewhere, according to law, both legal and physical. Anxieties over the missional conflict is expressed in 16:17, where Paul appeals against divisions and obstacles contrary to doctrine; however, this appeal is in vain as such unanimity is impossible in any economic system, whether material or spiritual. As Derrida explains, law (*nomos*) does not only signify the law in general, but also the law of distribution (*nemein*), the law of sharing or partition (*partage*), the law as partition (*moira*), or the law of participation in the protocols of these processes (see Derrida 1992b, 166). Another sort of tautology already implicates the economic with the nomic as such. As soon as there is law, there is partition: as soon as there is -nomy/*nomos*, there is economy. Besides the value of law and home, of distribution and partition, economy implies the idea of exchange, of circulation, of return. Once a system is in place, there is economics, because most systems involve distribution, sectioning off (partition), boundaries, and, most significantly, the perception of cycles or circulation. Therefore, even God's distribution cannot escape economy. So we begin our study from the point of view that the relationship between God and the believer is a system, like a household, and is at once legal and by implication economic. Taking Derrida at face value, this is enough to carry the thesis of the present chapter, but that is not sufficient, so we continue to look at the other subdivisions of this economy of faith.

In terms of God and Abraham, there is a notion in Rom 4:3–5 that righteousness is currently delayed. Furthermore, the important promise from God to Abraham that he "will account righteousness" is an even more delayed form of future-realized righteousness, which the believer, unlike Abraham, is consciously aware of because they are told so by an apostle,

Paul. The promise of righteousness is no different than most economic systems in which physical goods equating to a given value are substituted by currency—itself a promissory note. Trust in this case is not only a process of transferal of trust in the text, but it is the transferal of a commodity of trust (represented by the noun *pistis* in 4:5). Abraham delivers to God a commodity called trust, not unlike the earthly financial setting where someone's trustworthiness is indeed a commodity that can bring greater financial gain than the one who is less trustworthy—loans, for instance, are more beneficial to those who have a good history of paying them back or who own a lot of property or money to secure it. What is most important, though, is that Abraham provides something to God in an active way.

The unfulfilled status of God's accounting righteousness shows he enters a protracted debt with the believer that places him under duty to them. Simultaneous to their power, the lenders Sarapion (P.Oxy. 3.486) and Admetos (P.Rein. 18) could be seen as having a duty to care for their borrowers to fulfil their obligation to provide credit and the financial flexibility that comes with it. The official Menches in P.Tebt 1.14 has a state sanctified duty to protect Heras's land, even though he exerts power over the latter's affairs in the meantime. Likewise, Abraham and the believer's expectations of God to return, along with God's commitment to return in 4:3 and the incomplete nature of Abraham's own provision, which is not given all at once but over a period of time, places an onus and duty of care on Abraham and the believer toward God. The delay and deferral between God and the believer and their state of owing each other creates a tension in the spiritual and material economy in which they intersect and divide.

As God is accounting righteousness to Abraham in 4:3, it seems instead that God is not directly giving Abraham righteousness at all but instead suspending it in an account. Righteousness is itself a nonpresent thing, because it, like a financial status, may be used like a physical commodity, but it is not physically concrete and does not have the perceived stability of an asset. The status of righteousness is a controversial site of debate. Scholars divide fairly evenly on the matter as to whether any believer has been accorded righteousness immediately through faith or whether this righteousness is developing and only accorded properly in a final judgement. There is also debate on the status of righteousness of Abraham and the believer and whether it is current or future—as has been discussed already with reference to Bultmann and others.

However, others claim righteousness is potential and future, and some say Abraham and the believer exist in a combination of both statuses.

Commenting on verse 4:24, Leon Morris (1988, 214) remarks that *mellei* ("about to") here "could refer to the future converts on the basis of justification as a present reality in 4:25 and 5:1, or it could refer to the final consummation of salvation on Judgement Day." However, the economic pattern we are tracing shows a lack of fulfilment in the exchange cycle, just like the promissory statement on a bank note assures that somewhere there is something of the value of, say, £10. God therefore accounts righteousness to Abraham; that is, he banks it in a trust account. Likewise, the borrowers in the papyri, who cannot pay their lenders upfront, can only promise full payment by adhering to an agreement with installments or interest. The lenders therefore do not receive the full benefits of their lending straight-away but piecemeal. In similar fashion, Abraham and the believer are not yet righteous and do not yet have righteousness, but they have some of the benefits and qualities of having and being righteous. In 4:11 we can locate the currency, or promissory note, used by God—the sign of circumcision while Abraham was still uncircumcised; although he did not have physical circumcision, he had this status accounted to him.

As well as a metaphorical association with currency, circumcision is also described as a "seal." In the ancient world, letters, including ones involving finance, might have their senders' identity mark stamped in a wax seal as authentication. A seal would only have value if the sender was trustworthy, so if a letter involved a business deal or promised payment, the receiver could judge whether the sender could honor that financial resolution. Similarly, coins in Paul's time had the face of the emperor on one side to provide authority and authenticity since they were not bullion and often debased, meaning they were worth less than their ascribed value. As such, use of currency involves trust in the economy of the state minting them.

There is a sense of delay and deferral with currency and seals, in that a promise to fulfil is linked to the reputation and trustworthiness of the user or their superiors. With the sign and seal metaphor in Romans in mind, the position of the believer in relationship to God is empowered through this delay and deferral. Abraham and the believer are promised righteousness by God and receive a subsidiary—the sign and seal of circumcision. God bargains too, not insisting that the believer physically has circumcision performed as a mark of their trust in him. God's concession here contrasts to the right of the believer to assess his trustworthiness. P.Oxy. 3.486 and P.Rein. 18 describe lenders making an active assessment of a borrower's ability to meet payments. The lenders in the papyri have not yet received all of the payments, meaning they hold a degree of power and authority over the borrowers, who in turn are in their debt. By comparison, the believer and Abraham have legitimate expectations of God, who owes them righteousness. The believer is the one who demands the authentication of the delayed benefit that God will provide to them and is equivalent to a banker who calls in a loan.

Pistis as Trust Rather Than Belief

Most crucial to the argument of this chapter of this book is its position on the economic sense of *pistis* with *pisteuein* in the syntax of 4:3–5 and 4:23–25. Our near-contemporary papyri texts use the same word—*pistis*—that we find in our Romans texts. In P.Oxy. 3.486.7, *pistis* is used in the sense of a *mortgage*, much akin to the meaning it holds today in terms of bank loans used to purchase homes, land, and even yachts. P.Tebt. 1.14.9 uses *pistis* to refer to property being kept in trust, which is ironic considering that we use this English word financially to mean safe accounts in which money is stored for some benevolent purpose. P.Rein. 18.10 uses *pistis* to mean something offered in guarantee, which in today's terms means an asset or proof of money of sufficient value to cover the cost of any payments not met due to unforeseen circumstances. In all these three ways that *pistis* is used in the papyri, there is one common aspect: the person giving *pistis* is having trust in the ability for someone to honor both financial and related ethical obligations. These papyri intertexts are of importance because they show that financial meaning could not be far from the minds of the hearers of Romans.

Philo's paraphrasing of Gen 15:6 in *De Abrahamo* appears to draw upon the economic sense of *pistis* as a notion of repayment and being obliged. Philo describes how "God marvelling at Abraham's faith [*pistis*] in Him repaid him ... with faithfulness by confirming ... the gifts which He had promised" (46.273; trans. Keck 2005, 119). Philo's reading draws out a vision of the relationship between God and Abraham as one of exchange rather than of one-way transferal, as God is depicted by Philo as repaying Abraham. Such reciprocity also goes for the believer in 4:23–25. This provision of trust from Abraham to God also positions the former as a benefit giver and the latter as an obligated recipient, thus empowering Abraham in the relationship. Just as the providers of mortgage, trust, and credit in the papyri set the recipients in debt and empower the providers to be able to expect obligations to be met by the recipients, Abraham's provision of trust to God provides God with the recognition and acknowledgement he presumably requires, while at the same time obliging God to make return and empowering Abraham to be able to expect such.

In 4:16, it is asserted that the promise to Abraham depended on faith but also rested on grace/gift. There is a tension here because faith—*pistis*—can be very financial! Many scholars omit a discussion of the financial-economic sense of *pistis* (see Williams 1999; Witherington and Hyatt 2004; Schliesser 2007). As with *logizomai*, some take pains to avoid an impression of reciprocity through the economic imagery, asserting God's sovereignty (Osborne 2004, 384; Achtemeier 1985, 78; Keck 2005, 121; Ziesler 1989, 124). These approaches see our text as retaining limited financial aspects of *pisteuein* and *pistis*, such as that of good faith and giving the benefit of the doubt to a borrower and emphasizing the sense of obligation by situating the believer as the obligated party.

The retained senses are compounded into a form of blind faith, which Abraham and the believer are seen as being obliged to have in God due to the latter's superiority. Elided are some of the financial aspects of *pisteuein* through *pistis*, such as the provision of credit, loans, and mortgages and the wielding of financial power and duty that could represent the provision of trust by Abraham in God and the associated power, onus, and responsibilities that come with it, as well as the obligation that God is put under by receiving this trust. The one-way transferal that is presupposed can be aligned with the grace, or gift, represented by *charis*—physical gift or generosity—which is contrasted to the result of works and is represented by labor wage (*misthos*) and things owed (*opheilēma*) in 4:4. In this relationship, the believer and Abraham can do nothing to affect the quality, timing, or quantity of this gift, and neither can they do anything significant to return or reciprocate such a gift. The only thing they can do is to express *pistis* as a form of inadequate link between himself and God and as a reflexive recognition of God's superiority. The importance of *pistis* is picked up on at various points throughout our analysis.

Trust, or provision of trust, is also active, just as the actors providing trust in the form of mortgage, financial protection, and credit in the papyri show. In P.Oxy. 3.486.7, Sarapion has provided credit, or *pistis*, to Dionysia through a mortgage. With P.Tebt. 1.14.9, Menches is looking after the property of Heras (who is being tried for murder) and thus is keeping it in trust. In P.Rein. 18.10, Admentos-Chestothes has provided trust to Dionysios and his mother who borrowed land from Admentos-Chestothes, promising their land in guarantee. P.Oxy. 486 and P.Rein. 18 both imply an active assessment by the lender of the borrower's ability to meet payments, and P.Tebt. 114 recounts an active assessing process.

What unites all three papyri testimonies is the fact that none of the uses of *pistis* convey any notion of blind faith, belief, or trusting without making assessment and calculation. In the petition of P.Oxy. 3.486, we find a precedent in terms of a person being able to assess, actively, the reliability of another through the concept of *pistis*.

Assuming it is possible that Dionysia was mortgaged the land, some important observations can be made about her relationship with Sarapion and his father. First, Sarapion and his father are providing benefit to Dionysia, and she is in their debt. Second, these men wield a certain amount of material and legal power over Dionysia, and she is under obligation to them. If we align Sarapion with Abraham, or the believer, who provide God with *pistis*, and Dionysia to God, who has received it, we open the possibility for thinking about the faith of Abraham and the believer in Rom 4 as being something provided under loan, with not only an obligation placed on God to return but also placing God in a position of a debtor. The believer in this instance thus becomes an active participant in a relationship in which they assess and come to trust God, like those offering financial trust or credit in these papyri do to those borrowing.

The Agency of Economy in Romans

As we shall see, *pistis* in its economic sense allows us to question the traditional sense of the relationship between God and the believer being a one-way transferal—as is the consensus of scholarship. The traditional argument goes like this: God accounts potential righteousness to Abraham—a transferal is consistent with grace, as represented by *charis* in 4:4. We also have a kind of self-reflective loop rather than a transferal: Abraham not transferring faith to God but, by having blind faith in God, responding to God's effect by being changed from unfaithful to faithful. This trust may or may not be in response to God's promises made to Abraham, but even so it is seen as blind, passive, and submissive. It is not a commodity that benefits God, like righteousness, and instead is only beneficial to the believer and Abraham. God's accounting of righteousness is, however, seen as a commodity that benefits the recipient, as well as being a status, and the potential and results of God's judgement and assessment of them.

The reading of one-way benefit, however, relies on the acceptance and control over the metaphoricity of *logizomai* and the neglect and ignorance of the economic potential of *pisteuo* and the other words with economic senses. Once the economic senses of the other words are appreciated through a deconstruction approach to *usure*, we can produce a different model of the relationship between God and Abraham. Similarly, in verse 4:23 the Septuagint phrase from Gen 16:6 "it was accounted to him" is cited and then in 4:24a the term "accounted" is used again in the context of widening the position of Abraham to potentially include all believers, prefiguring the past (Jewett 2007, 340; Keck 2005, 130). The believer's faith here is in the death and resurrection of Christ rather than the compendium of promises God made to Abraham. Likewise, the picture is of a relationship between God and the believer, which is linear, simple, and one-way: of God is able to account righteousness to the believer based on their faith in Christ's death and resurrection.

While the believer is not as obliquely stated as believing or trusting God as in 4:3, he or she is described as believing or trusting in God through a long noun phrase: *epi ton egeiranta Iēsoun ton kurion ēhmōn ek nekrōn*. This phrase seems to define the identity of God around the act of raising Christ, as if to intensify the indebtedness of the believer to God. Thus, God is providing the promise of future righteousness *and* having already provided the resurrection of Christ from the dead. Conversely, the believer is not seen to be able to provide return of equivalence of any kind for this. God is thus the only active party, the only provider and the only one giving benefit, and the believer, like Abraham, is merely a passive recipient of overwhelming and formidable grace in the form of the option to gain righteousness through belief in Christ's death and resurrection. However, this passivity unravels when we analyze the semantics of *pistis* and other aspects of the economic metaphoricity of Rom 4 in the context of other economic imagery in Romans as a whole.

Our papyri texts affirm reciprocity through their use of *pistis*. In Rom 4, the believer is the one doing the trusting, or *pistis*. Conventional scholarship tends to position the believer as a passive recipient in a relationship framed by economic metaphor; however, our papyri texts are at odds with this. If Sarapion has loaned land to Dionysia in P.Oxy 3.486, then he has trusted her and assessed her ability to return. Heras, in P.Tebt. 1.14, trusts Menches to look after his property legally and financially. Admentos-Chestothes has loaned land to Dionysios and his mother in P.Rein. 18 and has based his assessment on their ability to promise their land *in guarantee*. If the believer is aligned with the lender and God with the borrower in all these three cases, then we find that *pistis* in Rom 4 cannot assure a one-way transferal and must involve reciprocity and mutuality.

Superiority can be dependent on who initiates an interaction or exchange within a patriarchal relationship. Moreover, initiation sustains the view that there is an all-powerful prime mover in any relationship in which onus and power is delegated from the top downward. To this end, this issue is linked to the economics of the relationship between God and the believer, with the former positioned as the ultimate initiator. Traditionally, a monarch would reserve the prerogative to speak first at court, and subjects would respond to commandments and questions, never requesting, only responding and beseeching. In 4:3–5 and 4:23–25, Abraham and the believer trust God and could be seen to initiate the transferal. This is very important as it positions them as the drivers of the relationship, much in the same way as the papyri discussed above, in which the actors providing financial *pistis* are also the ones who initiate transferal in the exchange process.

Of course, in any financial interaction an actor is always already subject to someone or something prior, and so it is fair to say neither God nor the believer is the instigator and both are responders. God does not enjoy the status as an original instigator of the relationship between him and the believer. He is not the only one with the prerogative and power. Instead his activity is one part of an ongoing chain of exchanges. We see this in P.Rein. 18, where Admetos is providing a type of guaranteed credit to Dionysios. Admetos is therefore in a position of power in his relationship with Dionysios. But as we have established, Dionysios is buying this credit from Admetos, having something to secure this loan with, and she becomes imbued with a level of agency in the process.

So let's explain how this relates to our text. In the first instance, believers trust (*pisteuousin*) in God that he has raised Jesus Christ from the dead, carrying the sense that the believer has provided God with trust in an active process. The believer responds to God in that they are basing their trust on something prior that God has done for them—raising Christ. However, if the raising of Christ is a security or proof of worthiness rather than a prior gift or provision, much like the lands (or mortgage on lands) used as security in P.Rein. 18, then the believer could also be seen as initiating the relationship and God could be seen as the responder.

In the second instance, it is stated that God will account righteousness (*logizesthai*) to the believer who believes that God raised Jesus Christ from the dead, just as he did Abraham for believing in his promises. As we have discussed, the financial aspects of *elogisthe* are accepted as established by most scholars, yet due to the financial aspects that increase in *logizomai* along with the active and empowering financial senses of *pistis*, our interpretation cannot lead us to one in which God is transferring and the believer is only receiving. If the believer is initiating the giving of benefit, then God must be responding by accounting righteousness. The status of righteousness is not only a product of a process of according righteousness, but it is also in its financial setting arguably a commodity. Thus, we could say in the case of Rom 4 that God is transferring to Abraham or the believer this financial commodity of righteousness. Anything God does is part of a chain of exchanges, and he initiates nothing. Why does God need to raise Christ for the trespasses of humankind unless there is something prior that he needs to rectify and his own interests are dependent on such balance? Has humankind accrued a debt for God that subjects him to something else, such as the cosmos or the chaos of material reality? If God requires faith—*pistis*—from the believer, does this not place him in their debt too?

Financial Empowerment of Owing and Being Owed

Debt is often seen as being oppressive and binding, and for most cases it is in practice. However, there is another aspect to it that is liberating, for the reason that it implies that when something is paid back, then the financial dynamic is leveled somewhat (even if not equalized). The creditor is not necessarily just the person lending money either. It could be argued that an employee who has worked a day and not yet been paid is a creditor and their employer a debtor, thus retaining some power over an actor who is traditionally thought of as being superior. So, the less powerful can find themselves exerting power over superiors through the process of debt.

For many scholars, the implication that God is in debt to anyone or anything is so horrendous that it leads to a mixing of confessional and scholarly beliefs, where the latter are undermined and the former become oppressive. Consensus exists that *logizomai* is used metaphorically in Rom 4, and scholars identify the financial-economic connections of the word (Witherington and Hyatt 2004, Keck 2005, and others). Dramatically, David Williams (1999, 183–84) explains Abraham's faith in Rom 4:3–5 as "entered on the credit side of God's ledger in lieu of another entry, his righteousness" and exclaims "all God asks of us is that we trust God's accounting!" However, how this might position God as in debt to a trusting believer is not explored. For Karl Barth (1933, 121), the use of this word affects an "analogy" that evokes a ledger on which "life entries are transferred by God from His account to man's account," although he makes pains to show that men attempting to carry out reckoning is a form of fraud and an impossibility. Some limit the damage of comparisons by distinguishing accounting from the sovereignty of God, such as Schliesser (2007, 336; invoking Luther; see also Heidland 1942, 293–95). Some do not directly acknowledge the metaphoricity of *logizomai* (Stuhlmacher 1994; Ziesler 1989; Osborne 2004; and Leenhardt, 1961). While many scholars retain certain financial aspects of the word *logizomai* in their interpretations of Rom 4, others are elided. One aspect retained is that of keeping track, taking stock, or counting. The aspects that are lost are the specificity of money, the notion of payment, the idea of being owed, and indeed the legal right to receive what you are owed. Furthermore, what is elided is any notion of reciprocity.

Since being in debt, whether as the more or less empowered actor, places one in subjection to the creditor, it becomes important to avoid being in debt, at least in a long-term or problematic sense. So, if I have a huge loan whose installments cannot be covered by my monthly wage, then I am hardly empowered. However, if I have a credit card debt that I am able to manage and that, through correct use, brings me benefits—such as being able to purchase items for my business that help me make more money—then I am empowered. Being in functional debt means you are not beholden to anyone; as long as you honor the debt, nothing else is expected of you.

However, by contrast, being the beneficiary of gift giving is unquantified and dangerously open. There is no specificity about what you need to do to return the generosity, and you could find yourself perpetually beholden because of this. This practical reality is betrayed in 13:6–7—quite in contrast to the spirit of 4:3–5 and 4:23–25. Here it is stated: "for the authorities are ministers of God.… Pay to all what is owed to them: taxes to whom taxes are owed, revenue to whom revenue is owed, respect to whom respect is owed, honor to whom honor is owed."

In our papyri, it can be argued that debt belongs to both parties, to the debtor and the creditor, who both have suspended and unfulfilled obligations to each other. In the cases of P.Oxy. 3.486 and P.Rein. 18, the borrowers Dionysia and Dionysios must continue paying installments and the lenders Admentos-Chestothes must continue allowing them to use the land or property. In the case of P.Tebt. 1.14, the trustee Menches must continue to safeguard the financial and legal affairs of Heras's property and Heras, as the trusting party, must consent to him to do so as per the law. But debt in these three cases is empowering because it does not presuppose the eternal deferral of resolution that holds someone under obligation, as gift does. Dionysia and Dionysios retain the right and ability to resolve their loans of land, and Menches will eventually, if Heras is absolved, transfer the properties in trust back to him. Once resolution occurs, there is the perception of the end of obligation between both sets of parties.

In Rom 13:6–7, Paul aims to show believers in Christ how to live in a world that is not consistent with their values. Rather than condemning that world, Paul insists that taxes—the mechanism of Roman imperial subjugation—are owed and thus must be paid. This is not because Paul sympathizes or consents to such oppression, however. Instead, the reason is that being *in debt and paying it* is liberating and removes you from indeterminate obligation to your creditor. This principle transcends the material sphere through to the ethical and spiritual too, as respect and honor are reasoned to be paid—to none other than those pagan powers who minister for God. As these non-Jewish powers are ordained, they are aligned with God, so it jars somewhat with the idea in Rom 4:3–5 that believers are recipients of grace that never needs to be paid back but yet still, according to some scholarship, paradoxically demands unquestioning faith. The contrast between the demand for a liberating compliance with the financial-spiritual pagan world, which is God-ordained, and the grace that never needs to be repaid, which is from God through Jesus, is paradoxical. Yet it shows that there is a difference between the principles of functioning in the material world and its necessary exchanges, on the one hand, and the profound grace of God, on the other. The function of *pistis* in the material world is to prevent a conflation between debt and generosity in a power structure that determines theological authority and to affirm a situation in which the enforcement of taxes and dues is more liberating than continued owing or unresolved generosity. To this effect, to reach the spiritual heights of receiving God's grace, the believer must embrace the materialism of the world.

In Rom 4, wage and debt are helpfully conflated, because wage is an indebtedness of an employer to an employee, especially from a Marxist perspective. As we have established, just as a worker is subject to their employer, an employer is subject, albeit to a lesser degree, to their worker in that they are required to pay them for their labor.[8] Wage is not a gift because it is not a surplus or luxury or an excess (see Agamben 2005). In Rom 3:24, the claim is made that God makes people righteous through the gift of the redemption of Christ Jesus, and, in Rom 8:23, redemption of the bodies of the believer is pledged. Redemption as a gift is oxymoronic, with the former meaning a payment and the latter supposedly altruistic. Gift contrasts to Rom 4:24 in which those who believe will have accounted to them righteousness if they trust in God raising Christ from the dead—this gift becomes economic.

Vengeance becomes a form of payment too in Rom 12:19, and though this is expressed as a metaphor, it could be economic justice, especially in terms of how wrongs can be settled through legal or extrajudicial compensation. There is anxiety expressed toward people gaining financial retribution here, and such onus is seen to be God's alone: "vengeance is mine, I will repay, says the Lord." Conversely, the believer is tasked with being altruistic in Rom 12:20, in that they should feed and satiate enemies without expectation of return, which juxtaposes with God's forced altruism in 4:3–5 and 4:23–25. In these texts, God is the ultimate giver, and the believer cannot be economically expectant of him. Of course, the economic power of purchasing (paying for a service) and being owed stays with God in that picture. However, this view contradicts with the direction of Rom 4 and places God in the vulnerable position of needing to repay something. More importantly, it is in paradox with God as the only source of pure altruism through justification, a status that is undermined by *pistis*, because those who offer this facility in our papyri texts are those who would expect payment: Sarapion from Dionysia for his mortgage in P.Oxy 3.486, Heras in P.Tebt. 1.14 for his property to be paid back by Menches if he is found innocent, and Admentos-Chestothes in P.Rein. 18 to be paid in land from Dionysios and his mother should they default on their borrowing of land. Consequently, it could be argued that believers, by offering *pistis* to God, are expecting some kind of payment.

A major theological repercussion of this is the pervading insistence of the economic framed by Paul at the beginning and end of his letter. In Rom 1:11, Paul longs to impart "some spiritual gift" to the Roman churches. The same word (*charis*) is used here, which undermines the purity of God's

---

8. Unless the worker is enslaved, which we must factor in to discussion of the ancient world.

altruism further on when Paul, as a slave of Christ, then states his hope he and the Romans can be "mutually encouraged" by each other's faith in Rom 1:12, thus destroying any notion of his spiritual gift along the example of Christ and God.

Spiritual gift is further undermined by Paul's intention to "reap some fruit" among the Romans, showing a link, even if indirect and suspended, between what he intends to give them and what he hopes to attain from them (even if communal). Paul's wish for fruit may be spiritual in parts but has a physical dimension in the light of Rom 15:22–29, showing how the spiritual and material are intertwined in a way that is unacknowledged by many scholars. Paul shames the Roman believers by telling them that those in Macedonia and Achaia have given to the poor believers (saints) in Jerusalem (Rom 15:26–27) and then contradicts this claim of altruism by identifying it as something owed (Rom 15:27). Such a claim is reasoned in Rom 15:27b by the assertion that, since gentiles have shared in the Jerusalem saints' spiritual blessings, they ought to provide them material ones in return. This assertion undermines the metaphorical binary contrast generated in Rom 4 in which wages and owing are aligned with the wrong idea about the relationship between God and the believer, on the one hand, and altruistic giving is aligned with the grace of God through Christ, on the other. Spiritual and material, economics and gift, are therefore all entwined to an indistinguishable degree.

Another aspect of debt that is important is God's potential to be in debt to and thus affected by something else—another actor or entity. Other sections of Romans use metaphors that have financial and economic implications that inform our texts of focus in Rom 4. To start with, we have Rom 11:4. This is the only text in the New Testament that directly refers to Baal. Reference to this Ugaritic god might seem irrelevant, but Julia Kristeva's (1980, 15) work explains the transportive effects of intertextuality, where signs and their systems are relocated between texts with new annunciations. Some have shown that Ugaritic god language, including the names Baal and El, might be adapted by those talking about the god of Abraham, and, indeed, Yahweh has a prior life as a polytheistic god (see Aaron 2001; Cross 1973).

At one point in the cycle, Baal is a dying god who is consumed by Mot in an act of theophagy, with Mot reported as saying "I approached Mightiest Baal / I took him like a lamb in my mouth / Crushed him like a kid in the chasm of my throat" (*CTU* 1.6, ii.19–23). Baal realizes the might of Mot and his allies, including Lotan and Sapas, and so he acknowledges his subordination to Mot. Baal then surrenders to his fate and rains down on earth and thus dies. In the aftermath of his death, Anat, Baal's sister and consort, laments him alongside El, his father. In rage, Anat attacks Mot, and the king Athtar the Terrible is appointed as protector of Baal's domain. Anat viciously cuts open Mot to free Baal, and then Mot is dispatched to the underworld. Baal is alive again; then he rains down and is victorious in battling Athtar to remove him from position. Mot reappears to challenge Baal, deciding to dispose of him. While Mot is excessively stronger than Baal, he cannot win because Baal must be able to function and descend as rain. So, Sapas finally intervenes in an effort to end the conflict and shows Mot, no more than Baal, can check or alter the course of nature. Sapas descends to the underworld for winter and takes Mot with her. Mot is brought up again every autumn as the corn, ready for sowing. As Mot is present in the seed, he is also able to be present in the upper world too, and his role in fertility is thus preserved. The battle has strengthened Mot considerably and made the seeds very fertile and virile. Baal now dominates; however, his triumph has resulted in the rise and strengthening of Mot.

This cycle is evoked in the catena in Rom 3:11–18, particularly 13 and 14: "their throat is an open grave; they use their tongues to deceive. The venom of asps is under their lips. Their mouth is full of curses and bitterness." Some link these verses to Mot, who had a "voracious appetite" (see Lewis 2002, 184). This cycle of consumption and provision reveals both ecological and economical pragmatism, shows gods as vulnerable and subject to nature, and reveals the need for balance, which sheds light on our texts of focus in Rom 4. In Rom 4:24 and 25, God, like Baal, is part of this material ecology-economy because he raises Jesus from the dead for human justification after he was delivered up for humankind's trespasses. This raising resonates strongly with the Baal cycle, albeit inversely, with God participating in a cycle in which Jesus, like Baal, is consumed into the depths of death and then raised up again, like Mot as a crop—alluding to the intersection between ecology and economy: agriculture.

In any relationship, the dominant actor is always subject to another preceding one. In our papyri texts, Sarapion would only be able to lend land to Dionysia on mortgage if wealthier and more powerful actors guarantee this. Admentos-Chestothes would only be able to make his arrangement with Dionysios and his mother if there is a financially motivated legal system to enforce this—he has no power on his own terms as a monarch would. Heras would only be able to entrust Menches if there is a precedent and a system of enforcement to ensure Menches does not exploit his wealth. So, the notion of delivery for trespass also reveals an economy to which even God must conform. God, like Baal, Sarapion, Admentos-Chestothes, or Heras, is thus subject to something else around him. Even if scholars reject a God in debt to humanity, here is a God who must pay a debt to something to even things out. This something owed need not be another god or entity but physics itself—the forces of a nature that must by definition precede God to be fathomable. If God is subject to *a priori* reality then he is not the original interlocutor in the relationship between him and the believer. Through this context the relationship between God and the believer becomes much more reciprocal through the trust aspect of pistis.

Questioning Authority and the Onus of the Believer

Implicit in the economic metaphors in Rom 4 is the notion that only God has the right to question, critique, or judge. In Rom 9:16–18, the story of Pharaoh and Moses is referenced, and God's mercy is favorably contrasted to human will. The hardening of Pharaoh's heart is actually his refusal to accept that he should not question the authority of God. The relationship between God and Pharaoh, rather than one that is pathological, stands instead as an albeit dysfunctional model of the push and pull between God and the believer, with Pharaoh representing the latter's onus and rights. With power being vested in economics, the perceived power in a financial relationship can maintain authority, and this has been transferred by scholarship into the spiritual authority of God. Authority, from this perspective, is located only with God and must retain the confessional stance that is so important.

The argument made by Paul in Romans does not overtly locate authority with the believer; however, such a view does emerge when we situate it within the context of the intertextual evidence from the papyri. The right of the believer to question authority in Romans can be read alongside the situation in P.Tebt. 1.14. This papyrus shows that while one party in a relationship may appear all-powerful, on closer inspection, it is not this simple. Heras's ownership of his land has, due to his trial, been transferred to Menches. Heras must be able to prove his innocence in order to regain the full rights of ownership just as a debtor or mortgagee must keep up with their agreed payments or settle their balance. Menches is in a position of power, whereas Heras, as a recipient of this justice, is subordinated. For conventional scholarship, this document might affirm the unique power and authority of God.

However, the power and authority of Heras is overlooked. Menches has not acquired Heras's property through an arbitrary intervention of might or through the prerogative of a monarch. Menches is as subjugated to the law as Heras is. The fact that Heras may have committed an offence and is more restricted than Menches does not necessarily mean he has less rights in principle. Menches has a responsibility to protect Heras's property while he is under arraignment, and Heras has the right to expect that these duties are met. Heras, presumably, would have recourse to legal action or tribunal if his property is disposed of or managed improperly. Menches, despite being the agent of state power, is also a servant of Heras, however troubled the latter may be. Just as Heras relies on Menches to care for his property legally, the believer relies on God to be just. The resulting implications are that the believer has expectations of God, just as God does of the believer. God's justice and might is not arbitrary and at whim, like a monarch's but according to a due process in which the believer is a stakeholder, not a subject. The believer retains the right to question, appeal, and challenge the authority exerted on them, even if their own moral and legal standing, like Heras's, is under scrutiny.

Trust, in the context of this debt, involves the believers and Abraham making a judgement of God's reliability as a divinity. Just as Sarapion and his father will have made a judgement about Dionysia's financial and moral standing before providing her this mortgage, Abraham's trust is not blind faith because the active aspect of the financial sense of *pisteuō* and *pistis* in 4:3, 4:5, and other parts of Rom 4 allow for an activity on Abraham's part that is akin to assessing and judging someone's reliability. Abraham gained assurances from God that he would be a leader of many nations despite the barrenness of Sarah's womb and the fact he was about one-hundred years old (Rom 4:16–19) and his faith "grew strong." Similarly, neither does the believer have mere blind-faith, because the active aspect of the financial sense of *pisteuō* in Rom 4:24 and throughout Rom 4, as well as *pistis* (which appears most frequently in Rom 4), allows for an activity on the believer's part that is akin to assessing and judging someone's reliability. The evidence consists of the promises God makes, which Abraham is consciously aware of as God told him. The believer delivers to God a commodity, *trust*, based on evidence of something done by God.

In our financial lives, we will have to show, against odds, that we can raise money and prove our wealth and reliability to honor repayment. This could be through paying a lump sum or a deposit, putting something up as a security, or having something valued. If something goes wrong, we must show we can cover the loss or respect our duty to the debt in the future. We are saying to our lender, or trustee, that if something goes wrong, we have the means to cover the financial damage or will endeavor to do so. While a financial actor can show evidence of wealth to prove they have sufficient means, by raising funds, God can raise the dead as a form of proof. God says, "I have the means to overcome death by lifting my son out of Sheol, so I will do it, and you owe me one." In Rom 4:23–25, it may be the case that God's having raised Jesus Christ from the dead (*egeiranta Iēsoun ton kurion ēhmōn ek nekrōn*) places the believer in his debt prior to the believer having faith or God accounting righteousness. Yet surely this raising also shows God to be under obligation to something prior if this gesture is needed. We see that any financial or economic exchange is simply one among many others prior—with any actor in a relationship possibly subject to the implications of a prior exchange, even God himself, albeit to a lesser degree than the believer.

Importantly, power is not held only by one party initiating a transaction. We are all subjects to a prior power. Many readings of Romans assume the complete powerfulness of God at contrast with the total passivity of the believer. This is enforced by readings of the potter and clay metaphor in Rom 9:20–21, which reveals priority of the potter over his material, the clay, in order to affect the same in terms of God and the believer. However, further analysis shows this metaphor does not work as simply as some think. A potter is an artisan craft-worker—not an elite person—who would have been subject to someone else—a patron, customer, or even boss. The pots he makes are not determined only by his will but that of other, more powerful people. The allegory of a potter thus places God as part of a chain of power relations of which he does not initiate or hold unique and singular powerfulness. Furthermore, the clay is not entirely passive to the will of the potter either. Clay has a set of properties that limits the action of the potter, such as its type, consistency, quality, resistance, and time-limited malleability. The potter therefore responds to the clay as the clay does to the potter, even if not equally. There is an eventual firmness and brittleness to clay, in which its form dries, and it cannot be further manipulated. Yet equally, the potter also has some power in relation to his clients and social superiors—his terms of service, his right to be paid, and his generic legal rights. Similarly, the believer, as the created, is not an eternally passive medium of the will of God but has a resistance through its own agency. At the same time, the potter relies on the clay practically and economically—it is a resource and an asset. The clay is from the earth, and its qualities are determined by the processes of nature that the human potter is working against through his artisanry. Perhaps the potter is oblivious that eventually the pot he makes will decay and return to the earth to fulfil its part in a geological system, with his attempts to create something permanent being futile in the end.

The potter and clay metaphor to represent God and his people could be seen to work, against the movement of posthumanist analysis, in that there is a difference between the agency of the potter, a human with intentions to make something, and the clay, which is a subject whose level of consciousness cannot be determined. However, humans are not like clay; they show signs of awareness and conscious intention. This metaphor may be problematic for those upholding a one-way relationship between God and the believer because they expect the believer to be aware of the transferal from God to them. Some may also think that the financial metaphor in Rom 4 upholds such an exchange relationship in the same way as the potter and the clay, but it does not, and posthumanist theory can show us why. Actor Network Theory (ANT) in the work of Bruno Latour (see particularly 2005) posits that agency can be attributed to nonhuman entities and that human actors' own agency is not necessarily superior.

For ANT proponents, agency is not equivalent to intention; however, I wonder if such distinction can always be made. For instance, there are actions I take every day that I do not think about overtly, such as moving my eyes or walking; yet, they contribute toward an overall aim and intention. Similarly, one could argue that a leaf has no less intention than a human unless they credit humans with constant conscious awareness, which they do not have. Key to my argument here is the ANT notion that no item or entity, whether human or nonhuman, is above the system or network in which it exists. Where ANT becomes most interesting is when we move away from this more visual potter and clay allegory into the more abstract and ambiguous financial metaphor. These two images may appear equivalent, but ANT shows that the relationship between the one giving trust and the one who is trusted is not quite as binary as it seems, especially when, as in Rom 4, the latter is also accounting. It is not as easy to place the actors in a grammar of active and passive. The potter and clay allegory impacts on Rom 4:3–5 and 23–25 in that the believer is not economically pathetic to God but is empowered through *pistis*, and this is illustrated by the use of *pistis* in our papyri texts. However, we can go beyond the simplicity of the grammar of the potter and clay allegory to show that there is a system—call it economy—in which neither the believer nor God are superior; both are at constant tension.

Let us examine our papyri to demonstrate this reciprocity and tension of influence. In P.Rein. 18, Dionysios has in effect transferred a mortgage, another debt, to Admetos, not ownership. This means that both of these actors are in debt and have received credit from another agency, perhaps another, wealthier person or institution. If Admetos is aligned to Abraham and the believer through this use of *pistis*, then this places Abraham and the believer in a position of power and duty in terms of their relationship to God. God, aligned with Dionysios, as the recipient of *pistis*, could be compared to a debtor and thus under obligation to pay back this faith to Abraham and the believer, yet also as a client of credit and thus in expectation of financial justice. Just as the actors in P.Rein. 18 are both, no matter who is more active and in power in their relationship, subject to a prior creditor as the latter has been passed the mortgage from the former, it could be argued that God is subject to the demands of death. God's raising of Christ from the dead is marked more acutely by God's subjection to the realities of nature than to his superiority to the believer. For this act of raising Christ to be God's strength, there has to be a presupposition of working against another force. God proving something to the assessing believer implies struggle, which shows God as being vulnerable and needing the believer to acknowledge him. God's supposed benevolent and awesome act is still part of an exchange.

The believer has an onus to continue giving God the recognition and acknowledgement he desires as well as providing the spiritual and moral space and flexibility for God to return this provision with righteousness. These recipients of credit in these papyri thus retain a secondary power, although their creditors, as initial active givers, are arguably more empowered. From such an interpretation, Abraham and the believer are empowered by active and initial giving of trust to God, and yet they are also like a service-provider or financial official and God a client, customer, or empowered citizen. In Rom 4, however, Abraham and the believer are, in the visible sequence of the text, initially givers and thus the ones empowered the most at that moment, although God's retaining of a return power is not necessarily inferior due to not initiating exchange, but also not necessarily superior because there is no assurance he makes an original and fundamental movement. By way of a return transferal and, importantly, in response to Abraham and the believer, God accounts righteousness to them.

The financial implications of *ethlogisthē* are accepted and seen to be clear to most scholars. However, due to the financial aspects that increase in *logizomai* along with the active and empowering financial senses of *pistis*, this does not mean only God is transferring and only Abraham and the believer are receiving. If Abraham and the believer are initiating the giving of benefit, then God is responding by accounting righteousness. While our present argument does not rely on *dikaiosunē* having a current financial-economic sense, the process of exchange between God and Abraham as possible through *logizomai* and *pistis* positions *dikaiosunē* as an exchangeable commodity.

Summing up the Anaylsis

The etymology of words is often oversimplified in that words are seen to lose senses of meaning and gain others. However, the understanding of words is always relative to context, intertexts, and history. If we transpose *pistis* from economic texts to theological ones, we cannot assume that the economic senses that are inconvenient will vanish! This is the principle of Derrida's *usure* and *retrait*. The economic ramifications of *pistis* therefore allow the notion of exchange to reemerge and compromise the theology of Rom 4 and challenge the assertion that God is all powerful and the only initiator and active player. The papyri we have used show that the economic aspects of *pistis* cannot be easily subjugated because the force of their contextual and intertextual traces are overwhelming. If *logizomai*'s financial metaphor is accepted and *pistis* is understood in Romans as being about trust, then the economic aspects of *pistis* as trust must be addressed, as should those of other words, such as justification and wage. The active financial power of someone providing *pistis* will be present in the understanding of a hearer of Romans even if at an unconscious level. The chain of exchange cannot be escaped, even by God!

The Implications of the Power of the Believer

There are many positive implications for thinking about the believer as an active agent. In terms of Rom 4, we find a believer who is empowered and has an interest in God's eschatological project. We can summarize these implications according to our analysis of the text.

The reality of division and delay of economy can be embraced.

Division and delay in economic and theological exchange needs to be rehabilitated, and any paradigm of final resolution of debt can be exposed as introducing into the theology of Romans a harmful infinite obligation on the individual believer. We can acknowledge that the economy cannot be escaped and that it involves inequalities and imbalances, divisions and separations, to allow it to develop and grow. Absolute resolution has been exposed as a mirage that is at paradox with the infinite deferral of the so-called altruistic gift. By rejecting the power of this paradigm of top-down economy, we allow for a faith that is negotiated and shared. The economic turn allows the believer to interact through their power and onus according to an endlessly ambiguous delay and deferral rather than a closed infinite reference to authoritative obligation cloaked as altruism. Delays and deferrals punctuate the cycles of power and resource, and it is the role of the individual to orient these and help determine fate. From here we can deal with and acknowledge these dynamics to allow fairness to occur. We see that if we pretend there is charitable altruism, then helping becomes self-righteous and oppressive. We can trace that whatever is given must lead to a return, without moral outrage. When an actor pays, they do so because of a prior stimulus. From the principle of reciprocity, which can be positioned as godly, even God is subject to making payment, even if this is much greater than anything the believer can offer.

Difference and division can be negative—few would doubt this. Contested and enforced boundaries between ethnicities, tribes, castes, classes, wealth, nations, languages, cultures, social systems, politics, ideologies, and religion, among others, have been sites of violence, oppression, or terror. However, to respond to this by homogenizing everything under the cloak of unity is abusive and detrimental to the onus of the person to be an individual within a society they identify with. Economy, like ecology, involves inequality and imbalance which is fueled by desire and dynamics for resolution which, at the same time, must be deferred to keep the system going. The saying "money makes the world go round," exemplified in the musical Cabaret, is not so much about ambition, but the mechanism that allows relations between actors to develop and change. Without imbalance, change could not occur—equilibrium and entropy are a stillness and a death. As Derrida observes, the term *economy* is the tautological "law of the house."[9] The house can be the world, church, economy, nation, or society—any way of conceptualizing the relationships between peoples and resources. The house is the metonym of space physical or spiritual, and once law is present, there are at once divisions and thus economy. Some of the divisions of laws are helpful to maintain order and peace, but some must be contested to be revised.

Divisions imply a need for systems, distribution, and mechanisms to ensure movement and play, which will include lack and surplus. Blanton describes how Paulinism, rather than a revolution, involved minor transformations within the imperial regime that nonetheless produced remarkable difference (Blanton 2014). The messianic is lived through the individual making small changes every day, with division and delay powering this movement to last rather than be a one-time explosion that soon turns cold. Beyond ethics, the economy is not intentional or conspiratorial; it is unconscious without being unanimous. The role of the individual is to orient this inequality and live out the life they want to. The role of the community—church, society, or state—is not to confine or control the individual but to prevent autocracy and increase empowerment. Such a view has no place for authoritarian politics or religion in which believers are supposed to subscribe fully to an authorized doctrine. Our top-down hierarchies in all institutions, including religions, have to be radically reaugmented to accommodate the right of the members to question and argue. Unity must stop being used as a cover for autocracy and control, in which an elite, or even one person's, way is forced upon the masses. Much of the abuse in religion and associated politics is caused by the forcing of the individual to conform to an authorized group, with the binary of heresy versus orthodoxy at work in this. The reason people maim and kill in the name of politics or religion is because they cannot accommodate eccentricity or difference—they have been convinced that a certain orthodoxy is the absolute and universal truth. Such concern is not just a matter for extremism but for mainstream congregations and assemblies. Through our economic reading of theology in Romans (and Rom 4 in particular) we can gain enhancement from the realism of the economic turn and embrace the realism of division and difference, so that delay is repurposed as opening opportunities for mean-

---

9. Ecology is "words of the house," existing as a tautology with "economy."

ing to be negotiated through deferral rather than perpetually closed in deference to an authoritative power.

Pistis should be read in Romans as trust and good faith between interpretation and imaginative trust.

Pistis should be recontextualized in our readings as having the semantic range to encompass interpretative assessment and trust in which the individual has the freedom and imagination to develop good faith. Agamben (2005, 118) shows how Paul does not set *pistis* against *nomos* but allows for *play* (what Derrida would call *jouissance*) between them. It is here that we find the spiritual depths of *oikos-nomos* ("law of the house"). Economic *pistis* allows us to reconfigure the role of an adherent of religion as someone who can make an assessment using their imagination and rationality within a territorial unit they have a stake in, from a home or a village to a state or a corporate entity such as a church or worship body. Such a rendering of *pistis* is empowering because it turns the believer from the passive assembly member into someone who can hold the authority, of whatever religion, to account. Removing unfortunate sticking points that descend from poor hermeneutics and inaccurate translational approaches will help reduce extremism, because the extremist elements within mainstream faith will struggle to maintain accountability when their motifs are challenged. For instance, another issue that needs addressing in another work is that of the semantics of sin in the biblical texts. I propose (for another work) that this English translation of the Greek word *hamartia* has set the theology of this concept way off course into treacherous seas of shame and guilt that have harmed generations of believers.

The economic sense of *pistis* dissolves the union of blind acceptance and spiritual faith and permits the believer to determine their relationship with God and their religious community. This freedom allows theology and faith to grow and prevents replication of oppressive prescribed and proscribed belief. When we dispense with blind faith extremism in our own Western spiritual culture, we also prevent corruption and harm. Some of our religious assemblies hold that the Bible, Qur'an, Torah, or the institutions of those faiths, such as church, priesthood, rabbinate, Sharia, and so on, hold ultimate unquestionable authority. The scandals of sexual abuse in the Anglican and Roman Catholic church, the Jehovah's Witnesses, and in mosques around world is largely a result of such perception where authority of belief is erred upon over human rights. Yet through rereading *pistis* in the activity of the believer, the breadth and depth of spiritual awareness in our texts and traditions can be fully realized and lived. Counterintuitively, in some ways, holding the text as authoritative is better than deference to a religious authority as long as we have a healthy approach to reading that invites variety. For some faith communities, their texts remain sacrosanct, and certain guides to reading exist that dominate the initiate. Sometimes the tendency to preserve tradition or praxis rather than text—a movement often packaged as liberal—is oppressive. There are many practices that are intrusive, exploitative, or harmful, such as arranged marriage, female circumcision, underage sexual activity and marriage, refusal of medical treatment, teaching of creationism, advocacy of violence, and so on, that are tolerated under the guise of religious tolerance. At the same time, there are mores and ethics forced upon other nations and cultures by the West under the principles of democracy, which smuggle in neoliberalism and judgmental superiority that harks back to colonialism. Through our reading of *pistis*, we can rehabilitate the text from intellectual elitism and empower the reader to resist authoritarianism in faith by demanding the right to interpret with openness.

Going back to the text charged with such openness can be the healthiest way to negotiate our faith, because in the text there is never an absolute—there is always a possibility of revision of views that can lead to a change of policy and doctrine. Such reading requires that at every instance, and for every person, we not only tolerate but expect different interpretations. Disagreement should not be an anomaly to be risk managed or contained, but something to be encouraged to elicit good theology. Every time we engage in an act of study, worship, or preaching, we can start afresh in our ministry with countless new possibilities for enlightenment. So *pistis* offers the text as an emancipating force over the doctrine of absolutism of all kinds, whether mainstream or marginal. From pistis we open the eschatological project of God to the scrutiny and creativity of the believer, whose gaze is paramount.

The agency in economy should be realized so the participant is an active stakeholder.

Inequality of power is inevitable and not all of it is bad, even if some is. For instance, the power of a parent over a child, a business owner over their employee, a judge over a defendant, a minister over a worshiper, a political leader over a citizen, a teacher over a pupil, or a human over an animal pet, can be necessary. However, in each of these hierarchical constructs there is accountability of the more powerful actor to the lesser. Through revisiting agency, we can propose a distinction between hierarchy and authority, in that some hierarchies are not always aligned to the direction of authority. In truly democratic societies, the legitimacy and capability of politicians and even presidents and prime ministers is questioned by society and the media to the point that those in power can be compelled to act differently or even resign. A parent can be a servant to their child, sovereign to their subject, leader to their citizen, and, as the agency of *pistis* teaches us, *God to the believer*! Jesus encapsulates this with his service and sacrifice—commissioned by God—to humanity. Due to this questioning of the direction of servility, the agency of the one lower in the hierarchy becomes more pronounced. Just as the subject and citizen has agency and retains authority, the believer exerts onus in their relationship with God.

Our contextualization of Romans within economic and even political agency provides a scriptural basis for the reassertion of the power and onus of the individual believer, citizen, or member. It repositions intellectual sovereignty with the individual so that, even if they do not have the physical power to assert this, they retain freedom and witness. No more is there validity to the model in which the ordinary person is a mere congregant or subject. We can reexamine the semantics of the Greek word *ekklesia* as church, as the calling out, or parliament, of the citizens from their homes to give their opinion on what should happen in the town or village. The myth of the divinely ordained monarch or minister, which translates from feudalism to globalization, from kings to business moguls, from the Pharisees and high priests to the priests, pastors, rabbis, and imams of today, can be fully rejected. With Romans we have an argument against the tradition that your ability to rule and preach is based only on your ordination, accident of birth, how much money you can make, who you can influence, or whether you are considered righteous.

The power of owing should be recognized as well as of being owed.

Obviously a person who lends money, property, or services is in a position of power both to decide whether to loan them in the first place, to decide terms, and to enforce repayment. However, we must recognize the power, if asymmetrical, of the borrower as well, and we can do this through an appreciation of the economic turn in Romans (and Rom 4 in particular). The borrower might, for instance, initiate this arrangement, negotiate terms, choose a lender over others, and demand service. The lender may rely on the custom of the borrower for their own financial wellbeing—think about how people rent homes, shops, and land to cover their expenses. Those lending money may have a stake in the concern for which it is being used or rely on the interest they earn from the loan to cover their own bills. The debtee also relies on the debtor to be financially successful themselves to pay the instalments of the debt as necessary. The debtor therefore has power as much as the debtee, and this even translates into the patron-client system, which, as well as being oppressive, offers the lesser party some influence, however little that may be. Remember in current English we use the terms *patron* and *client* to mean customer, so we could even say that both actors in such an arrangement are beholden to each other!

From an adapted approach to economy, we should adjust the way we read *pistis* and other economic words in Romans. Through a more even reading of *pistis*, we can dispense with this notion that the person transferring some form of value is the only powerful actor and see the recipient of that value as able to transact back as a debtor. Both the debtor and debtee hold responsibility and duty to each other; neither is ever superior by absolute. They both owe to each other finance, service, and loyalty. If everyone owes, then this means that no party is presumed abounding in their provision—not even God. Abounding provision is used by regimes to enact oppression and justify illegitimate authorities, both in church and the state. Even if we hold to the superiority of God's grace (as distinct from human altruism), we need to approach our theology with an equitable economy in order to make it work in the world we live in. God becomes accountable to the believer through their good faith and trust, which creates righteousness. Rehabilitating the power of owing allows the believer to be enlightened in the eschatological project of God as an important contributor, offering change and direction.

Economic circularity emboldens and affirms the power of the believer to question authority.

When we recognize the attributes of economy discussed in the previous paragraphs of this section, we can begin to affirm the power of the believer to hold religious, and indeed temporal, authorities to account. The constantly readjusting economy, its ebbs and flows, its swings and roundabouts, its benefits and disadvantages, its liberation and restriction, all contribute to a reading that the believer has a mandate. Any idealism of economy as resolved, or as altruistic, merely adheres to oppression. Circularity and cyclical economic transition allows for feedback as well as input. It shows the individual has something to offer according to their skill, knowledge, and imaginative faculties. We can reject accepting someone's authority based only on their power or status and open our hearts and minds to the unique expertise of the individual. Paul recognized that each of us offer something crucial and unique to the church and that we should be mindful of the specific gifts that we and others bring (1 Cor 12:4–14; Rom 12:3–8). Such addition of an individual skill or identity to a given system means that there will be a new expression rather than a replication of something before. Individuality added means that every expression of an idea or theology is never the same but is different. Individuals or groups may be excluded or rejected; however, their influence remains even if external or distant.

Furthermore, circularity means that there is an opportunity for the individual to struggle for and affect change in the wider system by way of return and continuity. The cyclical struggle of Mot and Baal examined earlier in this chapter was essential for stability in that religious system, rather than being a definitive site of permanent change. While non-Christian religious myth might for some be indicative of pagan or even demonic misguidance, in the economy of our reading it is representative of a reciprocal nature of being between God and the believer at ground level, literally. Such feedback may be neoliberal in some circumstances, but I propose here that the agricultural pagan motif of the natural cycle imports the realism of reciprocity back into the theological dynamics of Romans.

Conclusion

In this chapter, Rom 4 was examined with near-contemporaneous economically oriented papyri, under the guidance of a deconstruction theory approach to etymology and semantics. We saw how critical the economic associations of *pistis* are for understanding the exchange of faith in Rom 4. We also discussed the importance of *logizomai* and *diakiō* related words, although the latter two would warrant further study in another work. I analyzed our Romans texts within the context of near contemporary papyri texts that use *pistis* and related words. In doing so, I rejected the idea of *pistis* as blind faith and traced an understanding of this term as good faith and trust. We saw that the trust, credit, mortgage, and assessing aspects of *pistis* as shown in the papyri reaffirms the activity of the believer in reciprocity and exchange in their relationship with God. While God accounts for the righteousness of the believer, he or she, through faith, assesses God's trustworthiness to make such judgements and provisions. Rather than a one-way transferal, the relationship between God and the believer is part of a chain of cycles from which even God is not exempt as a subject, linguistically or philosophically. Both God and the believer can give and receive, initiate, and respond. While the cycle is asymmetrical, there is difference between the believer and God: the believer also has agency and power through their faith that helps to shape and determine God's projects.

2
GRACE

For what says the scripture? "Abraham trusted God and it was accounted to him for righteousness." Now, to the one working, the wages are not accounted according to gift, but according to debt-owed. But, to the one not working, but believing on the one justifying the ungodly, his trust is accounted for righteousness.
—Romans 4:3–5

For the gifts and the calling of God are irrevocable.
—Romans 11:29

On what condition does goodness exist beyond all calculation? On the condition that goodness forgets itself, that the movement be a movement of the gift that renounces itself, hence a movement of infinite love.
—Derrida, *The Gift of Death*

Altruism is selfishness out with a pair of field glasses and imagination.
—Christina Stead, *House of All Nations*

Altruistic gift-giving serves as a form of grace in Rom 4 and seemingly undermines the power of the believer in his or her relationship with God. This chapter focuses on the metaphor of gift-giving in Rom 4:3–5 and its place in the paradigm of "altruistic gift as grace." I challenge the movement of some biblical scholars, who, following the reasoning of Seneca, attempt to affirm gift-giving as a purely altruistic act. Furthermore, I reject the extension of this argument that such giving is removed from economic exchange. I argue that, even if material items are not returned, the expectation is that loyalty and gratitude will be reciprocated as economic paybacks. The social act of giving hides the attempt, whether conscious or not, to place a recipient under perpetual obligation. In order to achieve the objectives of my argument, in this chapter I look beyond the propaganda of Seneca to the writings of near contemporary ordinary people (as documented in P.Oxy. 12.1481, P.Oxy. 42.3057, and P.Mert 12). These texts enable us to trace the reality of gift at the ground level. I focus on *charis*-related words for simplicity and to keep the study focused on our Romans text at the word level.

Previous readings of the gift allegory in Rom 4:4 suffer from a contradiction between the concept of gift-giving in the widest sense and its reality in the ancient world. The word *charis* as used in 4:4 is often translated as "grace" rather than "gift," and *charisma* is more typically translated as "gift."[1] However, the two words are often used interchangeably and, when we contrast *charis* in 4:4 to the Greek word typically used for labor wages (*misthos*), as well as the Greek word that typically indicates "things owed" (*opheiēlma*), it becomes clear that, not only does *charis* mean "gift" in this allegory; it also aligns God's grace to a gift freely given. Some confessional scholarship understands *charis* as a purely altruistic gift from God to humankind, but in doing so they remove the financial realism of gift-giving in the Roman era from the use of *charis* in Rom 4:4. The importance of the ancient concept of the gift and its effect on the hearer of Romans cannot and must not be ignored. Through the papyri, we see how the so-called altruistic gift is always economical. We see that benefactors offer gifts against a perceived background of austerity, but we also witness how recipients try to reassert their agency and avoid dependence, often by gestures of thriftiness and mild dismissiveness.

Separating the altruistic gift from grace prevents us from importing dependence theocracy onto Romans and avoids the view that the believer is only a passive agent. By rejecting austerity and altruism of thought and belief and affirming the economic thrift of individual perceptions, we can start constructing a theology of the believer that is analytical and discerning. We can reject the imposition of massly produced doctrine and develop an individual relationship with God. Only when we are honest about the irreducibly economic insistence of gift-giving can we expand grace to a reciprocity of power, albeit uneven, between God and the believer.

---

1. Romans 5 uses the word for free-gift *dorea* together with *charis* and *charisma*, compounding this struggle around the meaning of "gift." There is not space in this argument to examine *dorea*, but this would be a useful study.

Argument

I argue that scholars and religious communities are too attached to the idea that ancient altruistic gift-giving is a fit analogue for God's perfect grace of God, not because of theological or ethical commitments, but because of incorrect assumptions about ancient economics. In effect, this reading transposes economic oppression into the theological field. Instead of this reading, I draw upon ancient and seemingly mundane letters about gifts to prove that gifts are never altruistic; they are always economical, even when read into a metaphor of grace in Romans. This reading is bolstered by the practical challenges described by Paul himself in Romans. If Paul is spreading the gospel of Christ in an earthy way, then surely the challenges and limitations he faced influenced his discourse and should be welcomed rather than obscured. Indeed, they add a necessary realism and value that the temple elite ignored. An economy in which gift-giving is an act of grace, I propose, enhances the gospel and empowers those commissioned to spread it. I argue further that pretending altruistic gift-giving affirms God's grace denies the individual economic autonomy by imposing upon him or her perpetual, unresolvable debt. In doing so, the analogues deny the believer his or her own theological autonomy. A more realistic understanding of gift-giving—in which the gift is a delayed form of economy—is more indicative of the relationship between God and the believer, which is eternally deferred yet open and constantly changeable. Let us speak of grace, I propose, as something unknown that we do not need to define, as an eternal sign that is never fully resolved in the material world. In short, let us leave grace with God and stop pretending we can know absolutely and universally what it means.

The Problems with the Concept of Altruistic Gift-Giving

The three problems I identify are: (1) the economic aspect is elided from the gift; (2) dependence is preferred over agency; and (3) the essential is conflated with luxury. We will see as the chapter develops, how each of these problems in the paradigm and metaphor of altruistic gift impacts on the theology of Rom 4:3–5.

The economic aspect is elided from the gift.

In a lot of the scholarship on the New Testament and Paul in particular, we find that discourse on gift-giving suffers from an aporia in terms of economy, that goes back to the propaganda of Seneca. (This is evident in Peterman 1997, for example.) Such discourse forgets that Seneca's *De Beneficiis* is not a moral compass or reliable historical witness for altruism; it is just another text, the motives within which must be questioned. Seneca is valuable only as an example of how contemporaries *perceived* their social conventions, not as a reflection of reality in totality. Seneca's bias toward the regime he was invested in will likely have skewed his judgement—he "has a dog in this race." Imagine if historians of the future considered Donald Trump an ethical leader because it says so in Breitbart.com or that the European Union was deficient based upon Nigel Farage's memoirs! Of course, Seneca, being a philosopher, was much more sophisticated than Trump or Farage, but he was also a propagandist and a polemicist who had a stake in the Roman hierarchical and patronage system in which he was a subservient client of the Emperor Nero. How ironic that he is reached for to support oppressive Christian theologies! The assumptions of the biblical studies academy has been that we take on face value the true altruism of gift-giving in the ancient world, and we consider expectations of gratitude to be moot or irrelevant to the relationship between the giver and the receiver. Let's bring this close to home: at Christmas and Eid, for example, the convention is to give and receive presents or money. Often, people agree, or at least feel obliged, to get each other or each other's children items and decide upon a maximum—and minimum—value; it is an exchange disguised as a gift. The problem with the resulting altruistic-gift paradigm of grace is that the gift becomes forced and oppressive. Altruism is used to cover the institutional fear of empowerment that economic exchange can bring. The myth of the altruistic gift cloaks a perpetual debt that is unresolvable. In this chapter we see how the altruistic-gift-as-grace paradigm affects faith in a way that oppresses the rights and powers of the believer.

Dependence is preferred over agency.

The surprising rehabilitation of Seneca in some of the more confessional biblical scholarship also elides the enforced dependence of gift giving from the altruistic-gift-as-grace paradigm. We only need to look as far as the patron-client relationship for it to be evident that gift giving in this context, both formal and informal, emphasizes the dependance of the recipient on the giver, while ignoring the dependance of the giver on the recipient. Of course, the status of a powerful patron is dependent on the support of their clients, each of which, with their own impetus, will influence the patron's agenda to some extent. The receiver of a gift who is socioeconomically inferior will have a level of agency and power in comparison to the patron. Indeed, it is interesting that in the English language, the two words used to create a contrast of power between the actors in this relationship are words that would both translate easily to mean "customer." Whilst the word *patron* does denote superior or elite benefactors—such as supporters of artists or poets—it has been rehabilitated in our capitalist modernity as a form of customer. Certainly, *client*—the inferior in this ancient binary—as an English word is synonymous with customer at a more sophisticated level (law, business, etc.) and refers to someone who is empowered and has definite agency and control. As such, we can implode the vision of the fully altruistic gift-giving ceremony and see how the expectation of dependence gives way to that of individual agency, a paradigm in which everyone is able to have some kind of influence, no matter how much they lack material power. This chapter aims to emphasize the role of agency in faith over that of blind dependence on received belief.

The essential is conflated with luxury.

The third problem is how the gift-giving tradition disguises the essential as luxury. As I have stated, biblical scholarship has sought to show that the gift is truly altruistic, with no expectation of return. If a gift is altruistic, then it must be luxury or oppressive; this is because the recipient of something essential will want to know that their ability to access it is regular and sustainable, requiring it to be economic and economical. Only when it is considered within the economy is it assured, because the giver will be more likely to be able to afford to give it if they have a return from the recipient. However, the downside of the economic gift to the giver is that they lose the supremacy of being perceived as being wealthy, powerful, and generous. It is therefore in the interests of the giver to engage in the cycle of giving but disavow its economy through the illusion of altruism. One way of doing this is to reduce what some consider to be essential and rightful to luxuries, so that everything becomes part of this illusion of the altruistic gift of luxury, even the food we must eat to survive.

A good example of this is in Charles Dickens's *Oliver Twist*. When Oliver first eats at the workhouse, he finishes his food and asks for more, causing the Beadle Mr Bumble to be outraged. This is because the pauper was supposed to be grateful for the shelter and food of the workhouse.

It was an undeserved gift, not a right. What is modest comfort to the upstanding member of society is made into luxury to the resident of the workhouse, as shown in the juxtaposition between the sparse meal of the orphans and the feast laden table of the officials of the workhouse. Similarly, biblical scholars adhering to Seneca's propaganda of the gift and the genuine gratitude of the recipients is part of this will to elide the liberty of economy. The tension between what is luxury and what is essential are fundamental to our argument. We have seen in recent Western right wing politics how a call to austerity has been disguised as individualism when it has instead reduced empowerment. When an essential is presented as a luxury, the recipient is disempowered. It prevents an individual from being able to criticize the quality or availability of it. I argue in this chapter that this gets transposed into the theology of the believer, who is seen as a recipient of a divine luxury that he or she has no alternative response to except to show unquestioning gratitude and loyalty.

Some Tendencies in Biblical Scholarship

As indicated, there are tendencies in biblical scholarship to deploy the gift metaphor to paradigms about justification by works, on the one hand, and justification by faith alone, on the other (Witherington and Hyatt 2004, Jewett 2007, Schleisser 2007). This has been moderated somewhat by Dunn (2006), who makes it more palpable within the context of reading Judaism as a religion of faith rather than a religion of works. The metaphor of gift-giving, its contrast to economy, and the subsequent paradigm of altruistic-gift-as-grace becomes so important to this line of scholarship that the tradition of the altruistic gift must be identified, established, and defended. Scholars such as Troels Engberg-Pedersen (2008) reach for Seneca and align uncritically with his propaganda so that this paradigm prevails. We see in John Barclay (2015) a recent conservative attempt to appreciate the circularity of the gift exchange that helps to open up the possibility of economic connotations in gift-giving. The problem with the altruistic-gift-as-grace paradigm is that it only prevails if the gift metaphor is obedient to perceptions of how scholars have interpreted it. However, the underlying metaphor will not necessarily work in the way intended. On the contrary, it has the potential to produce different effects. It is undermined by the reality of gift-giving in the world, including the ancient world, as we will see through the insight provided by the ancient papyri. I would go as far to argue that while there are few fundamental principles, one is that there is no such thing as altruism and that every relation, transferal, or exchange is economic, whether material, intellectual, or spiritual. In my view, this is ethically beneficial, as we shall see.

The argument that gift-giving is something special outside of economics is resisted in "Given Time" (Derrida 1992b, 161–87). "Given Time" begins with an amusing epigraph about how a grande dame of letters complains that the king takes all her free time (thus an economic argument), and she would rather give the remainder of it to a charity for impoverished young women if she could. So, the woman, as an elite person, is limited by an economy of a monarch; she should have unlimited resources but is subject to the law of time. Furthermore, the monarch cannot be generous with the grande dame's time, because he cannot control time and is thus also subject to the economy of time, just as the grande dame's generosity is restricted within the monarch's needs within time, which require the return to be sustainable: "apparently and according to common logic and economics, one can only exchange, by way of metonymy, one can only take or give what is *in* time" (163, emphasis original).[2] Once a system is in place, there is economics, because most systems involve distribution, partition, boundaries, and, most significantly, the perception of cycles or circulation. Derrida strips away all the idealistic layers of the altruistic gift down to that of time—an economy that cannot be overcome even with the best intentions.

Ancient Papyri and Deconstruction Theory

As in the previous chapter, I am calling upon the wealth of the Oxyrhynchus papyri in this chapter. While the majority of the documents are practical and administrative, there is a personal nature to the letters I focus on regarding gift-giving. Even though such documents would

---

2. "Among its irreducible semantic predicates or values, economy no doubt includes the values of law (nomos) and of home (oikos, home, property, family, the hearth, the fire within). Nomos does not only signify the law in general, but also the law of distribution (nemein), the law of sharing or partition [partage], the law as partition, moira, the given or assigned part, participation. Another sort of tautology already implicates the economic with the nomic as such. As soon as there is law, there is partition: as soon as there is nomy, there is economy. Besides the value of law and home, of distribution and partition, economy implies the idea of exchange, of circulation, of return" (Derrida 1992b, 166, emphasis added).

not be considered literary, the binary between literary and official is not straightforward. It could be argued that every text has a literary element, from the writing on a shampoo bottle to an invoice for a delivery. We can discover through such functional documents the individual situations of people and the drama of their lives. The authors and recipients of these letters are ordinary lower middle-class people[3] dealing with the effects of politely imposed altruism, which muddles their social and professional spheres. They display a respectful and proud resistance to the obligation under which more wealthy, powerful, and influential people seek to place them. The Oxyryncchus manuscripts we are using date from around the third century BCE to 640 CE. There are many other texts in this papyri corpus that would inform our study than I have identified, but my aim in this chapter has been to focus on a more limited number at a sentence and word level, as I have done in my biblical exegesis. As these papyri are touchstones for our textual ground-level reading of Romans, I provide an outline of each one.

In our first papyri text P.Oxy. 12.1461 from the early second century CE, a soldier in camp writes to his mother, reassuring her about his health, acknowledging the receipt of various presents, and expressing his general satisfaction. In this letter the soldier Theonas addresses his "lady mother" Tetheus, beseeching her not to listen to stories of his ill-health: "I was much grieved to hear that you had heard about me, for I was not seriously ill; and I blame the person who told you." There is an implication that Theonas feels that others communicating with his mother have embellished accounts of his ill-health to exact obligation from her and him. He continues: "Do not trouble to send me anything. I received the presents from Heraclides." Further on he says, "do not burden yourself to send me anything." Based on the mention of the gifts from Heraclides, this suggests Theonas is concerned that people might be sending valued items through her, on his behalf, thereby holding her obligated as well as him. Key observations we can make before we bring this text into our analysis include: there is not necessarily ease and trust in accepting gifts—there is often apprehension; when third parties (such as Theonas's mother) are implicated, it exposes the social and structural obligation a gift places someone under; altruistic giving presupposes a weakness or misfortune in

---

3. This anachronistic assumption is based on the subjects discussed and the fact that ordinary working class people or peasantry would not have been able to afford the wherewithal for papyrus and postage.

the recipients. This letter, therefore, points us toward some of the problems we find when discussing the altruistic-gift-as-grace paradigm in the letter of Romans, in that the believer receiving grace within the altruistic-gift paradigm is obligated without room to negotiate, is not able to consent to their obligation, and is forced into a communal structure in which they are expected to accept authority by proxy and never have a chance to critique or determine it.

In our second papyri text P.Oxy. 42.3057, a letter dating from the first to second centuries CE, an Ammonius acknowledges receiving items from his associate Apollonius but appeals to him not to send further gifts Ammonius cannot afford to repay, emphasizing that the two men should continue to offer each other their friendship instead. Ammonius informs Apollonius that a crossed letter, a portmanteau (compartmentalized luggage case), cloaks, and reeds have arrived. However, he insinuates that some of the items are not the best quality. The reeds "not good ones," and the cloaks, with a barbed compliment, are "old ones" that he considers 'better than new." It is possible he is trying to ratchet down the value of these items to reduce expected and unspoken obligation placed upon him by Apollonius, without insulting him directly. Ammonius appeals to Apollonius not to continue to "load" him with these "continual kindnesses" because, he says, "I cannot repay them." It is worth noting at this point that Ammonius seems to be resisting an attempt by Apollonius to obligate him through the falsity of altruism, but, as he cannot escape the reality of his own social or economic inferiority, he appeals to pride and spirit. He subtly rejects the condescension of being sent old reeds and cloaks, as well as a crossed letter (where papyri is reused with writing written at right angle across previous text) by reframing them in terms of kindness. Ammonius discloses that he cannot return the gifts with the same value but maintains emphasis on the friendship between them. In this way, Ammonius avoids the altruism and imposed austerity of an oppressive friend and reaffirms his own pride in how his material thrift reflects spiritual morality of kindness. Bringing this to our reading of Romans, this letter connects the economic reality of altruistic gift-giving with the control of understanding by the religious elites and authorities. It shows how the altruistic-gift-as-grace paradigm prescribes belief and limits the believer's interactions under the guise of a valid authority, such as that of the church. It offers overly simplistic or flawed doctrine as something the believer should be grateful for, while denying the believer's input. While the believer may be inferior to the power of certain structures, he or she can appeal to the validity of their own intellectual and spiritual thrift to reject some codicils of doctrine passed off as grace and affirm others.

In our third papyri text, P.Mert. 12, dated at 29 August 58 CE, a certain Chairas writes to his friend Dionysius that he was delighted to receive Dionysius's letter as it made him feel he was at home. Chairas mentions that he and the others with him have "nothing," which may be an absence that is material, social, or emotional. Chairas states how he will dispense with writing to Dionysius with a "great show of thanks" because, he reasons, such thanksgiving is only necessary between those who are not friends. It has been claimed that this reasoning indicates a parity between the two correspondents, who are both physicians (Bell and Roberts 1948, 52, quoted in Peterman 1997, 75). However, this assumes that two men in the same profession would be equal in status, and this may not be the case; Chairas may be wanting to invoke friendship through his rhetoric so that his thanksgiving is not understood by Dionysius as part of an obfuscated patron-client relationship. Chairas has received a prescription of plasters from Dionysius, which could indicate that he is in some kind of difficulty, and I propose that he may have been a battlefield surgeon or, at the very least, a physician attached to a military unit. Under this light we could infer that Chairas's reference to having nothing emphasizes a pride in his service and the spartan situation he is in, which surpasses any material advantage Dionysius may have. Chairas's serenity and small return thus becomes quite noble and subtly rejects any sense of patronage attempted by Dionysius. Chairas frames Dionysius's communication and prescription as an "affection" rather than a necessity and in doing so humors and exposes Dionysius's attempt to present a necessity as a surplus. If I am wrong about the military context of this letter I propose, my observations about the dynamics still have a high degree of accuracy.

These papyri teach us that gift-giving is impossible apart from the reality of our lives, which are always economic, as Derrida argues.[4] If they exist, gifts interrupt the economy and cannot be circular or be involved in exchange; they must remain anaeconomic (Derrida 1992b, 166–67),

---

4. "If there is a gift, the given of the gift (that which one gives, that which is given, the gift as given thing or as act of donation) must not come back to the giving (let us not already say to the subject, to the donor). It must not circulate, it must not be exchanged, it must not in any case be exhausted, as a gift, by the process of exchange, by the movement of circulation of the circle in the form of return to the point of departure" (Derrida 1992b, 166).

which makes sense in the relationships described in these papyrus texts. It could be said that the circle of economy relies on what is outside, the spirituality of pure gift, to create disruption of "circularity, relation, reciprocity and reappropriation" (Spitzer 2011, 135–36), and we see even friendly and caring interactions as reciprocal in the papyrus texts too. Gift-giving, however, cannot be fully foreign to the circle; although associated with the outside, with status removed, gifts are still associated with the circle of economy. Thus a "familiar foreignness"—the distance, and yet at the same time connection, between gift-giving and the economic cycle—is oxymoronic, making the gift impossible to determine either as one-way altruism or coordinated exchange within a timeframe (Derrida 1992b, 167). We find, therefore, that gift is only possible where the "paradoxical instant … tears time apart" (168). If gift-giving could be separated from the circle of economics, its exteriority would not be "simple, ineffable … transcendent and without relation"; rather they would stimulate the turn of the circle and set the "economy in motion" and necessitate that an account of the gift be given (185–86)—thus making the true gift be perceived as economic and thus annulled! As such, "gift and economy are mutually dependable" (Spitzer 2011, 145). In our papyri texts, we find generosity is never truly altruistic despite good intentions. Generosity is always ulterior and exterior to the dynamics of socioeconomic reality; this does not, however, undermine the genuineness of relationships between people who may care about each other but be of differing powers and means. This paradox of gift-giving is also at the heart of the economy in theology, a fact that is undermined if we view the gift of God's grace as an altruistic gift.

So is gift-giving altruistic by intention, as some argue through Seneca? When a recipient "gives me back or owes or ought to give me back what I give him or her," this annuls the gift. To keep the notion that there is a gift, restitution occurs as part of a "complex calculation of long-term deferral or, if you like, *différance*" (Derrida 1992b, 170). Derrida goes even further and asserts an even more extreme stance on the matter—even the perception that something is a gift annuls the gift (171), because the "simple consciousness of the gift right away sends itself back the gratifying image of goodness or generosity," which is a kind of "auto-recognition," "self-approval," or "narcissistic gratitude" (179). We see recognition being used in our papyri texts not to show ingratitude but to prevent perpetual obligation, which, while of the best of intentions, is oppressive and aggressive, presenting what is necessary and owed as a surplus benefit. So, there is a violence inherent, one that allows illegitimate sovereignty of powers over the labor of the worker (Tofighi 2017, 50–51), enforcing their wage as a gift rather than something owed! We can extend this into theology by saying that gift-as-grace provides permission to enforce religious authority over believers, with very little space for them to resist or revise this.

Ancient Giving and the Place of Romans

Every social relationship in antiquity had an economic factor to it (see Donlan 1981–1982, 139). Moreover, since the Stone Age, every transaction was a "monetary episode" in a long chain of social relations (Sahlins 1972, 185). Prestige valuables such as jewelry and precious stones, for example, were exchanged between members of the elite, and these payments were separated from the trading of more mundane goods, such as foodstuffs and other necessities (see Aarts 2005, 3–4). Ceremonial exchange reserved agency for the more dominant and limited the ability of ordinary people to decline gifts that would place them under obligation (Aarts 2005, 4). Twenty-first century readers tend to idealize gifts as being selfless and without any expectation of return, and maybe this is due to the emancipation of Western society over the twentieth century (a point made by Barclay 2015). Contemporary westerners are able to indulge this illusion. However, we know that many forms of gift-giving in the first century were most likely tightly entwined in the economic system and exerted control over less powerful actors.[5] In Romans, Paul's mission is spiritual, but it still has practical aspects that are subject to finance (Rom 15:22–29), and tensions between necessity and generosity are revealed in Rom 15:26–27, where it is stated that churches in Macedonia and Achaia made contributions to the Jerusalem church with pleasure (15:26) but also due to obligation (15:27). Complicating the situation even more is that of Macedonia's and Achaia's reception of spiritual blessings from Jerusalem, which places them in debt materially, such as obligating them to provide financial support.

The elephant in the room for the first-century Pauline world is the patron-client relationship, which involved gift-giving within an unequal yet reciprocal construct in which more powerful actors subjected the

---

5. Various in-depth studies have been conducted on this area, most notably by Andrew Wallace-Hadrill (1989), Ernest Gellner and John Waterbury (1977), Walter Donlan (1981–1982), Anthony R. Hands (1968), Paul FW Danker (1983, 1988), and more recently, Gerald W. Peterman (1997).

less powerful through gifting. This tradition jars somewhat with Seneca's altruism. Another system—benefaction, in which a person would have an honor bestowed upon him for carrying out an act of generosity for a city—was also a well-established tradition long before Paul.[6] Mutual obligations between individuals and groups of differing status were normal (Peterman 1997, 4) and included power negotiations, which were often unequal. Certainly, Paul needed to use his apostolic superiority to discipline assemblies who he felt went astray, and he wanted recognition for his efforts.[7] We also have examples from history of authorities wanting to limit or control altruism in order to prevent others from gaining influence. For example, in the "The Gift" (1969)—an essay that influenced Derrida's "Given Time" (1992b)—Marcel Mauss analyses potlatch, a feast tradition that forms the basis of certain indigenous economic systems. In these feasts, elite people in tribes would give away or destroy value items as a maneuver to exert their influence and wealth. Issues of economic significance were negotiated, such as land, fishery, and forestry rights. The Canadian government banned the practice between 1885 and 1951, as it often involved chieftains asserting their influence by trying to outdo each other in generosity, thus leading to a worrisome redistribution of resources that could lead to certain people becoming more wealthy and powerful than is convenient or predictable for a Western capitalist government. Institutional giving may have also reminded Western authorities that its own supposed benevolence is motivated by profit, not altruism. Potlatch compares to Roman patronage in that it is economic and not altruistic. Paul's missiological housekeeping in Rom 15:22–29 shows an anxiety about whether resources will reach the places he thinks they are meant to be and thereby avoid an imbalance that might undermine his authority over the rightness of the gospel.

---

6. Bruce Winter (1988, 88) offers an example of a benefaction inscription from the second century BCE in which Dion, son of Diopeithes, deems that Agathocles, son of Hegemon of Rhodes, is rewarded with citizenship with its associated grants and admission to various tribes, including the Essenes and Bembineans, as a reward for noticing the high price of corn and philanthropically selling his corn below the market price. In an inscription from Ephesus, Skythes of Archidamus is awarded a gold crown for his various acts of welfare for citizens.

7. For example, Gal 1:11–17; 1 Thess 2:6; 4:2; Rom 11:12; 1 Cor 3:1–3; 4:17; 7:17, 25; 9:1–2; 11:17, 23, 34; 12:27; 15:8, 10; 2 Cor 1:5, 13; 6:13; 12:11–12, 14; 13:10; Phil 2:22; Phlm 10; among others.

The charitable aspect of gift-giving is used to oblige others: the refusal of a gift could be taken very negatively, as an insult (Marshall, 1987, 255), and this is reflected in Rom 11:29. Between so-called equals, such an obligation might be used to establish friendship or to seek social approval, but between two unequal parties it could have the effect of establishing the more wealthy or powerful as superior to the less wealthy. Such a power relationship would raise expectations of return, or obedience, from the inferior party to the superior one, with no limits. In addition, it would expose the superior party as not being as self-sufficient and powerful as they might seem, in that they need and rely on a return from the inferior party, whether that be return of goods or merely deference and acknowledgment. Consequently, the inferior party would also retain some power in the relationship, even if that power is far less than that of the superior party. The way these two parties relate, however, is through exchange, not charity or altruistic gift. To put this in terms of rhetoric about God's grace, just as Paul relies on the contributions of his planted churches over the Mediterranean, God also needed support, even if this is not equal to the support he provides to believers.

Contrast between the Agency of Wages and the Oppression of Gifts

Biblical scholarship has often sought to preserve a contrast between gifts and wages (or debt) in Rom 4 and its associated contexts in order to perpetuate the idea that God's transmission of grace to believers is a one-way process. However, in *Cher.* 122–123, when speaking on the relationship between Abraham and God, Philo is more realistic about gift-giving than Seneca is in *De Beneficiis*. In this text, Philo argues that in the real world the ones who might give gifts[8] are in reality selling items or services, and those who receive gifts, in reality, purchase these beneficial items or services. The givers seek repayment for the gift given, and the receivers of the gift are motivated to make a return or profit. This means that what really occurs is a sale, not an act of giving. Philo calls out the economy of gift-giving, although he does so to contrast material giving to God's eternal grace. In this text Philo also fails to give insight into why God gives, and he does not acknowledge that, if there is a reason for God to give, then God needs to give, thus rendering the gift of grace as economic as the material

---

8. Using a *charis*-related word.

world. In Philo's reading, the material is uncoupled from the spiritual to avoid linking the idealistic altruism of gift-giving in the world to the grace of God. The metaphor of gift-giving is therefore upheld in spite of the idealism of Seneca and protected by a more realistic Philo.

Other ancient texts also question one-way altruism. In *A.J.* 1.183, Josephus makes an argument against conceptualizing unlimited one-way grace as a gift. In this work, Josephus reimagines part of a conversation from the book of Genesis in which God praises Abraham's virtue. In Josephus's words, God says, "Thou shalt not however lose the rewards thou hast deserved to receive by such thy glorious actions," to which Abraham replies "what advantage [*charis*] will it be to me to have such rewards [*misthos*], when I have none to enjoy them after me?" (Whiston 1895) This dialogue implies, perhaps counterintuitively, that God's *charis* or gift is given in return for, or in expectation of, Abraham's virtue and his deeds. The return is styled as a wage (*misthos*), which frames the relationship as a kind of employment rather than patronage. Not only does this analysis undermine the altruism of the gift, but it infers that Abraham initiates the exchange instead of God. Even in this significant scriptural story about Abraham, the notion of wage or debt persists.

The gift metaphor is loaded with a convenient psychology of altruism, which involves a disavowal, or amnesia, of economy. *Laissez-faire* economist Milton Friedman once said "there ain't no such thing as a free lunch," and there is a progressive truth that can be salvaged from this draconian austerity.[9] The description of God's eternal grace as a fountain in Philo's *Cher.* 123 is an interesting metaphor in this regard. A fountain is something through which water passes. Rather than signifying eternity, the water is ephemeral. Water in fountains must go somewhere and be replenished. Fountains are artificial and rely on a mechanism to control the water flow. As water distribution is a major contributor to prosperity, this metaphor becomes economical beyond Philo's intentions. While the artificiality of fountains might be indicative of God's design and action, the artificiality betrays grace's connection to the economy. Since fountains show security and prosperity in a settlement, Philo's allegory indicates economic circulation of return rather than one-way altruistic flow. A metaphor of a waterfall or even a natural well might have allegorized

---

9. A sustained exploration of the similarities between these Derrida and Friedman can be found in Tratner 2003.

eternal grace more effectively because nature is prior to artifice and God is seen as the original creator. Yet even natural waters betray their ecological limitations, since water depletion, carbon footprints, and climate change have become reality in our twenty-first century world, denying the luxury of grace. Such emergencies persist as the payment for civilization's negligence of the environment.

The pattern of the allegory in Rom 4:4 is to create a contrast between gifts and wages or things owed (*charis* versus *misthos* and *opheilēma*), which in 4:5 is revealed to be aligned with the contrast between what comes from faith alone (God's altruistic grace) and what comes from works (nothing spiritual and only something earthly). Parallel to this is 6:23: "For the wages of sin is death, but the free gift of God is eternal life in Christ Jesus our Lord." In this verse, the Greek *misthos* is used for wage; however, another word is used for gift (*dorea*), which is translated, tautologically, as free-gift. A simple reading would be "do bad things and you will die (spiritually) but be grateful for God's generosity through Christ and you will live forever." However, this verse implies that trying to do things to affect righteousness is sinful and the payment will be bleak, whereas if you accept you are pathetic, that you have nothing to give, and that only God can save you through Christ, then you are saved. Some such as Barclay (2015, 492) recognize the economic turn of the gift, emphasizing how the efforts of the recipients of grace "produce obedience, lives that perform, by heart-inscription, the intent of the Law." While such a view appreciates the reciprocity of gift-giving and grace, it somewhat neglects the fact that, if this is a circular relationship, there is some feedback from the believer to God, and, if so, then there is also an efficacy going beyond what God surmises. Envisioning gift-as-grace, or grace-as-gift, forgets the realism of our material, spiritual, and intellectual exchange in the world.

The contrast between gifts and wages affirms that the believer cannot do anything to elicit grace from God and that they can only receive it by having faith. However, contradictorily, such faith is not instrumental, and only God can choose to provide grace. God is the actor with sole power and control in this transferal. In a similar vein, Moore (1994) highlights the problem of how in John 4 scholars try to view Jesus as the sole dispenser of wisdom and the Samaritan woman as a mere recipient, thus a one-way process. Scholars view a one-way process of pure gift from God to Abraham. The contrast between justification by works and justification by faith-alone in Rom 4:5 is paralleled by the contrast between employment economics and altruistic giving in 4:4 (Witherington and Hyatt 2004, 123) and confirmed in 4:6 through the authority of David in the midrash that follows and in the prelude in Rom 3:27–30. Such a view contrasts the one working (*tō de mē ergazomenō*) with the one not working *but believing* (*tō de mē ergazomenō pisteuonti de*); these are two types of believer: the former departs from the example of Abraham and the latter echoes it. Abraham's rectification is also presented as a "sheer gift" (Keck 2005). Labor is aligned with works and gift with God's grace through faith.

Various scholars use the distinction between *opheilēma* and *charis* to identify grace as altruistic gift-giving (for example, Jewett 2007, and Schliesser 2007):[10] economic labor is aligned with theological works; wage becomes attached to misconceived ideas of religious reward; and the notion of gift-giving is identified with God's grace. These alignments, however, are undermined by the use of the same word, *ergazomenō*, for the one who works in the economic sense in 4:4 and the one who (does not) work in the theological sense in 4:5, thereby blurring the boundaries between the two. The use of the same word (*ergazomenō*) problematizes the distinction between economic work and theological (non)work, which is not distinct from work but is an inverse category. Dunn (2006, 366) almost aligns those who do not work to the undeserving/ungodly when he reasons that this text "distinguishes a human contract from God's surprising mode of operation: he justifies the ungodly." Consistent with the New Perspective, Dunn claims that the resulting justification by faith message would not have been controversial to Jewish hearers. While the latter might be true on a conscious level, the distinction Dunn describes, between the faithful unworking and the unfaithful working, is undermined by the blurring of the economic metaphor in 4:4 with the theology in 4:5.

---

10. See Jewett (2007, 313), who draws on Thucydides, *P.W.* 2.20.4, where Pericles in his funeral oration recognizes how Athenians' sense of goodwill is different to those who owe the state a favour and thus act "not out of grace, but out of a sense of obligation (*ouk ex charin, all es opheiēlma*). Allied to this is the notion of *misthos* as being thoroughly economic and not at all metaphorical in terms of "religious reward" as in some other New Testament texts: Mark 9:41; Matt 5:12, 46; Luke 6:35 (Jewett 2007, 312). Jewett critiques some other scholars for viewing it this way and cautions that *charis* does not denote grace but "requires a neutral definition" as gift or favour (313). Schliesser (2007, 344 n. 905) argues that the metaphor is interrupted, for it follows the line of the Gen 15:6 quotation, and moreover Paul is disrupting the logical continuation of the image that might be "whoever does not work, will not receive repayment, except as a gift" (344 n. 906).

Such claims here rely on the metaphor behaving as it is supposed to behave, according to expectations of Paul, his followers, or even New Testament scholars. However, this metaphor does not necessarily work in the way intended. On the contrary, it has the potential to produce different effects. Indeed, "justification by faith" is an *aporia* in that it is conditional, meaning the believer is expected to have faith to be justified, which could be seen as an exchange, thus undermining the altruism of grace. One might ask why justification is not simply universal? In the traditional concept of gift-giving, we find the retention of altruism, generosity, fulfilment, and completion, but we also find at the same time an expectation that gratitude transcends time. We find delay, response, and the need for recognition elided from it; however, this is idealism according to the pattern of *usure* and *retrait* (see Derrida 1978b, 1982). In reality, gift-giving is an economic maneuver, whose presupposed return is obscured by delay, surprise, and unsolicited charity.

Culturally and politically there is inequality in the exchange of labor for wages (*misthos*). The economic system places more power and onus with the employer, who can choose who works for them and the terms by which the worker is employed, including wages, hours, policy, and so forth. Nevertheless, the employee, while subjected to the employer's choices, retains important rights under the law. The employee must be paid and treated fairly, safely, and with dignity. If not, then the employee can act against the employer through union strikes, protest, grievance, tribunals, or civil or criminal legal processes. The employee can whistle-blow if he or she witnesses criminality, and many states have a free media through which the employee can do this. Even in the first century, free workers retained some rights, although admittedly not as much as employees in democratic nations today.

Key to our discussion is that employees are owed a wage in this financial relationship, and if they are not paid their employer becomes in their debt. So, the use of this financial metaphor in Rom 4 involves the empowering financial aspects of *misthos*, such as the rights of the worker and the indebtedness of the employer; these are retained when the notion of justification is contrasted to *misthos*. According to the grace-as-altruistic-gift paradigm, the social inferiority of the employee and the superiority of the employer are elided in this contrast, because it is not good enough for God to be superior like an employer who still has duties and debts toward the employee. He must be *even more powerful* than this. Justification cannot be like a wage-labor exchange; otherwise this will be justification by works, and the believer will retain rights and powers. The traditional reading wants to argue that justification is not a wage-labor exchange, but it really is. The believer does retain rights and powers. However, one should not take this too far. The emancipation of workers only occurred after a long tradition of serfdom and slavery, the breakdown of the feudal system, and the emergence of mercantile capitalism in the later Middle Ages. Wage justice did not always exist and is not universal today in many parts of the world. An economic reading of Romans that recognizes that the believer retains some power but ignores the inequality in the employer-employee transaction reinforces the labor inequality still experienced by many. A reading that holds the believer to be powerless and pathetic collaborates with social injustice. Furthermore, altruism in the ancient and early modern eras was against the background of wage injustice, so integrity of the recipient was never possible. Today, it could be argued that charity given to the third world provides the donors with esteem despite the lack of fair wage and food equality between the third world and the West. The impoverished and oppressed are denied fair economic exchange or integrity. This shows it can be more just for exchange to be economic rather than charitable. This justice transposes into the realm of belief, where the believer is affirmed by being involved in a spiritual and intellectual exchange with God.

As we have discussed, in P.Mert. 12, Chairas expresses delight in receiving his friend Dionysius's letter and some medical items; the letter reduces his homesickness. However, discomfort is also described. My hypothesis is that Chairas is a battlefield surgeon or a physician attached to a military unit and that Dionysius is similarly qualified but more elite and with greater means. Against the grain of altruism that is implied when Dionysius sends a prescription for wound dressing, Chairas—the writer of P.Mert. 12—yearns for equilibrium. He hopes to maintain "serenity" by giving an "equivalence"; however, at the same time, he is diminutive of his own "small return" and renders Dionysius's letter and prescription as "affection" rather than something useful that will hold him under obligation. Chairas is trying to reframe the exchange—both of materials and epistolographic message—as an economic transaction, like a wage, rather than gifting-giving. However, equilibrium in the economy is as much a myth as it is in gift-giving. It is a symptom of an oppressive maneuver. Counterintuitively, Chairas tries to affirm economic exchange on the basis of friendship to prevent a formal bond, like a patron-client relationship. All exchanges, from the very formal to the very informal, include a tension between formality and informality. Mostly, the informal relationships tend to be the most usurious and the formal the more transparent. Yet no exchanges allow for equilibrium, full symmetry, or equality but are continuously negotiated or contested, whether by wages and debt or by gifts.

As stated in our earlier summary, in P.Oxy. 12.1481, a soldier in camp, Theonas, writes to his mother, Tetheus, reassuring her about his health, acknowledging the receipt of various presents, and expressing his general satisfaction. However, Theonas is concerned he has been placed under altruistic obligation by proxy through her. She has received a message that he is seriously ill, which he may worry is a sign of weakness. So he explains his delay in replying to her letter as his having been "in camp," thus emphasizing his usefulness to their society. For Theonas, this is perhaps a way to ward off attempts by others, such as Heraclides, to indebt him, by invoking the spirit of military function. He wants to be self-sufficient, rejecting the burden of generosity and reaffirming any transaction his mother has facilitated through the transparency of a debt he owes on her behalf.

In P.Oxy 42.3057, Ammonius acknowledges the receipt of items from his associate Apollonius but beseeches him not to send further gifts that he cannot afford to repay, emphasizing that they should continue to offer each other their friendship instead. Ammonius has, in my view, been subjected by Apollonius to an "embarrassment of riches" that the former wishes to understate. Ammonius uses vague sarcasm to deflect obligation to his friend Apollonius, who has sent him cloaks. Apollonius has attempted an altruistic blow on Ammonius, and Ammonius responds by describing the cloaks as old ones that are "better than new" due to the spirit they are given in. It could be that Apollonius is financially more advantaged and has sent the cloaks to Ammonius because he considers him inferior. Ammonius receives the cloaks spiritually, rather than materially, and in doing so does not need to account for his practical need for them. Instead, he returns pity, which might suggest Apollonius cannot afford to send new cloaks. Ammonius's return is therefore a gift that places Apollonius under spiritual or moral obligation by shaming him but showing "understanding."

The gift in Rom 4 contrasts to a wage in a way that upholds this injustice. You are not allowed to earn it, pay it back, or decline it, otherwise you will retain some power and rights. Idealism of the gift is also present in Rom 4, where God is the sole provider of benefit, and God retains all the rights and powers in the relationship. This reading relies on a notion of true altruistic gift in the human world for the metaphor to work. In reality there is no such thing as a truly altruistic gift, and giving is merely a delayed and detached stage in an economic exchange in which the recipient should be able to refuse or return the gift. The denial of the economy of gift collaborates with an oppressive insistence of patronage for domination.

Though scholars are showing how original hearers and worship communities today might interpret the theology, the economic sense cannot be used to support the theological sense and at the same time be divided from it as if it would not have further influence on its meaning; this metaphor has the potential to signify beyond these controlled limits. Economic senses of these terms, especially *charis*, affect the notion of grace more than we might think. Why? First, because the weight of the financial words studied in the first section of this chapter mitigates against the argument that *charis* is purely an altruistic and one-way transferal. Second, because the pattern of metaphysical *usure* is at play here too in the uses of the words *charis*, *misthos*, and *opheilēma*, certain aspects of the financial sense of these words are retained in their usage and certain aspects are elided, namely, aspects associated with gift-giving in the ancient world, but also gift-giving as a generic philosophical phenomenon. It is therefore a big mistake to argue that the relationship between God and the believer is based on God's grace as an altruistic gift-giving in opposition to a wage or a debt. The fallacy of this maneuver is to deny the worker economic rights of return and in turn to deny the believer a right to speak back to religious authority. Affirmation of wages or being a debtor ensures the rights of return—materially, intellectually, and spiritually. As we established in the previous chapter, even being a debtor is positive because it allows one power and onus in a relationship of exchange. There is more freedom in being indebted than being obliged for generosity.

A French proverb goes "one may say as readily 'to give a gift' as 'to give a blow'" (*donner un coup*) (Derrida 1992b, 171). Gift-giving was never selfless in the ancient world or even in the Pauline tradition; instead, it betrayed ulterior motives of economic control and oppression. Greco-Roman sources are rich with references to giving and gift-exchange that subvert the examples of altruism and charity presented by Seneca and endorsed by some New Testament scholars. Some of these include papyri texts of ordinary people, but many include the "textbook"[11] of gift-giving, Seneca's

---

11. For Peterman (1997, 52), *De beneficiis* is "methodologically … quite a valuable source to inform us regarding the social conventions of giving and receiving" that would have occurred in Greco-Roman environments.

own *De beneficiis*, which formalizes how society can gain cohesion through generosity and gratitude.[12] Seneca's main argument is that people in his era do not know how to give and receive benefits in the proper manner: *beneficia nec dare scimus nec accipere* (*Ben.* 1.1.1 [trans. Guglielmino]). Seneca argues that "people need to be taught to give, to receive and to return willingly and to strive to outdo each other in deed and spirit" (Seneca, *Ben.* 1.4.3 [trans. Peterman 1997, 4]).[13] In other words, Seneca implied that people need to be forced to receive and be denied agency. Yet while Seneca notes the presence of exchange and the obligation of the receiver, he claims it places equal demands on both. For Seneca, this is a social friendship not an economy. What we find in Seneca is the illusion of benign social obligation which, while involving exchange, is more about idealistic social cohesion in which obligations cause people to help each other in times of need. However, Seneca's benevolence is a cloak to oppression.

Seneca concedes that the reception of a benefit places a receiver under obligation (5.11.5) but does not view this to be one-sided and sees the reception as placing an equal demand on both parties (2.18.1) as part of a friendship (2.2.11; 2.18.5; *Ep.* 19.11–12). As such, this becomes for Seneca an "exchange of obligations" (2.18.2) within social reciprocity. In one sense Seneca is in tune with my argument—all giving is part of an exchange; however, Seneca is less aware of how protracted it is. Furthermore, since social relationships are interlinked with political and economic relationships, Seneca's idealism needs to be challenged more firmly by scholars such as Peterman and Endberg-Pedersen, who show awareness of his ulterior motives but do not push against him. In any act of giving, even between family or friends, there is a power dynamic, as well as connected personal, social, political, and economic aspects. No form of giving involves symmetry or full equality between parties. Either the giver, or the receiver, is in a position of greater power, even if that changes and shifts over time. When framed as an economic transaction rather than an altruistic gift, all that can be determined at any time in this dynamic is that neither party is the prime mover. Both are subject to something prior to themselves, and both have agency.

In the philosophical salon and political arena in which Seneca inhabited, there is an altruistic idealism that is undermined by the realism of

---

12. The Latin edition of Seneca I have consulted is Seneca 1967.

13. In the Latin edition this is found in Seneca 1967, which I consulted by way of comparison.

the letters of ordinary people. In P.Mert. 12, P.Oxy. 42.3057, and P.Oxy. 12.1481, reference is made to unsolicited material gifts received by the writer of the letters: wound dressing; cloaks, reeds, and a luggage case; and some unspecified present, respectively. These letters all suggest the authors are in situations where they have only basic comfort and resources, such as military camps or barracks, or they are in circumstances in which they may be perceived as being in need. Chairas in P.Mert. 12 mentions that he and others have nothing; however, he invokes friendship and resists any idea of being rescued by Dionysius, despite the latter sending the wound dressing. Chairas also focuses on his thanksgiving and wishes of good health to Dionysius, perhaps to evade the material gift he may feel is being forced upon him. Ammonius in P.Oxy. 42.3057 pleads not to be "loaded" with continual gifts he has not requested. Theonas writes to his mother in P.Oxy. 12.1481 to prevent her receiving unsolicited gift items that force him and her into perpetual debt.

Romans 4:3–4 and 11:29 involves an austerity in which altruistic gifts become pervasive and mandatory: "For the gifts and calling of God are irrevocable." This means you are under obligation to accept the gift of God. Where there is expectation to accept, there is economy, because there is need from the giver to exert their influence over the recipient. The gift of God as irrevocable is therefore oppressive. Since gift-giving in a human context contrasts to wages, it is a forced gift that ignores the role of the believer in the realization of God's work. Forced altruism is tautological, because all giving aims to surprise or embarrass the recipient at the behest of the donor. This is why some religious movements have resisted altruism so as to object to the ideological motives behind it. In Myanmar in 1990 and 2007, for example, Buddhist monks refused alms from the military out of protest against the regime, knowing this would damage its legitimacy; these gifts from the military were not selfless but motivated by a desire for power. Similar refusals have been made in other religious movements. It is clear that dominance is the agenda, even in some of the most well-intentioned circumstances, when the economic rights of exchange are denied.

Thrift versus Austerity

Economically, to make the receiving of gifts irrevocable and unlimited, there has to be austerity at play, because austerity manufactures the necessity for the enforced altruism. Such austerity is inflicted by the authorities on the poor, who are considered not entitled to wealth but lucky to benefit from it through charity. This is distinct from thrift, which is a personal control over one's own economy or, tautologically, their household economy (*oikos nomos*). Thrift is empowering and self-directed even if it can be too libertarian and individualistic, whereas austerity is disenfranchising and imposed yet almost always statist, whether reactionary, conservative, or communistic. The other side of the coin of austerity is, therefore, altruism, whether formalized policy or informal interventions by powers into the lives of individuals. Both altruism and austerity appear in ethics and politics; however, this is transferred into the theology of faith. An austerity of theological discourse allows for the altruism of prescribed doctrine that places the recipient under perpetual obligation. Thrift, in contrast, can be a rejection of imposed doctrine and an independent discernment of theological discourse. Let us see in the papyri how the contrast between austerity and thrift in the economic field can transpose into theology in Romans.

In P.Oxy. 42.3057, Apollonius has sent Ammonius a crossed-letter, a portmanteau, and reeds. Both of these gifts show austerity rather than thrift. The dissonance between different aspects of the text illustrates this if one reads carefully. A portmanteau case is a thrifty, or austere, item; it is a luggage case sectioned off for greater efficiency of storage. The reeds sent are also "not good," Ammoinius observes. Apollonius is, I assess, inflicting austerity on Ammonius, which increases the oppressiveness of the gift. By recognizing the spirit of the gifts and how they are better than new items, Ammonius is asserting thrift against the inflicted austerity, which increases the illusion of altruism in the gift.

Austerity is being exerted upon Ammonius in order to invoke altruism in a way that suggests that he is not worthy of anything better and should be grateful for even the very basic provision. Ammonius's thrift reaffirms his rights of exchange and refusal of perpetual debt. He renders his reception of the austere gifts as thrifty, suggesting he is used to newer and more decent ones. In P.Mert. 12, Chairas states, almost with pride, that he and the others where he is, "have nothing." In P.Oxy 12.1481, Theonas emphasizes how busy he is in order to assert his usefulness; he eschews anything beyond the thrift of his existence and urges his mother to reject any gift items that others may want her to convey to him. Austerity and altruism are therefore imposed from outside powers on to the individual, whereas thrifty economics flows from the individual and dissipates outwards. Austerity produces perpetual obligation and unworthiness so the juxtaposition of gift-giving becomes more powerful and generates perpetual and unaccountable debt that is cloaked by altruism.

Thrift is a self-induced act that makes all transfers accountable through transparent debt and an eschewing of problematic altruism that may perpetuate obligation infinitely.

Thrift, aligned with wages as something owed, represents the usefulness and agency of the worker against the machine of globalist excess. Gift and charity, against the backdrop of austerity and infinite production, diminish agency and deny the purpose and importance of the worker and the individual more widely. Gifts in the economy can be seen as the oppressive surpluses of capitalist excess Blanton critiques in *A Materialism for the Masses* (2014). Furthermore, in his afterword to Pier Paolo Pasolini's *St Paul: A Screenplay*, Blanton (2014 128) describes how Paul exposits "works and the weaponization of surplus against would-be workers." Both austerity and altruism are within the category of surplus, which ensures limitless production and protocol yet at the same time restricts agency of the individual as a worker. They reduce people to being segments in an endless factorial production line, in which their labor is not essential but replaceable. The role of the worker is diminished in that whatever they do can be replicated by someone else slotted into their place. Gone is the artist, craftsman, or artisan, and in their place is the operative. Alongside this is a duty to participate in this corporate machine, which originated in nineteenth century morality and has extended into globalism, with austerity positioned as a consequence of personal lack and altruism as undeserved assistance.

In Romans, Paul can be seen to expose Roman imperial market spirituality, in which excess production is gifted by the elite to the disempowered as an obligatory token of loyalty. Such patronage is upheld by the possibility of eternal life, which guarantees capital production in perpetuity. Surplus in the economy is weaponized because workers produce goods in abundance, some of which are processed and passed back to them under the guise of gifts when they are entitled to them. Inversely alongside surplus, austerity allows for a downwards restriction on the resource of the individual, making society's elite or moderately advantaged responsible for the charitable maintenance of the poor, and this also imposes forced altruism through charity. Similarly, the eternal abundance of God's grace, produced partly through the interpretation and imagination of the individual believer, is augmented and altered by the authorities—both temporal and spiritual—and dictated back to them.

Austerity denies the believer the right to interpret and develop their belief. Altruism enables the prescription of doctrine to the believer and oppression of them by the religious authority on the argument that the believer is pathetic and should be grateful for guidance and authority. Thrift, however, fosters a wise suspicion of enforced traditions and explanations, being open and unapologetic to the subjective force of the believer. From this analysis I argue that an authority guiding believers is restrictive and controlling, which leads to the continuous manufacture of a limited number of ideological algorithms. However, self-reliance of interpretation and a cynical prosecution of authoritative normativity is healthy and improves faith. From this approach, insular and prejudicial presuppositions that destroy and decay faith lose influence. Such critical individualism also enables a creative engagement with God that increases variety and diversity.

Gifts uphold a surplus that suspends the believer's economic and political rights in perpetuity. Among these rights is to be able to interpret, imagine, and believe, and such ideology finds its way into all aspects of life, including faith. Paradoxically, while neoliberal powers place limits on the interpretation of individuals, they rely on the surplus generated by the seemingly endless production of information, the main commodity of the digital age, where everything we write or participate in online is used to influence our thoughts and habits. In biblical studies, exegesis requests limitations on meaning, but the presupposition in traditional exegesis of boundless, oppressive grace is limitless!

Giving in Time: Delay and Deferral in the Epistle

In Josephus's *A.J.* 1.183, God needs to reassure Abraham that, even though the reward for loyalty is not immediate, it will be realized, thus showing that God needs Abraham's loyalty to continue. Such assurance may betray a sense that God is worried that another form of exchange could happen over time—the glory of the immortal God exchanged for images resembling mortal man, birds, animals, and creeping things (Rom 1:23). In eschatological and soteriological history, there is delay; believers must wait for God, who makes promises of future rewards which are framed as gift-giving. However, in *De cherubim*, Philo continues that "God distributes his good things, not like a seller vending his wares at a high price, but he is inclined to make presents of everything, pouring forth the inexhaustible fountains of his graces, and never desiring any return; for he has no need of anything, nor is there any created being competent to give him a suitable gift in return" (123). Some observations may suggest an infinite production-line theology in which the believer, like a worker in a factory, is unimportant, and authorities, under commission by God, convey an endless generosity the workers do not deserve. The metaphor of the fountain infinitely pouring forth already shows concern that the believer is given power. Reading against the grain, however, the economic and ecological reality of water fountains merely increases the power of the believer to determine their faith! There is no meaning owned by the authority that is immediately available like a constant fountain, and the believer has to interpret and create and apply their own meaning to their lives, just as someone has to gather the water from the fountain and use it. The fountain has to be maintained to work, just as the assemblies of believers in the world have to be maintained. The exchange between God and the believer is never immediately realized; it is always deferred and delayed through the negotiation of meaning.

Romans is called an epistle, or a letter by trendy preachers, although its historical context exposes a difference from what we think of as a letter today, a difference that is integral to the deferral and delay inherent in the message of Paul. Today we have systems of communication in which the only cause of delay in real time would be the prerogative of the respondent. Sometimes we can see if the recipient has seen our message and whether they are currently engaged in replying! In the last century, text communication largely took the form of letters delivered via postal service, but even these were usually delivered promptly in Western countries, give or take, with the sudden prominence of motor vehicles and then airplanes in freight logistics. Conversely, an ancient epistle was slower, taking months or even years to arrive. To understand the delay of epistle conveying in Paul's time, I suggest we imagine that we are stationed on Mars, trying to send electronic missives that may take a month or so to arrive back on Earth, then another month for a reply.

In order to understand Romans and the anxieties of the distance between time and space in giving and receiving, we must appreciate the delay, deferral, and difference of epistles. Before, after, and during the committal of words, a missionary such as Paul would likely have great concern and anticipation over how his text would be perceived by the hearers. Even the most articulate writer cannot overcome the changing circumstances in which their message is heard or control how it is understood. Derrida (1992b, 184) shows that the desire of gift-giving is powered by the impossibility of its resolution, and thus a gift exerts pressure on any text or speech that invokes the gift. The metaphysical "law of the economy is the circular-return to the point of departure, to the origin, is also to the home" (166). In many ways, Paul yearns for a safe return to his interpretive home in which his words are justified.

Having established the historical realism and limitations of correspondence, I am aware that we cannot instantaneously transport our physical bodies from one place to an extreme distance even on Earth. We cannot "beam" ourselves to a new location as on *Star Trek* or fly at speeds that break laws of physics. So even at the advanced stage of technological connection we find ourselves at, there is room for delay or difference in perception that generates anxiety. Even sitting across a kitchen table, you and I can talk clearly to each other in real time, but there is still a gap, a delay, and an anxiety that what we are saying may not quite convey what we want to, at the right time, in the right way. You and I are different, and our instances of sense are never fully transparent, however well we might know each other. This is a structural universal of communication. Instead, you or I may censor our thoughts in speech, and even if we were fully honest, we may not ever make a perfect transition between the two modes. There is always a delay, a deferral to a more ideal expression, and a constant difference between what is said, what is meant, what is heard, and what is understood.

Paul and his followers are clearly concerned about the potential for gaps between intended meaning and understanding. Paul's presence in the epistle might create an illusion of resolution,[14] but his absence is at tension with the expected resolution. There is a compulsion to protect the core meaning of the text from misinterpretation in a situation that is possibly different to where Paul is now or when he was last at the place of reception. Yet at the same time, Paul would have been concerned with making his message flexible and robust enough to withstand the uncertainty and inconsistency of the conditions of reception. Even at the level of the form of the epistle, there is both desire for absolute resolution and deferral of this lest it be insufficient or erroneous. Paul invokes gift-giving in the prescript and thanksgiving and by implication in the peroration, showing that for him the giving of his epistle anticipates a return in resolution that satisfies both he and the recipients on his terms. Yet while the metaphysical "law of the economy is the circular"—a return—"to the point of departure,

---

14. An Egyptian a generation after Paul exclaimed, "I rejoiced exceedingly as if you had come," when he received a letter from his brother (P.Mich. 8.482). See Richards 2004, 13

to the origin, also to the home," at the same time "*oikonomia* would always follow the path of Ulysses" in that a system of exchange is never really resolved by an equilibrium or equitable conclusion (Derrida 1992b, 166; my italics).

Delay and deferral obfuscates the reality of the economy, passing off the exchange as a gift. Not only can an original act of giving be divorced from the act of return, but an act of taking or injustice can be divorced from the return or justice. Any initiative, whether given or taken, can be detached from the next stage in the exchange through delay and deferral. In Plutarch's *Lucullus*, a scene is described where prisoners are released from jails after their loved ones thought them dead. This emptying of the jails is compared to a resurrection as well as a gift, which could be paralleled to that of Jesus and the resulting grace. It relies on delay in time, in that it is only perceived as a gift because it is late, and the relatives thought it would never happen; had it occurred promptly, then it may have seemed like a judicial right. Counterintuitively, delay usually obscures the exchange because it happens later and is not identified in connection with the prior gift. In this case, the families of the released prisoners will likely feel indebted to the giver of this gift in the future, with another delayed transaction. So delay both obscures the giving, the way something is received, and the motivations of the giving. Time increases desire and defers promised resolution. However, it does so in a way in which rights become passed off as generosity. We have the same difficulty in our papyri texts in that we cannot see what was sent before or afterwards to appreciate the reciprocity, but we can make intelligent speculation.

Such obfuscation occurs in the missiological and the theological, which, I propose, are indistinguishable in Pauline Christian thought. For Paul in Romans, the gift is not necessarily only material, but also spiritual, moral, or intellectual. In Rom 1:11, Paul longs to see the Roman Christians so that he can impart to them "some spiritual gift to strengthen" them or, as we could interpret this, to ensure they understand. In parallel, Derrida (1992b, 165) not only identifies desire as being central to the concept of the gift, he also goes further by saying that "desire and the desire to give would be the same thing, a sort of tautology." Paul mentions the mutual encouragement of each other's faith, perhaps in the same spirit of Seneca's idealist propaganda (Rom 1:12). However, in Rom 1:13, in a statement about his desire to visit in the face of travel problems, Paul says he intends to "reap some fruit [or harvest] among you as well as among the rest of the Gentiles." Fruit (*karpos*) becomes the antithesis of gift in Romans, undermining altruistic gift-as-grace (see also Rom 6:21, 7:4). *Karpos* is often used in the New Testament and other ancient texts as a metaphor for productiveness, and in our next chapter we examine the effect of the olive tree on missiology and eschatology. For Paul, the fruit might be the spiritual and financial support—both in finance and obedience—of the Roman church.

In another sense, it means a need for feedback that returns the gift of meaning. While Paul's mission is, as he proposes, human rather than divine, the reciprocal nature of the mission suggests that the relationship between God and the believer must be reciprocal if the world and heaven combine.[15] There is no total endless altruism, but at the same time there is also no complete resolution; an endlessly deferred reciprocity fills the relationship. While Paul's wish to give the Romans a spiritual gift and the intention to benefit from their fruits may not be specified as linked, they are nonetheless. If Paul will reap fruit on his visit, then the crop is already growing, suggesting he has planted seeds in his previous preaching, distancing the gift he may bring from the benefits he gains in time and space, making them seem unconnected. There is a tension between the desire to give, the need to receive, and the distance in time and place in the process of epistle communication. Epistles offer the question as to why we do not see the text of what they respond to or indeed the reply from the addressee. Even the curating of Paul's epistles indicates a tendency to suppress reciprocity, with scholars from the early church to today denying themselves the reciprocal discourse in the name of authority: we are told what gift Paul or God gives, but the significance of the fruit harvested is dismissed. This is apparent in the fact that only Paul's epistles survive into the canon of the New Testament, not the letters sent to Paul by the communities he addresses!

Gift-giving only seems different from an economy in that the return is delayed or obfuscated in a relationship. Return is not the same as resolution, however. The illusion—the sleight of hand—of giving depends on a delay in time where the return must be obscured or its responsiveness to the gift disavowed. Some scholars seek to justify the surplus of return for the gift as a spiritual enhancement of friendship through gratitude (for instance, Engberg-Pedersen 2008, 16). Even in an unequal relationship, the less advantaged party's will to return is considered gratitude, even if

---

15. After all, those raised from the dead will be bodily, not mere souls, as in Platonism.

they cannot provide a material return (20). Furthermore, for some Pauline scholars a hastened material return even shows a thankless way of thinking (20). However, as surplus increases, it causes unlimited anticipation of future resolution, which holds the recipient in thrall. Deferral of return obfuscates the connection between the acts of giving and return, to deny the economy. Furthermore, resolution of any return is never sufficient and thus perpetually deferred. While the inferred perpetual deferral of return is restrictive, the perpetual deferral of resolution is not—indeed it is empowering. Maybe the lack of resolution or the utterance that is outside of speech is grace.

For Derrida (1992b, 163), gift-giving can only take place in time, and economics is always time-bound. In Greek, "economy" is the law of the household, *oikos-nomos*, meaning all transactions in time, including those in business and family, and nation and home, are economic (166). The home in first century society was the microcosm of the cosmos and still is often treated as such via the nuclear family unit of Western nationhood. As time, organization, and participation are presupposed by economy, so too is distribution and partition. Life is the transferal of resources, both material and spiritual, between boundaries. Even biology adheres to this through osmosis, which is economical too. To manage this distribution, we require law, both physical (automatic) and legal (judicial), and as soon as there is law, there is economy and thus exchange. Even things we think are purely altruistic, such as parenthood, childhood, friendship, and sex, are economic over time. There is nothing outside of the economy. Gift-giving, like the economy, is never fully resolved either, because time allows for disavowal, denial, and obfuscation. Time is the factor that obfuscates the economy of the gift. The delay of giving, or receiving a return from the gift, helps assuage the myth of altruism. Furthermore, familial generosity remains economic through time. As such, God's giving as alike to, or set apart from, the political altruism of gift-giving and patronage culture, is rendered problematic. Therefore, God's altruism is subject to the same doubt as that of the analysis of these texts, and consequently there is always an economic circle. However, such doubt may be only in human perception, and so in faith terms there can be an outside of this circle outside of time, which is uniquely godly. When God interacts with believers however, it is always circular economics.

Chairas, in P. Mert 12, equates his receiving of a letter from Dionysius to being in his hometown, although time and space and the expense of sending this letter defeats this feeling. He intends his return letter to be a "small return" rather than an "equivalent": "and be able, if not to give you an equivalent, at least to show some small return for your affection toward me" (*kai ei mē ta isa soi paraschein, bracheia tina parazomai tē eis eme philostorgia*), deferring the return in time and betraying the convoluted economy inherent in the disproportionate power relation that inflates the value of Dionysius's letter, which is likely of the same material cost. He does not necessarily attempt to resolve the exchange but sends back a return that is both realistic and spiritual, refusing quantifiability that may show him up as not meeting the mark, yet also taking advantage of the deferral to perpetuate any judgement of his return due to his noble thrift. There is a need to resolve the transaction, not necessarily to close it, but to keep it open to further response, thus continually evolving and creating an ongoing relationship rather than a subjugation. The smallness and serenity he mentions becomes inverse, something noble, an affection that is open and not quantifiable but a fair return nonetheless.

In P.Oxy. 42.3057, the suddenness of the letter and the gift from Apollonius prohibits the receiver Ammonius from refusing it politely or planning for how to respond. Taken off-guard, Ammonius admits he cannot repay the gift and offers only feelings of friendship: "but I do not want you, brother, to load me with these continual kindnesses, since I cannot repay them ... the only thing we supposed ourselves to have offered you is (our) feelings of friendship" (*ou thelō de se adelphe ba - punein me tais suneches{es}i philanthrōpais, ... ou dunamenon ameipsasthai, auto de monon hēmeis proairesin philikēs diatheseōs nomi - zomen parestakenai soi*). However, the implications are that this debt is perpetually deferred and undefined, causing a spiral of moral and material debt, without giving Ammonius time to prefigure his role in the exchanges. Such suddenness of reception resonates with the problems of our own immediacy of communication today, albeit with less predictability. For instance, we receive emails or messages from people that infer a requirement for immediate response, even with an indicator for the sender as to whether we have read them in Whatsapp or Messenger. Ammonius's offer of friendship seeks to undermine the never-ending obligation of this giving with a spiritual proposal that defers his acknowledgement of the value of the gift and gives him space for self-justification. He further refuses the perpetual deferral of resolution implied by the gift but at the same time uses this perpetuity to defer his obligation by the injustice of the impudence of the unsolicited act of giving. By turning this perpetuity on its head, Ammonius demonstrates that deferral and delay can be empowering or oppressive or both, depending on whether openness or closedness is deferred. While Apollonius may have tried to set up a benevolence that is infinite, in which any attempt to maintain face is closed down, Ammonius refuses this catch, reframing exchange as an economic transaction—"I can't repay them"—thus deferring the resolution he cannot make with the abstract openness of acknowledging kindness without quantifying it. Believers cannot repay the ultimate grace of God; however, they can interact and retain some onus that is important in creating a relationship.

In P.Oxy. 12.1481, Theonas may be unwell or ill at ease but he dismisses this, accepting the life of camp as regular. He refers to his mother Tetheus as "his lady" (*kuria*), perhaps so he can elevate her status to defer accounting for any austerity or deprivation subjected upon him. I wonder if Theonas may be concerned about being obligated to the giver of the presents Heraclides, because he dilutes the generosity by focusing on how Dionytas delivered the gifts to him, including others in the generosity. Thus Theonas removes emphasis from the immediacy of the transferal and the continual deferral of return by opening this gift-giving to the creative reality of economic transaction. He tries to turn the perpetual deferral of return and obligation on its head for his own empowerment, lengthening the transferal of the gift and adding another actor—Dionytas—to undermine the oppressive altruism of the surprise gift and open its value to the spiritual, which cannot be quantified in a closed and conclusive way. Theonas's sign off is very revealing because he invokes "the gods ... continually." Rather than recognizing any implied closed value that he would need to return to resolve this unsolicited act of giving, he opens it up, spiritually, to divinity. Maybe it is here that we find God's grace powering an openness of benevolence in which religious authorities cannot dominate—a relationship with divinity that is perpetually evolving and changing.

The papyri show that it is crucial to distinguish between two types of deferral and delay—what I will call *infinite* versus *eternal*. Infinite is continual, repetitive, and closed, like the infinity of numbers moving up by one integer. Eternal is evolving and open, offering change, dynamics. and evolution. For instance in P.Mert. 12, Dionysius may want Chairas to be perpetually subject to obligation, which is closed to any form of return. However, Chairas wants their relationship to evolve around a respectful friendship that is constantly negotiated and open. As the economic, so is the theological. Deferral of resolution perpetuates closed and absolute meaning. It is the endless repetition of one person's or one system's idea, like a production-line economy. Its perpetuity is not creative but limited and restrictive. Deferral of meaning, however, perpetuates an openness that defies any claim for the absolute and opens up the interpretation and imagination of the individual believer. Grace becomes momentarily acute at the point at which the need for resolution drives the movement away from altruism and toward the acceptance of a universal openness. God cannot manifest in the dark expanse of infinite authority, but only in the eternal chasms of possibility.

Gift-Giving beyond the Material or Spiritual

Gift-giving is beyond the obvious material or sociopolitically ritual that feeds back into the material realm through long deferral. Implicit is a contradiction in which we find the material and spiritual contiguous but, at the same time, gift and grace separate. Nineteenth century ideas of charity framed human and social rights as benevolence in which the rich would gain moral credit and satisfaction for giving aid. This was compounded by a view that the individual's own responsibility is to stay out of poverty. A failure to do so betrayed a weakness of character, with books by Samuel Smiles ([1859] 2014) and Norman Pearson (1911) showing the popularity of such attitudes. Outreach to the poor and to the convicted arguably began due to a concern that poverty and criminality could spread hereditarily and pervade society, threatening the security of the upper and middle classes (Lombroso [1876] 2006). Those infected might lose their superior status. It was feared, in the aftershock of Charles Darwin's challenge to creation, that if life can evolve, it can also devolve (Byron 2000, 134). People wanted to appear to be higher on the evolutionary scale than others. Religious missionary motivations stemmed from self-righteousness and the need to confirm their status as good Christians because winning souls showed the superiority of a person.

In some ways this was a narcissistic marriage of social Darwinism and Christianity. Charity-as-a-gift was therefore not altruistic but preventative and protective, for the benefit of those who were not poor.[16] It was not immediately material but involved a moral or spiritual return, which afforded the giver a sense of superiority over the disadvantaged recipient. Even if the giver perceives their act as generosity, they have a return, albeit

---

16. Interestingly, Seneca, whose ideology of gift is critiqued in this chapter, also showed fear of poverty in *Epistulae Morales* (see 44.7 in particular).

not material. Derrida (1992b, 172) calls this "symbolic recognition." If the giver does not understand their giving as generous or altruistic or if they forgot these thoughts and emotions, they would still retain unconscious memory of it, thus annulling the gift. However, if we dispense with the altruistic baggage of altruistic charity and embrace the economy of the gift, we can have useful discussions about what kind of social, ethical, and religious ideology we want to shape. Maybe we can invert the self-righteousness of giving to show that material charity, when rephrased as economic, can prefigure an ethical agenda that is accountable to individuals as stakeholders. Such giving can be economic in the philological, cognitive, and spiritual. Gift-giving is not simply material or reducible to materialistic or ritualistic value. There are other ways in which giving entails a return beyond the material and the ritual. Sometimes these returns are narcissistic in terms of recognition; however, maybe this powers the creativity of the individual.

To demonstrate this symbolic recognition, we turn again to our papyri texts. In P. Mert. 12, when Chairas thanks Dionysius for his letter, he uses the word *Xairein* for "greetings" alongside wishes for his "continued health." Further, he says he writes with "great thanks" (*magalas eucharistias*), thus rendering a gift-related word in the concept of returned recognition. In this papyrus text, even thought-as-a-gift places the recipient under the obligation to return with another thought. Ammonius, in P.Oxy 42.3057, has received old cloaks from Apollonius, and he acknowledges they are not new, but he recognizes the spirit of the gift. There is recognition, but this is mixed with dismissal of material debt. He then pleads with Apollonius not to send anything else as he cannot repay and then reaffirms their friendship. There is tension here between the material, on the one hand, and the emotional and spiritual, on the other. Theonas, in P.Oxy 12.1481, suspects maybe that his mother Tetheus's loving generosity toward her son is making her indebted to others. He is concerned for the material implications of her letter and presents and wishes this not to be intertwined with emotional implications, but it is. So, too, is it with Paul and the recipients of his letters. Paul negotiates the borders between the spiritual and material worlds, with one being translated into the other and then becoming inextricably linked.

The materials used to create ancient letters—the papyri and ink—are themselves value items, but they are positioned as mediums for salutations, thoughts, and recognition, thus highlighting that even the conveyance of a thought has economic ramifications. The cost of sending a letter in this era is significant, meaning that good wishes and kindness, as a luxury, is a myth; they are economic. Even speaking to someone to tell them good wishes may have implications that need to be offset, such as considering whether this person's opponents may have a dim view of your kindness. Travelling to speak to someone to give good wishes in ancient times necessitates energy and cost that must be budgeted for or rationalized, thus annulling the gift. Today, if we send a text message, Messenger or Whatsapp message or email, we calculate how doing so affects us and consider how it may be perceived within the context of our personal lives and careers. We send messages to assuage our own consciences or to feel like we are good people. We might send messages against our feelings and in coordination with what we think is most beneficial to us or those we love. Sometimes we take risks to do this or compromise allegiances with others. All of these factors show that the effort of giving or responding to kind messages is not purely altruistic but to some extent calculated and economic, and we do not need to give material gifts for this to be the case.

In Rom 15, the altruism of gift-giving is undermined in a part of the text often seen as only missiological. In the opening of the letter, Paul shows his desire to impart spiritual gifts to the Roman church, yet in Rom 15 he implies this comes at a cost. Romans 15:22–33 details Paul's plans to visit Rome, in which he aims to make a collection for the church in Jerusalem. Macedonia and Achaia, Paul says, have made their contribution, and Paul points out that the citizens of Rome owe it to Jerusalem to do so as well. He continues in 15:27: "For if the Gentiles have come to share in their [the Jerusalem saints'] spiritual blessings, they ought also to be of service to them in material things." The paradox here is that the grace of the spiritual benefit of the gospel appears to come at a material price, which undermines grace and the gospel! If, however, we distinguish altruistic gift-giving from God's grace, a more honest theology can appear. Mission requires personal sacrifice and material cost, as we see from Paul's example, the story of the apostles in Luke-Acts, and even the activity of the disciples of Jesus. The realism of the mission adds a progressive and liberating economic dimension that increases individual rights in the commission of Christ. The practicality of the church as a physical corporation is revealed here—it must be resourced. However, the church is also a spiritual cosmological entity too (see Lincoln 1981). In order to build the church, therefore, believers have to do and give things. The spirituality of God's church thus relies on the physical and material work of the believer. The spiritual support—even that of an apostle of Christ—needs to be funded and sustained, so the gift of Paul, extending to the grace of Christ, depends on the contributions of the believer. This undermines traditional scholarship's attempts to split gift-as-grace from the worldly economy—there is no fountain of grace as Philo perceived but instead a river tamed by humankind. In mission, as in any relationship, the giver often needs the evidence of need from the recipient. This mimics God's need of the expression of need from the believer, in which their rendering as unworthy becomes the return of the gift. God's grace must, therefore, be outside of this.

The material and spiritual therefore merge or are indistinguishable in a way that does not allow a special pleading for divine gift. However, this does not mean we have to abandon a sense of God's grace. Counterintuitively, to fully experience God's grace, we must dispense with its mandatory connection to altruistic gift. Of course, the metaphor of God's grace-as-gift is unavoidable and even logical and serves an important purpose in understanding. It should come with the caveats this chapter has identified. Ultimately, God's grace must become something unquantifiable that we cannot fully define, however not something that demands exhaustive and unquestioning devotion. In the material world, it can only be thought of through the economic turn. Attempts to align God's grace to a sense of gift as truly altruistic and superior result in oppressive theology that defies grace entirely.

The Gift as Supplement

Let us propose that the singularity of grace is the blind spot in the contradiction in which the gift is both essential and supplementary or even luxurious. A tension between luxury and necessity permeates the gift. The gift is a supplement, which is defined by Derrida (1976) as something that seems to add by way of surplus yet may at the same time compensate, replace, or substitute. Eroticism and love are supplementary to marriage, onanism to sexual intercourse, laughter to seriousness, literature to philosophy, metaphor to proper, absence to presence. How many marriages survive without love and eroticism? How can democratic governments be held to account without the hilarity of satire? How can philosophy be expressed without the description of the poetic and dramatic? How much can anyone write without needing to use a metaphor—even a cliche? How do we know what is present if we do not consider what is not—darkness/light; hot/cold; good/evil. The metaphysics of presence refers to the superiority of the present speaker over the absent writer of a text, and it renders writing a supplement to speech. Yet in some of the confessional traditions of biblical studies, scholars yearn for the original text from the lips of apostles, prophets, and disciples! The search for the original text is pinned upon the actual vocal words of people transmitting the words of God or the voice of God himself! We should note at this point that there are many movements in biblical studies that do not seek authoritative authorial finality and are open to plasticity and plurality of interpretation. In this radical spirit, I ask: what if grace is that moment at which we admit things we cannot speak of, the gaps in the meaning that drive our need to interpret and imagine in our own right, not relying only on the gifts of the previous thoughts of others? What if grace is the moment before we leap into the precipice of meaning?

God's grace is best placed away from the necessity of the gift despite the latter being the paradigm for the former—both necessary and in excess. In *De communibus*, Plutarch argues that gift-giving is only real if the receiver needs and finds use in the gift. However, something supplementary or excess is also necessary. Seneca polemicized that only through an exchange of official good deeds is one able to live in security (*Ben.* 4.18.1) and that the interchange of benefits strengthens life against unseen disasters (4.18.2) so that the obligations felt between friends will cause them to aid each other if one of them is in distress. The reality is that Seneca's idealism of benevolence is exposed as economic and useful. For instance, Seneca states that it is not possible for a man to live outside of human society, which is a system of "exchange of good deeds" as Peterman (1997, 55) observes of *Ben.* 4.18.1. Seneca's statement here undermines biblical studies' use of Seneca's work as a proof text for gift-giving as a form of generosity outside of economy. Here, there is a tension between the essential and supplementary because, in the illusion of biblical studies, a gift is both luxury and necessary, friendly and formal, decorative and useful. Yet, at the same time, maybe grace is outside the circle of the gift's economics, powering it along.

Gift as a denial of the economy is undermined by the process of givers identifying things people may need to impress or subvert them and potential recipients eliciting things they need through the rigmarole of giving. However, it also means power can be exerted through the process where a gift is positioned as a supplement. Embracing the economic while at the same time accepting the power of grace can be liberating. In P.Oxy. 12.1481, Theonas wants to emphasize his usefulness and wants to clarify the facts of his personal health and finance, but at the end of the letter he invokes the grace of the gods through his thanks. In P.Oxy. 42.3057, Ammonius is very uncomfortable with being given an unexpected gift by someone, because it puts him in debt. The writer praises the cloaks he receives as "better than new" due to the spirit in which they were sent, which is a return to the giver, Apollonius, who will acknowledge his own generosity. This seems nice, but Ammonius (the recipient) implores Apollonius (the giver) not to issue these continual kindnesses, because, he says, he cannot repay them. He concludes that all he can offer back is "feelings of friendship." This exposes the gift's economy, but also acknowledges grace at work outside of the cycle; it is not simply an altruistic gift. Ammonius disrupts the exchange with the grace of friendship, which he elevates as going beyond altruism. In P.Mert. 12, the spirit of wishing good health may be the grace rising above the posed altruism of the letter and prescription of plasters, with a need for equivalence to be reached by a health salutation being returned by reply.

For Agamben (2005, 124), gratuitousness "manifests itself as an irreducible excess with regard to all obligatory service" and while "grace does not provide the foundation for exchange and social obligations," it instead "makes for their interruption." Gift as gratuitousness therefore disturbs the perceived resolution or equality that is often attributed idealistically to economic exchange—where the receiving party might be presented as not being obliged because they are owed or have provided something of value to justify being paid, for example, workers being paid for labor they have provided or a shopper paying money to a shopkeeper because they have obtained wares from them. Gift-giving attempts to move outside of this exchange structure in order to defer resolution and oblige the recipient, so that he is perpetually under obligation. Agamben notes that George Bataille defined an "excess of grace in his theory of the sovereignty of the unproductive expenditure (dépense improductive)" (124). In doing so, he "transforms gratuitousness into a privileged category of acts" (including "laughter, luxury, eroticism, etc.") that "stand in opposition to utilitarian acts" (124). Gift or gratuity relies on this opposition to be able to exert influence and place the recipient under obligation, but the irony is that this opposition also draws its justification from economy, because the luxury and privilege of gift cannot be altruistic, and the giver expects return of some sort. Grace-as-gift, however, can be seen instead to interrupt both the economic and altruistic to increase the awareness of the believer of God's grace transcending the time and sequence, but not the dignity of, exchange in the world. The manifestation of God's grace in the world is therefore found within this set of tensions, where the believer's power and onus is both necessary and supplementary to the will of God in his eschatological project.

Gift as Distinct from Grace

One of the major takeaways of this chapter is that despite the etymological connection in Greek, gift and grace are distinct. Indeed some etymological links such as these do become oppositional rather than similar. The Greco-Roman and latterly Western tradition of the proffered altruistic gift that is not really a gift and is really economic, is not the same as grace. The metaphor of God's grace-as-gift is not insufficient or deceptive but just another metaphor that needs analyzing as all metaphors do—with deficits and excesses of meaning. Defects with this metaphor are not an imposition more than any others. All metaphors contain as much contradiction and paradox as they do similarity. While Derrida is essentially silent on his own faith in that he refuses to declare atheism or theism, I would like to extend his work by factoring in Agamben to show where God's grace can appear in theology. In short, it is a mistake to consider earthly gift-giving, especially that from an elite or superior source, as equivalent to God's grace even though the comparison is essential in this paradigm. The interaction between God and the believer must be raised above this pretension while at the same time embracing real economy. Altruism is a form of economic oppression cloaked as a benefit. Gift remains economic, whereas grace is outside of economy, willing the intended generosity on. Altruism hides and oppresses reciprocity whereas God's grace allows it to flower.

According to Agamben (2005, 124), "for Paul grace cannot constitute a separate realm that is alongside that of obligation and law," and "grace entails nothing more than the ability to use the sphere of social determinations and services in its totality." For Agamben, God's grace, through gift and gratuity, cannot exist outside of a relationship with both faith and obligation (see 119–21 in particular). In other words, God's grace can never be purely altruistic, and the generosity of gift-giving only extends to allowing the recipient an entry into a privileged form of economy. This holds to our present argument that grace does not justify the altruistic gift. Grace rehabilitates the economy and exchange, even though it rises above it. If we pretend that the gift is altruistic, we become blinded to God's grace and oppressed. Through an affirmation of economic exchange the believer can experience the power of God's grace from outside and transition into a two way relationship with God. Grace is lifting and empowering through economy, of which altruism is a subdivision of, not through a nonexistent idealistic pure altruism.

As such, we may say that God's grace does not provide a one-way flow of benefit from God to the believer, but instead, and at best, offers the believer an unconventional invitation to engage in exchange with God, albeit a delayed and deferred exchange. Agamben is more positive than Derrida on altruism, however, and while he denies that gifts can ever be removed from the economic cycle, he sees Paul's gospel as signaling a messianic rupture in *charis*, which transcends the authority and allows the individual sovereignty to distribute their own grace without regulation by law (drawing on Rom 5:15–21 and 2 Cor 9:7–8; see Agamben 2005, 120–21). Grace therefore lies in this messianic calling, not in a cascading divine altruism from God to the believer via self-ordained authorities.

This present chapter may feel cynical to the reader, as if God's grace is being denied. However, this is not the case; instead I am denying that God's grace is equivalent to the human gift tradition or altruism. In all three of the papyri, we have a sense that the gift is being mistaken for grace, that the giver is being altruistic, and that the recipient benefits greatly from this generosity. However, all three recipients are anxious toward the obligations these gifts place them under. Generosity will only ever be equitable when it involves an acceptance of economy. While the New Testament metaphor of gift-giving in contrast to wages undermines grace, the outcomes are very positive combined—the power of the believer and the limitless grace of God through Jesus Christ. The key is that the latter relies on the former. Without the power of the believer there can be no grace whatsoever, because grace relies on the reciprocity between God and the believer, not an idealized altruism. Grace is abundant. It is just that our metaphors, indeed our use of language, need to be checked and challenged.

For Derrida, "grace is what surprises us in the gift" and that "beyond calculation or narration, it is the meeting of our conscious decisions and the chance of an unforeseen future" (see Shakespeare 2009, 162–63). Grace is therefore the result of the borderline point of faith, between the known and the unknown. The economics of *pistis* emerges as a calculation and assessment, yet at the same time contains a contingency—prayers in the darkness. When you lend money, allow someone to babysit your children, or look after your house for instance, there is always a risk, however much you manage to reduce it through informed assessment. It is in this space that God's grace emerges. This may seem cynical again, but the rationale for that decision can be filled with spirit.

Rather than assessing whether to lend money based on whether we profit from interest, we can do so on the integrity of the person and if they are using it for ethical good. Selecting who cares for our children can be a decision made on the lovingness of the person rather than their austerity. If we let someone use our home, we can do so out of hospitality rather than expecting them to adjust to our mores. We retain the right to assess, but we have a responsibility to interpret fairly and lovingly where there is room for doubt. Derrida (1992a, 123) says that preconditional to grace must be "chance, encounter, the involuntary, even unconsciousness or disorder," on the one hand, and "intentional freedom," on the other, and these two conditions must "miraculously, graciously—agree with each other." This precondition for grace allows for the chaos of love within the onus of the individual to assess this. Grace must not be an economically calculated transaction cloaked as altruism, such as with patronage or potlatch culture. Instead, it must be simultaneous and open to contingency or the risk of betrayal or default. The heart of the person dispensing or receiving grace must be open and intending not morality or conformity, but that the outcome of the transaction assures the freedom of the other with whom they engage, even to their disadvantage. Abraham and the believer's trusting in God is therefore not akin to the receiving of a gift in line with Seneca or Roman patronage, as some traditional biblical scholarship argues. Instead, it is an unconsciously driven maneuver made in the spirit of an intention for liberty, within a moment in which these two opposing poles coincide. Righteousness to Abraham and the believer is, conversely, given in the spirit of God's grace, within the same window of contingency and risk, in which the intention of the believer to trust God coincides with God's own intention to empower the believer as a vehicle for his glory. Grace is thus driven by the reciprocity of God and the believer in gift, not the gift itself.

Summary of Analysis

So far, I have challenged the presupposition that ancient gift-giving is purely and truly altruistic, and I have contextualized these traditions as far as I can within a context of the economy. The contrast between the wage and the altruistic gift has been thrown into doubt by acknowledgement of the economic turn of gift-giving, albeit delayed, and the exposure of oppressive intentions of benevolence. Altruism has been aligned with austerity, with the latter being imposed increasing the self-righteous maneuvers of the former, whereas economy has been aligned with thrift, which contrasts to altruism in that it is a form of self-management that retains dignity of the individual. From these contrasts and alignments we can trace a believer who is not subject to other authorities but able to take ownership and determination of their own interpretation, creativity, and faith. We have seen that delay and deferral obfuscate the economy of the gift, which, on one hand, can close possibility, and, on the other, can open it out to endless variation and diversity. It has been shown that gift is beyond the material versus spiritual binary and instead involves creative economic feedback between these two fields. Through the supplementarity of the gift, we can trace the faith of the believer, who is both necessary and extra to God's will. Then, from here, while recognizing the prevalence and necessity of this metaphorical paradigm of gift-giving as grace, we find a distinction between an altruistic gift and God's grace.

The Implications of the Power of the Believer

Acknowledgement of the economic is empowering to faith.

As stated earlier in this chapter, the first problem of the altruistic gift paradigm of grace is that gift, and then grace, becomes forced and oppressive. Altruistic giving, however well-intentioned, can be demeaning and used to restrict. Psychological studies show that people tend to be more suspicious of people who attempt to be altruistic when there are identifiable benefits to them (*tainted altruism*), than those who are completely selfish (Newman and Cain 2014, 648–55). This is significant in that it shows how the necessity of survival is thoroughly economic, and we know that religion is shaped by the emergence of society and efficient deployment of resources through agriculture, such as the raising of animals, the diversion of water, and the husbandry of plants, such as olive trees in our allegory in Rom 11.

Other psychological studies show that helping behaviors are aimed at helping the Self as well as the Other, meaning that altruism cannot be separated from selfishness (Krebs 1991, 139); psychological anthropology shows that our human ancestors who placed importance on getting help for themselves increased survival and forged cooperation (Finlay and Syal 2014, 615–17). Some social philosophy questions whether altruism is true without self-interest (see Badhwar 1993, particularly 115–16). Behavioral theory experiments show that self-interest promotes an altruistic outlook

(Chan 2017, 667–73), and I wonder if this is not only due to the communal binding but to the fact that the recipient is aware of the benefit to the other and is not under obligation. Without affirming selfishness, concern for one's own wellbeing and sustainability empowers us to be fulfilled enough to be caring. So, the rejection of pure altruism does not mean kindness and generosity is denied, but it involves return through recognition and comfort, as well as reassurance that there is social order and justice for all.

A major problem of the posed altruistic gift is that it is not freely given but forced and violent. Walter Benjamin (1996) shows that the real violence is the obscuring of the difference between types of violence. For Benjamin there is the proletarian strike, which presupposes the righteousness of unfair law, and the general political strike, which is messianic and divine because it overthrows unfair law and government. The proposed altruistic gift is proletarian violence because it aims to correct injustice according to a restoration of a prior unfair law, whereas an economic rendering is prototypically divine and messianic in that it has the capacity to topple a regime by empowering an individual through their rights to return beyond the limitations of predetermined sovereignty. Paradoxically, the general political strike does not destroy the economy; instead, it perpetuates the cycle of exchange in the material realm, including the mental and spiritual that interacts with the material (such as pride, esteem, righteousness, honor, etc). It does, however, destroy the infinite neoliberal altruism that is not even disrupted by the proletarian strike and closes in on the individual and perpetually delimits their agency and onus.

For Paul, the law is not abolished in the messianic age but becomes stripped of altruistic perpetual oppression, which closes the potential of the believer and is opened up through the affirmation of its economy in the empowerment of the believer. Rather than the obligation of law in the economy—the law of the house—restricting the theological thought of the believer, the obligation of the law instead sustains the rights and onus of discourse both ways, between God and the believer. It opens interpretation and imagination—the factors of the composite of faith—and makes genuine meaning out of the eschatological tension between the heavenly and the earthly. It allows for empowerment of the believer for the realization of true grace.

Economic agency is a paradigm for real faith.

The next problem I identified was that emancipation is seen as dependence in the altruistic paradigm, whereas the self-determination of the individual is condemned as unsocial and unethical. There are many moral and ethical arguments that set communal dependence and personal agency at tension. Obsessions with transporting democracy and capitalism involves subjugating the recipient state to an altruistic clienthood and committing the recipient to a moral obligation that they submit to austerity. Both these forces remove the ideological identity of the subjugated. There is a presumption in European and especially United States neoliberalism that capitalist democracy is normative and should be replicated even at great economic and humanitarian cost (the austerity). Even the powerful empires of France, Britain, and Spain were honest, to some extent, about their superiority and their claims to the right to colonize, however unethical those claims might be. The problem with contemporary neoliberalism is that it positions itself as morally superior and beneficial to the nondemocratic countries it intervenes in. This has been evident in the contentious wars in this and the previous century, which have promoted the national interests of dominant countries without acknowledging the benefit to them (Dixon 2019, 820). Such certainty about what human rights are in postcolonial occupation leak into religious and cultural issues, with the veiling of women being presented in opposition to women's liberation, for example, based on problematic presuppositions (see Tofighi 2017, 95–126). There is a danger that every other culture becomes subsumed by self-righteous altruism into a neoliberal structure that is positioned as infinite. Banning of veils, types of circumcision, theocratic governance, corporal and capital punishment, and other practices are examples of such altruism, which aims to restrict features unique to other religions and cultures under the pretense of Western moral and political superiority. Suspending for a moment the ethical problems of some practices, it is worth noting that Western moralizing merely exposes the severe inequality inherent in the neoliberal consensus. Such consensus denies individuality under the pretense of equality, which is actually corporate universality.

While Romans shows the believer to be part of an organic body of Christ, we have to avoid dissolving the individuality of what the believer brings to the conversation, theologically, through our economic reality. Everyone has something to give, no matter how poor or insignificant they may seem. In Rom 12:6–8 Paul says: "We have different gifts, according to the grace given to each of us. If your gift is prophesying, then prophesy in accordance with your faith; if it is serving, then serve; if it is teaching, then teach; if it is to encourage, then give encouragement; if it is giving, then give generously; if it is to lead, do it diligently; if it is to show mercy, do it cheerfully." Romans is not consistent with altruistic dependence because the believer is identified as part of the gift matrix, which is economic rather than altruistic. This means that the believer is not merely dependent on the wider body but is instead an organ that is integral and has agency in that body.

Reappraising the gift as economic is not to be materialistic or immoral but realistic and honest. Relations between parties should not be about generosity and charity but equality and mutual exchange that reinforces agency while at the same time increasing cooperation and minimizing dependence. Viewing Romans through the economic lens affirms the ethics of Christian faith and the rational expectations of the believer in all Abrahamic religions—to seek knowledge and radically apply it to life (as per Cullman 1951). To see gifts as economic rather than altruistic allows the believer to engage deeply in their faith and their relationship to God with agency rather than dependence on authorities. Radical application allows them to steer away from the illusory generosity of one-way reception and toward reciprocity. Herein lies the real grace.

The binary between the essential and the supplement is dissolved.

The third problem I identified is the presupposition that what is essential and what is supplementary is clear and established when it is instead highly subjective. We saw that the dichotomy between the essential and the surplus justifies austerity because it strengthens and altruism because it is benevolent. Conversely, we found through our readings of the papyri letters that thrift acknowledges the economic dimensions and increases the self-determination of the individual. Thrift, as distinct from austerity, helps the believer dispense with the oppressive paradox of altruistic gift-giving being both essential and at the same time excessive. From here we can recognize the *jouissance* of Derrida's notion of the supplement—across a continuum between the fundamental and the superfluous poles, rather than fixed as something extra, luxurious, or ornamental.

Dissolution of the binary between the essential and the supplement removes the control of the theological authority over what a believer must think, know, or believe and what they should not. The deeply unhealthy idea of the irrevocable gift can be reframed as an (albeit asymmetrical) exchange between God and the believer, with the believer having power and onus. The power to reject a gift allows the believer to develop their relationship with God and the affirmation of the economic recognizes the believer's rightful place in the economy of the eschatological project. The believer can earn, pay, or return to God in the eschatological economy, in the only way they can affect reality, leaving grace outside of this mechanism as their conscience commands. The economics of gift-giving can point the believer toward grace in an honest way, in which they are not excluded by corrupt authority, and can relate to God in a way that unites them in enlightenment.

Conclusion

In this chapter I have argued, counterintuitively, that the insistence on the anaeconomic gift is symptomatic of oppression. In denying the notion of the altruistic gift, however, rather than being pessimistic, I have argued that the economic and materialistic reality of gift can liberate believers from the yoke of oppressive powers, including churches and governments. Readings of gift allegory in 4:4 in biblical studies have been far too lenient with literary sources of the ancient world, such as Seneca, and scholars have abandoned historical-critical faculties in their acceptance of these sources. In reality, we can see that gifts in the ancient world are entirely economical and rarely altruistic, so while we use the gift as a metaphor for God's intervention, we cannot expect it to coordinate with grace. Readings that contrast *charis* in 4:4 to labor wages (*misthos*), as well as the more generic "things owed" (*ophelema*), attempt to align God's grace to altruism and condemn payment as a materialistic, inferior process yet they undermine the social justice of grace itself!

To show that the altruistic gift must be separated from grace, I have focused on near-contemporary papyri to show how the so-called altruistic gift is oppressive rather than helpful or liberating. One papyri I turned to was P.Oxy. 12.1481, where Theonas tries to convince his mother Tetheus that he is not ill nor in need and acknowledges presents sent through her from others and hopes she is not obliged or burdened by this. Another was P.Oxy. 42.3057, where Ammonius tries to underplay several gifts and the letter sent to him, yet at the same time infers obligation and an inability to pay back such gifts. Another was P.Mert. 12, where Chairas affirms the importance of friendship to ward off obligation, highlights his thrift, and indicates a need for resolution to attempted altruism. My analysis of these papyri showed that gift-giving in the material world is never truly altruistic, and its oppressiveness can be shown by the recipients' often polite attempts to reject or downplay it.

I assert that *gift-giving* is not the same as *grace*. Gift-giving necessitates the reciprocity of the economic turn, although it involves an attempt to obscure it in a way that allows oppression. Grace, on the other hand, is something obscure that we cannot quantify or assess yet, from outside, drives the cycle of exchange and mutuality between God and the believer. I have scrutinized and challenged the traditional confessional approaches. I have shown that only when we honestly appraise the ancient concept of the gift and its effect on the hearer of Romans can we truly understand grace. Furthermore, I posit that altruistic gifts and grace are not the same and are at tension, despite being within the same metaphorical composition. The so-called altruistic gift disavows a liberating economic turn if it is justified by the likes of Seneca or other polemicists and propagandists of the Roman Empire. Reading gift-giving through the papyri, away from altruism, acknowledges the economic and offers a much more empowering relationship between God and the believer, which is empowered by grace from outside this cycle. Grace emerges through a messianic rupture that ensures the individual is sovereign and their giving is done with mutuality, reciprocity, and dignity.

3
GRAFT

POLIXENES
Say there be;
Yet nature is made better by no mean
But nature makes that mean: so, over that art
Which you say adds to nature, is an art
That nature makes. You see, sweet maid, we marry
A gentler scion to the wildest stock,
And make conceive a bark of baser kind
By bud of nobler race: this is an art
Which does mend nature, change it rather, but
The art itself is nature.
—Shakespeare, *The Winter's Tale*, 4.4.88–97

But if some of the branches were broken off, and you, a wild olive shoot, were grafted in their place to share the rich root of the olive tree, do not boast over the branches. If you do boast, remember that it is not you that support the root, but the root that supports you. You will say, "Branches were broken off so that I might be grafted in." That is true. They were broken off because of their unbelief, but you stand only through faith. So do not become proud, but stand in awe. For if God did not spare the natural branches, perhaps he will not spare you. Note then the kindness and the severity of God: severity toward those who have fallen, but God's kindness toward you, provided you continue in his kindness; otherwise you also will be cut off. And even those of Israel, if they do not persist in unbelief, will be grafted in, for God has the power to graft them in again. For if you have been cut from what is by nature a wild olive tree and grafted, contrary to nature, into a cultivated olive tree, how much more will these natural branches be grafted back into their own olive tree.
—Romans 11:17–24

Religious and cultural identity is used to limit the power of the believer by showing that one culture's ideology transcends and supersedes another. The third chapter of this book takes the argument from word level to pericope level; it looks at the meaning of the famous olive-tree allegory in Rom 11:16–24. One prominent view of this text is that it is a deliberate inversion of Theophrastus of Eresius's instructions on grafting. In Theophrastus, branches of cultivated olive trees are grafted onto wild ones; in Romans, wild branches are instead grafted onto cultivated trees. This inversion seemingly signifies that the "wild" gentile believers are either wanting or in need of reproach (Davies 1984, Esler 2003a, 2003b, Nanos 2008). Another take on the tree allegory is that it portrays the "wild" gentile believers as morally rejuvenating the seemingly "cultivated" Israel (Bryan 2000, Dunn 1988b, Baxter and Ziesler 1985, Ramsay 1906). Within this second view, some see the allegory based on practices explained in texts by Roman writers Columella and Palladius, in which shoots from wild olive-trees are indeed grafted onto cultivated ones to revive and refresh the latter, thus advancing this argument for the gentile believers rejuvenating Israel (Baxter and Ziesler 1985, Ramsay 1906).

In this chapter I reject the prominent view that this text inverts Theophrastus of Eresius's instructions on grafting branches. At the same time I challenge the view that this allegory portrays the gentile believers as morally rejuvenating Israel. I further refute the presupposition that the text is primarily based on practices explained in texts by Theophrastus and Columella. Instead, I find that the allegory of the olive tree shows the wider dimensions of mutual exchange.

Argument

As with the previous two chapters, I use ancient intertexts and contexts to situate Rom 11:17–24. In this chapter, however, I do not use papyri but practical horticultural intertexts by Theophrastus, Columella, and Palladius, alongside Derrida's own metaphor of the graft as writing, to emphasize mutuality. I also use Jacob 5 in the book of Mormon because I see this as an interesting revisiting of the allegory in Rom 11:17–24. I show how some standard readings emphasize some form of one-directional benefit between graft and tree, gentiles and Israel. I survey some of the problems with this approach and how it creates problematic attitudes on the relationship between faiths and cultures. I show that implicit in the ancient and other texts focused on in this chapter is a sense of an exchange, albeit an asymmetric one, rather than one-directional benefit from tree to graft or graft to tree. I discuss how the graft is an artificial intervention into nature and show that explanations about the intent of the grafting are undermined by the intertext inherent to the wider exchanges of nature. At the same time, I demonstrate that the purity of nature is undermined by the glance of the conscious person viewing it—their attempt to interpret the world around them. The exchange between subject and object is ever evolving.

I will show that eschatological Israel is not merely a kingdom, country, or ideology but an ever-evolving and ever-growing site in which there is an exchange between God and the believer. This site must interweave with other cultures, traditions, and faiths. If not, then how can it be an international religion in which people can be inducted? Christianity, in the spirit of Christ, must be inclusive as well as inductive, evolving as well as structured, ecological as well as economic. Thus from a discussion of the power of and onus on the believer through their faith in their direct relationship to God in the previous chapters, we move in this third chapter to a different aspect of the believer's power and onus in their faith. The previous chapters showed how the believer assesses and reads evidence in order to develop their belief. Each believer makes an individual reading and assessment, meaning that each believer's belief is different and varies from another's. This chapter examines how the individual characteristics and qualities of the believer, rather than being adjunct or detrimental, are factors that empower the believer in their relationship with God and thus enhance the existence of the Christ-believing community. We then see how discourse and interfaith relations can be improved from an inclusive, mutual perspective.

The Problem with One-Way Benefits

Theology must be grafted onto a hermeneutics of mutuality, or vice versa. Maybe in this chapter I cull from theology a one-way transferal of benefit—even breaking off branches; however, we should never deny the influence of these texts and their impact on our tree of interpretation. The traditional mainstream adherence to the one way transferal of benefits, from olive tree to wild graft and thus from eschatological Israel to gentile believer, provides theological justification for divisive and exclusionary ideology. At this point, I wish to trace out the superiority and oppression that such readings can, both deliberately and unwittingly, support.

Then, later in the chapter, I highlight the benefits of alternative readings of mutuality.

Grafting as one-way benefit is framed to favor superiority over mutuality.

The first problem is how the olive tree grafting allegory has been positioned to create a sense of superiority and supersessionism. Nevertheless, we must make an effort to try to understand this reading of the olive tree allegory rather than simply condemn it as insufficient. To begin this task, we must first question notions of superiority even where they are deemed absolute. Christianity, despite never being distinguished from Judaism by Jesus or Paul, has too often been viewed, by those within the tradition, as superior to all other faiths, superseding them. The dominant imperial forces that underpinned Christianity failed to respect and appreciate the contributions of subjugated cultures to their story. Religion in the West, particularly Christianity and Islam, have been interlinked with imperial powers that define themselves as absolute universal entities. However, in reality, the boundaries that these empires and faiths have attempted to set are not impermeable: they are as influenced by the colonized traditions as they influence them.

Some have questioned the suitability of using biological metaphors, such as tree metaphors, to represent the textual tradition of the Bible. Yii-Jan Lin (2016, 150), for instance, argues that other metaphors, such as cyborgs, may be more effective. Of course, we must caution that the olive tree allegory in Romans is not just representative of written texts, but the wider religious and ethnic identities the texts represent,[1] including oral traditions, ritual, behaviors, worship, discipline, fellowship, and much more. I share Lin's concern about the use of biological metaphors, particularly those related to the tree, and its impact on ideology; however, I am more vexed by how the interpretation is based on a flawed understanding of the ontology of natural physical entities and their relationship to their environment. I also think it is a mistake to separate nature from culture and coordinate their vehicles to tenors, such as comparing text to cyborgs because both are artificial, because the contrast between these values reflects a continuum rather than a binary. In our olive tree allegory,

---

1. Taking care not to oversimplify or conflate these terms in anachronisms (see Esler 2003a).

as we see further on, there is a paradox in how nature and culture are deployed. In some ways the understanding of this allegory is unscientific, and in others, it is encouraged by scientific purism, as we shall see further on. However, it is important to note that the olive tree metaphor is based on a very limited philosophical and scientific ontology, which perpetuates a supersessionist view of Christian authority. In *La connaissance de la vie* (1969), Canguilhem notices how in the beehive, new cells are built upon old ones that are obsolete, and he compares this to new scientific discoveries and principles superseding former misconceived notions. It could be said that the principle of science follows this pattern of religious revelation, especially from the covenant through the Torah, gospels, and then the Qur'an. New Atheism could be seen to be part of this supersessionism, too.

The need to control the olive tree allegory by traditional mainstream scholarship is indicative of an autocratic church and political authority. Parts of the allegory are cherry-picked to match presupposed theology, and other parts are ignored in a pattern of *usure*. The complexities of the unconscious and intention are miscalculated. Authority becomes invested in an authorial singularity that upholds hierarchy and superiority. The result is a denial of the importance of the individual in making meaning and contributing to the theological and ethical journey of an entity, such as the church, government, state, or community. This denial is apparent in the authoritarian ecclesiology of top-down hierarchy and the prescription of belief and opinions by those with power to those without—this is not limited to one ideology but exists in all religions, denominations, and political movements. Such superiority leads to an exclusion of other identities, particularly cultures or faiths that are Othered by religious imperialism or proselytization. In particular, it denies the importance of people from other faiths and traditions by superseding their contributions. It also denies the uniqueness of every individual's personal faith journey and cultural background.

A uniform corporate is prioritized over the individual in a community.

Individual identity is threatened by the corporate despite both being needed. The basic unit of identity, the individual or the believer, is so often denied in favor of a corporate entity that wishes to dissolve it under the pretense of cooperation. However, any corporate identity relies on the sum of its parts and, more importantly, their value. Too often the larger, greater corporate identity is dictated by a monarch, oligarch, or theocrat, ignoring the import of the parts—the individual or believer. This goes for political states and religions. While the existence of the corporate entity relies on the individual, their power and onus is often repressed, leading to a bland uniformity rather than variety and difference. Identity is presented as unanimous and static—leading to a rigid and uncompromising idea of faith—whereas in reality it is fluid. Christian, Hindu, and Buddhist fundamentalists, as much as Muslim extremists, foster an ignorance of the influence of other traditions on their texts and cultures. They also ignore the changeability of doctrine, doxology, exegesis, and hermeneutics. The olive tree allegory should offer an organic and changing structure, but instead it is used to present faith as static and unmovable.

Exclusion is seen as a definer of outside and inclusion as inside.

The third main problem raised by the olive tree allegory is the question of who is included and who is excluded—a question that is more ideological and discipline based than the previous two problems discussed above. Too often, the condemnation of heresy or apostasy is used to show who is included and who is excluded, not only in religious faith but in wider ideology. In the section above we discussed the problem of how identity is framed as static rather than fluid, whereas here we focus on the events of inclusion and exclusion. In our allegory we see acts of kindness contrasted to severity, with the former aligned to those "not fallen" and the latter to those "fallen." Also aligned to the former are those left in the tree or added later, and to the latter, those left out or cut off. Of course, in the long term, these excursions and inclusions form part of the fluidity and evolution of faith; however, in the moment, they are experienced as sharp changes and departures from the norm.

There is a suggestion that severity is unceasing condemnation and kindness is unconditional affirmation. This is a problematic value judgement because we are never fully or perfectly at adherence with any ideology, whether it be political, social, or religious. The olive tree allegory relies on an absolute and static definition of a tree, in which only a superficial notion of its ontology is accepted—root, trunk, branch, and leaf. In accordance to the pattern of *usure* this static definition ignores the fact that much of the function of the tree is reliant on symbiotic organisms, that the microclimate of the air above its leaves and the soil around its roots are integral to its existence. It also ignores that the tree we see today is substantively different from the tree that could be seen a few years ago. Parts of the tree that we saw last week may be in the clouds or dissipated into the soil today. There are chemical processes, including osmosis, respiration, excretion, nutrition, and photosynthesis, related to the leaves and roots that cannot be seen or defined. Where the tree begins and ends is not simple; however, such simplicity has been transposed onto the theology of the olive tree allegory in Romans. Such allegorization has reduced religious discipline to a binary of in and out, in which those who are "in" are saved and justified and those who are "out" are eternally rejected and condemned. The effect is fundamentalist Christian thought that is mainstreamed yet feeds into extremist doctrine, rejecting the difference and variation between believers and denying them their unique relationship to God through theology. However, such an erroneous ontology ignores the organic nature of trees, in which matter can be excreted and reintegrated, where the boundary between tree and the rest of the world is not as clear as some may think, despite its recognizable structure.

Intertexts Used

While I do not use the ground-level papyri of Oxyrhynnchus and other similar corpuses here, I do draw upon practical horticultural sources that offer a contextual reality to Rom 11:17–24. These sources are essentially horticultural and agricultural handbooks designed to assist gentleman farmers of the era farm their land and increase productivity for the survival of themselves and their dependent relatives, staff, and slaves. These texts are enlightening because there is something sublime about keeping a farm, which is a microcosmic paradigm of the world and humankind's attempts to live within it and shape it. The authors of these texts have experienced the struggles and joys of agriculture and horticulture firsthand. They are not urbane metropolitan elites using unrealistic tropes, such as Seneca's propaganda on altruism that I criticize in the previous chapter. Furthermore, the earthy realities of ecology offer a lot of potential to the growth of missiology and eschatology.

The first of these ancient texts is *De causis plantarum* or *Historia plantarum* (*Peri phyton historia*), by Theophrastus of Eresus (371–287 BCE). Theophrastus—perhaps the first ecologically informed botanist—was trained by Aristotle in natural history, and this work sits alongside his mentor's *Historia animalium*. It is worth noting that Theophrastus's ten-volume work,[2] completed between roughly 350 and 287 BCE, was never completed, although the practical style of it suggests it was for reference and instruction rather than literary merit. His work, particularly this text, was translated into Latin, first by Greek scholar Theodore de Gaza (ca. 1400–1475), and was significant during the Renaissance. It has been noted that Theophrastus was aware of plants in their environmental context— with climate, soil, elevation, light, and water being factored into their propagation. Similarly, we are using Theophrastus in our analysis to place Rom 11:17–24 in its environmental context by placing the text within its locality of practical horticulture rather than lofty literary and philosophical motifs.

The second ancient text we are using is that of Lucius Junius Moderatus Columella (4–ca. 70 CE), who was a trailblazing Roman agriculturalist and much more contemporaneous with Paul. As with many high-level veterans in the army, Columella devoted his postmilitary time to farm his estates at Ardea, Carseoli, and Alba in Latium. It is said that his main work, *De re rustica* (twelve volumes surviving in full), was not widely distributed or read (see Peck 1963, 383–84). Despite a flourish of verse imitating Virgil in book 10, *De re rustica* seems to have been a practical handbook with literary merit, rather than a literary performance to impress (Kenney 1982, 973). The third ancient text in our study is by Rutilius Taurus Aemilianus Palladius. The work we draw upon is *Opus agriculturae*, which is a manual of farming in fourteen volumes written in the late fourth or early fifth century CE. The work acts as an almanac in books 2–13, with subdivisions covering crops, vegetables, fruit trees, and livestock. Book 14 provides an early form of veterinary medicine. The exact part of the text we focus on is a kind of appendix to book 14, a poem, *De insitione* (*On Grafting*), which is made up of eighty-five couplets of elegiac verse that contains detailed instruction informed by field observation. One of the stanzas of this appendix details olive grafting.

It is worth mentioning at this stage another text I draw upon on, Jacob 5 in The Book of Mormon. The Latter-day Saints movement arose in the Second Great Awakening of the nineteenth-century Protestant revival, in which there is an attempt to rehabilitate the divine potential of humankind. The Latter-day Saints movement derives from the Protestant movements that emigrated to North America and relied on effective farming

---

2. Of which only nine volumes survive.

for survival, probably even through to the time of Joseph Smith's mission. Regardless of whether the Book of Mormon is considered an authentic religious text, I consider it an important book in terms of biblical reception, and the reworking of the allegory in Jacob 5 contains practical agricultural sense. Early settlers in North America would have needed to be aware of the reciprocity between plants and their environment. From this perspective, it makes sense that a Latter-day Saints reading of this allegory in Romans affirms the notion of exchange between God and the believer.

Theory Used

Approaches that restrict or question the vehicularity of the olive tree are flawed, because metaphor is both economic and ecological in its shapes and processes. Deconstruction ideas on metaphor and intertextuality are therefore used to show how the olive tree allegory functions to show the relationship between individuals as sites of meaning-making. Metaphor itself is a kind of grafting, of one theme into another, with reciprocal effects, as Derrida explains in another essay that we shall pick up on further on in this chapter. Both metaphor and grafting involve the transferal of material from one context to another. As all language is arguably metaphorical and all text is intertextual, the idea of pure sources from which something is taken and inserted into is therefore too simplistic. Instead there is a strange paradox where an utterance, when taken from one context and placed into another, is both at contrast and integral. As hearers bring these contexts together, they construct texts based upon their own understanding; the believer then becomes a carrier of utterances from one context to another. What is more important than pinning down the allegory, as an analogy with all its parts allocated to a missiological framework, is the process of grafting and how this signifies the continual transference of the cultural, literary, and theological reciprocity of Pauline missiology.

Usure is not only connected to the metaphysics of etymology or the apparent wearing away of prior sense over time—that renders metaphoricity sterile. It is also connected to the way that metaphorical constructs elide, dismiss, or subjugate certain aspects of the metaphor—indicated usually through talk of how suitable a metaphor is for a given situation or how far we should be guided by it. However, whatever the specifics of their interpretation, most commentators and scholars accept certain aspects of oleiculture to be active and present in Rom 11's allegory. Those who believe that this context is important will have quite specific ideas about what oleiculture is and what it achieves, and they will use those stances to inform how the represented conceptual acts are understood. Yet such positions typically carry the assumption that all other ideas and stances on oleicultural science are irrelevant or would be absent from the consciousness of the hearer or that the latter's unconscious awareness of them would be null. If we apply the theory of *usure-retrait* to Rom 11:16–24 at a macro text level, however, it is possible and plausible to claim that the rejected aspects of oleiculture, which do not necessarily fit into the perceived theology of Paul in this text, can nonetheless exert an influence on the understanding of the nature of the relationship between the believer and the eschatological-Israel project of God.

Applying Derrida's concepts of *usure* (1982) and *retrait* (1978), it becomes possible to draw upon these traditions in Columella and Palladius mainly, but also in Theophrastus, and to see how this olive tree allegory operates and signifies beyond the possible intentions of the author and his followers and how it might be understood unconsciously and by hearers. Clearly, this allegory does not merely underline, emphasize, and enrich the perceived intended and authorized theology of the text; it also has ramifications outside of this. Deconstruction of the allegory enables us to look beyond an affirmation or condemnation of ethnicity in the supposed intentions of the text and to appreciate the role of the believer. The practice of olive-grafting represents the addition of a believer into the wider eschatological-Israel that the olive tree itself represents. However, a deconstruction approach, and an appreciation of what this allegory gains as well as loses through *usure-retrait*, compromises the idea that there is a one-way transferal of identity and influence from eschatological-Israel to the believer. Using Derrida's own essay on identity and grafting in *Dissemination* (1969), we can form an alternative picture of a mutuality of transferal, with the believer also bringing identity and influence, which contribute to the holistic identity of eschatological-Israel. This picture can be seen as a radical extension of some of the implications inherent in the works of Cullmann, Dunn, and Lincoln, as discussed in the first chapter of this book.

Established Views

I have categorized the six main views on the olive tree allegory text. In sum, the first five views have the same outcome of interpretation: the condemnation of the gentile world, either in contrast to the affirmation of

Israel or the emergence of Christianity through Paul. Such readings of the metaphor contribute to the problems established earlier in this chapter. First is the denial of the significance of the oleicultural context altogether. Johannes Munck (1967) and Douglas Moo (1996) fall into this group. This position holds that what Paul says is decorated with metaphors that are unimportant; it thus couples authoritative interpretation with a denial of the individual to engage creatively with the text. The second, covered by Williams (1999), elevates theology above language in the text and does not rely on the metaphor, which is illustrative. Such a position denies the interpretative rights of the individual and defers supremacy to theology outside of language, which is dangerous. The third—C. H. Dodd (1932) and others—holds that Paul was ignorant of oleicultural practice so the technical details of the metaphor are irrelevant. This, for my argument, inadvertently makes some sense, as we shall see further on, in that Paul emphasizes the grafting process more generally rather than limiting it to one technique. However, the intention of this theory is to explain the grace of inclusion of gentiles into the people of God. Dodd thinks Paul chose the wrong metaphor due to his inexperience of the countryside, which left his statement vulnerable to being mixed up. The confusion between the grafted and the graftee may lead people to picture gentiles being the benefactors and the people of God the ones lacking! These three positions assume that Paul's theology shows, in varying forms, the superiority of a renewed Israel in which the gentile world participates. The metaphor is excess to this and separable.

The fourth position is Daniel Boyarin's thesis (1994) that the metaphor in this text helps to erase ethnic difference, which I argue is well-intentioned but anachronistic and proposes a homogeneity of identity that is neither desirable nor real. However it is the fifth and sixth positions, both of which rely strongly on oleicultural intertexts, that help enlighten us most on the text. The fifth position considers that Paul deliberately inverted Theophrastus's method of grafting a wild olive shoot onto a cultivated tree in order to conclude that gentile believers are wanting and reproachable and that their boasting is condemned. W. D. Davies (1984), Philip Esler (2003a), and Mark Nanos (2008) share this position, although these scholars' views vary in some significant details. Davies believes that the grafting is representative of gentile believers being taken from the gentile world, as represented by the wild olive tree, and added into Israel, represented by the cultivated tree. As such, Davies's argument has more negative consequences for the perception of the gentiles and more positive ones for Israel. Nanos departs from Davies somewhat in that he does not believe Paul meant the wild olive tree to represent the gentiles as a whole, for this suggests too negative of an evaluation of the Hellenistic world. However, Davies (1984, 160) claims that, because the wild olive was notoriously unproductive, the fact that Paul aligns the gentiles with this image is "a most forceful indictment of their [the gentiles'] lives." Esler is willing to consider the metaphor as more than decorative but considers Paul's metaphor as an inversion of the standard practice of grafting rather than adhering to Columella's method (this will be explained further on). Consequently, Esler also follows the premise that the gentiles are found lacking compared to Israel.

The sixth position is that Paul's allegory positions the gentiles in a positive light. This position includes Christopher Bryan (2008), Dunn (1988b), and Stuhlmacher (1994). A.G. Baxter and J. A. Ziesler (1985), and William Ramsay (1906) hold a subdivision of this position, which specifically bases the allegory on another oleicultural method—that of Columella and sometimes Palladius—in which a normally unfruitful yet strong wild olive slip is grafted into a hole bored into a weakened cultivated tree. This creates a superior potential for fruiting, since the different strengths of both trees combine to allow fruitfulness where apart they would be barren. This position legitimizes the interpretation that the gentile believers or the gentile world in some way rejuvenate Israel, Judaism, or eschatological Israel, just as being grafted also benefits gentile believers.

Analogical Consensus

So let us begin our analysis where we can dare to say there is wide consensus, which is what the parts of the analogy might represent. Before this, let me quickly define allegory as "metaphor sustained, and developed" (as per Tambling 2010, 6). Allegories can be used to create paradigms, such as the medical paradigm of criminal desistance. For Romans, the allegory of the olive tree grafting is part of a horticultural paradigm in a theological argument made by Paul. The cultivated olive tree can be aligned to Israel, God's people, or the Christian church—what I prefer to call *eschatological-Israel*: Israel, as a spiritual entity, that has been widened to include the gentiles. The wild olive tree is the gentile world, or the world outside of God's people. The shoot from the wild olive tree that is grafted onto the cultivated olive tree either represents individual gentiles or segments of the gentile world, which are inducted into eschatological-Israel. The process of grafting is the addition of believers in Christ from the gentile world into eschatological Israel. These new believers are now identified with the latter yet at the same time differentiated. The cutting or breaking off of branches is the extraction of gentiles or existing Jews from eschatological-Israel if they cease to be believers. The grafting back in is the readdition of these excluded Jews or once-included gentiles, if they come back to belief. Such a consensus is a conflation with no common ground that affirms the role of the believer or the potential of the metaphor. From this analogical consensus a metaphysical consensus forms, which is supremacist and restrictive.

The Metaphoricity of Grafting and Romans

The metaphysical consensus that seeks to control the metaphor in the text can, however, be challenged by examining the ancient texts that may have been in the minds and collective consciousness of believers. The practice of olive grafting was prominent in Greco-Roman literature and horticulture, both as an ascribed reality and as a trope. It is worth noting that the earliest known reference to grafting, dated to 424 BCE, is found in Pseudo-Hippocrates ("On the Nature of the Child"). In this text the speaker opines about how the maturity of humans is analogical to that of plants. They say that plants can only fruit when they are able to draw a viscous liquid from the ground, and they only have the strength to do this when they realize a certain size. They continue to reason that it is beneficial when a less mature plant is grafted onto a more mature one, because the bark of the latter acts like a soil concentrated with nutrients, meaning that the less mature plant can benefit without having reached maturity yet.

So, hearers of Romans may have already been aware of a variety of grafting techniques and predisposed to metaphors about the grating process. In pseudo-Hippocrates the graft may have been added so a young plant could benefit from the sap of a tree's bark, but the tree must also have benefited from the graft; otherwise the process would not be done. The implication was likely that the wizened tree lacked the productiveness of the young tree and thus benefited from its fertility. This description has certainly been a fruitful ground for metaphorical comparisons. For instance, like the grafted shoot, the embryo, which is also discussed in this section of the Hippocratic text, is dependent on its parents for life; yet at the same time, the resulting child brings something fresh and revitalizing. Being careful to avoid a literalist supremacist view of youth over the aged, it could also be argued that the tree represents the status quo while the graft provides an alternative way of looking at things. The graft is a supplement in that it is both surplus and essential to the growth and identity of the tree. The act of grafting is both natural and artificial. We arrive then in Romans at a paradigm in which grafting is seen as an interaction between nature and culture rather than a straightforward trope of a fully wild tree. In Romans, there is wildness and technology—biology and cyborg (see Lin 2016).

Dunn's view that only the idea of grafting is important and that specific grafting processes do not exert an influence on the text does not suffice, unless you elevate the authority of an accepted theology over the creativity of the allegory. However, the view I espouse does not rely upon the claim that any specific grafting process was in Paul's mind when he wrote his text, which avoids the restrictive attitude of some scholars. All three grafting techniques discussed—those of Theophrastus, Columella, and Palladius—involve mutual benefit to the tree and the scion. The latter two techniques are especially important because they seem to accept the mutuality and reciprocity of benefit that inevitably occurs through the agricultural process of grafting. If one tissue is joined to another, it will exchange fluids and nutritional substances—the leaves of a developed graft will photosynthesize[3] and provide benefit for the tree, and the tree's roots will draw water and other nutrients from the soil, as Theophrastus and Aristotle both theorized.[4] It does not require a knowledge of twenty-first century biology to accept such mutuality. These principles must exert an influence on what this allegorical olive tree and olive-grafting is representing.

Some of the readings of this allegory, in the pattern of *usure*, elide these principles of mutuality and reciprocity, and this elision effects the reading of the text. Such positions emphasize readings in which either eschatological Israel or the gentile believer is the sole recipient of benefit, while the other party is the sole benefactor or giver. Others, which do not see the allegorical olive tree or grafting process as having any significant influence at all, allow for an interpretation that is bound up with prior theological presuppositions and that denies the ability of the hearer to be influenced individually by the allegorical image. Of course, it could be the

---

3. While photosynthesis was not discovered by Paul's era, it was evident that the leaves used sunlight to aid some kind of nutritional processing.

4. As seen in Theophrastus, *Hist. plant.* 2.2.11, 2.6.3, 2.7.3–4, 6.7.6, 7.5.1, 8.7.7; *Caus. plant.* 3.6.1–2, 3.9.1–5, 3.17.5, 5.15.2–3; and in Aristotle, *Plant.* 650a.20–26, "plants get their food from the earth by means of their roots" (trans. Smith and Ross).

case that Paul was using a specific grafting theory or maybe even none at all, but that does not rule out the ideas of reciprocity and mutuality, which are present in both Columella and Palladius, exerting meaningful influence on his own writing or on the hearer's understanding—either indirectly or unconsciously. Remember, in Romans, metaphor and theology are inseparable. Once metaphor is introduced to a text, the author opens a poetic transaction with the hearer that cannot be dominated by an ideal of what an author means or does not.

The role of the believer, the point to which the metaphor appeals here, must be appreciated as being *as prominent as its host*, (eschatological) Israel. Cullmann (1951, 230) claims that a "general ethical rule" for how the Jewish law is to be obeyed and applied does not exist. He claims that Christ's message was that "fulfilment of the law" is "not literal," that a "radical application" (226) of it was required, and that the believer had to make his or her own "ethical judgements" (225). Some of these radical applications and ethical judgements might be outside of the authoritative consensus of (eschatological) Israel or even very much in opposition to it, yet they are still relevant, important, and necessary. As such, even the believer who diverges significantly from the consensus retains power and onus to shape God and his projects. The reaffirmation of the metaphoricity of the text therefore aligns with the emancipation of the believer as an individual empowered to make judgement about the interpretation of texts and their ethics. Metaphor is everywhere, but when it is opened up as a paradigm, it requires the interpretation and creativity of the individual to make sense—this is the role of the believer in the theological text.

How appropriate natural metaphors are for theology is an unresolved question. Tree imagery, in particular, has the benefit of showing how things are related, but it also risks being monolithic. However, this is due to the problems with the way such metaphors are deployed and read. Another risk is the imposition of a hierarchy, such as one finds in a family tree, evolutionary or historical progression, flow chart, leadership, and so on—all of which use tree-like diagrams in an ideological way. Again, the problem is due to the way the metaphor is deployed. Hierarchal metaphors prioritize parts of a tree, especially those parts of the tree that are useful to civilization, such as trunks and fruits, or that are visually obvious, such as leaves and branches rather than the symbiotic relationship between the tree and less valued forms of life such as fungi and insects. Successful trees are seen, ideologically, as those useful to humans in that they produce wood and fruit. Human interventions, such as those through horticulture and agriculture, become viewed as more civilized and superior while the wildness of seemingly less productive trees are rendered as inferior. Yet at the same time, paradoxically, at a spiritual level, the natural purity of wild trees are romanticized as superior, beyond meddling human intervention. The simplistic ontology of a tree as just leaves, branches, and roots also provides a restrictive definition of what it represents.

Some have argued that tree metaphors in the religious text should be put aside for artificial and even anthropomorphic ones, such as cyborgs (see Lin 2016). In my view it is correct to acknowledge the problems with the use of tree metaphor, but I do not agree with the rejection of trees and roots (as per Lin via Deleuze and Guattari). For instance, as a probation officer, I note how some theorists find roots (rhizomes) to be more helpful metaphors of desistance than the journey metaphors (roads and paths), because they allow for the multidimensional representation of the simultaneity of progress and setbacks, rather than offering only linear simplicity. Such metaphors allow desisting offenders to evaluate setbacks constructively and accept there will be failures on the way as well as successes; journey tropes, however, compound feelings of failure or regression at every hurdle. I note that Lin (2016, 150) argues metaphors should move from the biological to cyborg. While mindful of the risks of poorly deployed and understood tree or grafting metaphors, in contrast to Lin I challenge biblical scholars to review their philosophy of biology rather than abandon such metaphors. Such revision is encapsulated by a discussion between Richard Dawkins and the Jainist monk Satish Kumar available on YouTube.[5] Kumar turns to the concept of "holism"—the connectivity of things in context as opposed to isolation—and uses an example of a tree. The tree, Kumar explains, is constituted not only of trunk, leaves, and roots, but less obviously, the soil in which it stands and through which it exchanges chemicals that were once part of its recognizable mass; the sunshine necessary for its photosynthesis and warmth; the air exchanged in respiration. For Kumar, there is an ethical and political implication to this paradigm of the tree's ontology. If you examine the issues of terrorism, religious extremism, or poverty, for instance, without the context in which they are situated and affected, you risk an impulsive reaction rather than a measured response. Indeed, this more expansive use of tree metaphor

---

5. https://www.youtube.com/watch?v=LrnwD_SE4jk&t=478s.

opens a significant opportunity for describing theological positions of inclusivity and relatedness.

Race, Religion, Ethnicity, and Grafting

One potential quagmire we can get stuck in is the contention over what was understood in the first century world by race, ethnicity, or even religion, and the appropriateness of biological metaphors to represent them. There is a long-established contestation over whether Jew, Judean, or Judaism is an ethnicity; whether Christ-following communities produced a new ethnicity; and how Jews, gentiles, and Christians relate. This book is not the place to add to this; however, some indication of direction is necessary for the reading of this allegory in Romans. Paula Fredriksen (2018, 206) argues that expagan pagans in Christ are "not-Israel," and their relationship with Israel is based on Levitical protocols and inherited kinship. However, our olive tree grafting allegory in Romans problematizes the division between being inside and outside of Israel, or any other entity. While I agree with Fredriksen that gentiles are likely not considered to be inducted into Israel, my reading of this allegory shows that the relationship between Israel and the other peoples or nations of the world operates on a continuum rather than a border. As such, there are characteristics of Israel and the Jews that are dependent on their connection with the gentile world, and vice versa.

Much of the recent argumentation in the area of ethnicity has come from Steve Mason, Philip Esler, and David Horrell, so it is worth situating my position within this dialogue. Mason and Esler (2017) have argued that while Jewish ethnicity is distinct, a Christian ethnicity is not. Others such as Horrell (2016) see Christianity as having ethicizing traits while not being an ethnicity in itself. I take Esler and Mason's point and suggest that comparing Jewish and Christian ethnicity is a bit like trying to compare an orange with a dog. At the same time, Horrell is right not to rule out a Christian ethnicity, although it should be noted in his response to Esler and Mason he denies claiming one is intact. Most importantly, Horrell's (2019, 1) claim that ethnicity is "multiple, fluid and hybrid in character," is significant to the direction of our argument here. Furthermore, Horrell sees ethnicity and religion to have another dimension of complexity to each other that is far more interlinked than Esler and Mason concede. Such fluidity does not, in my view, allow for a homogeneity but instead presupposes a constantly shifting relationship of traits. Ethnic identity is a vast matrix of signifiers that defer to limitless others. Trying to pin down identity through one moment of time or one ideological perspective is insufficient. Rather than seeing only corporate identities, we need to analyze at a more detailed level: that of the individual being and their function in context.

For Fredriksen (2018), a divine relationship bridging heaven with earth is paramount in ancient ethnicity, and this removes a necessity to create firm boundaries. The relationship of the believer with God becomes much more prominent and important to how ethnic status operates. From this perspective, unity is not about ethnic tribalism, dogma, and doctrine but inclusivity through a shared commission from God. Though such a view may be against the grain of theological readings of Paul, the allegory's force is that Israel is a changeable entity that sometimes includes Jews and sometimes gentiles, with both subject to being inside and outside, being original, included, excluded, and reincluded. In short, Israel is not an absolutely defined entity but an influence that pervades from its core and radiates eternally into the ether. The Jews may be considered by some to be exclusively "in," but what that means is unstable. The Jews and gentiles are neither in nor out but between the core and the eternal effervescence.

Reading the Text alongside Theophrastus

The emancipation of the olive tree allegory from authoritative biblicism will require various stages, or to use our metaphor, various grafts. Onto the history of this allegorical interpretation, I thus make my own first graft: of an ancient text. We begin with the method outlined by Theophrastus of Eresus (371–287 BC) in *De causis plantarum* that Davies, Esler, Nanos, and others rely upon in relation to Paul's allegory in Romans:

> It is also reasonable that grafted trees are richer in fine fruit, especially when a scion from a cultivated tree is grafted onto a stock of a wild tree of the same bark, since the scion receives more nourishment from the strength of the stock. This is why people recommend that one should first plant wild olive trees and graft in buds or branches later, for the grafts hold better to the stronger stock and by attracting more nourishment the tree bears rich fruit. If, on the other hand, someone were to graft a wild scion into a cultivated stock, there will be some difference, but there will be no fine fruit. (Theophrastus, *Caus. plant.*, 1.6.10.1–11 [trans. Esler 2003a, 114])

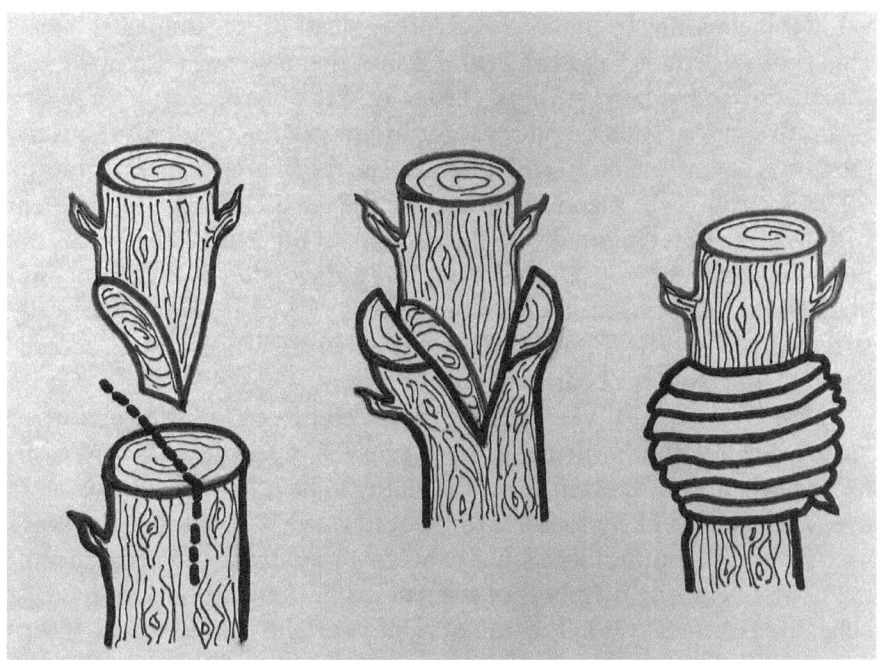

Fig. 1. Theophrastus's Grafting Process.

The rationale behind this process of grafting a shoot from a cultivated olive tree onto the branches of a wild olive tree is that the latter is hardier, with strong roots and more resistance to poor weather, while the former is more able to produce fruit than the latter. Oakes (2001, 21) observes how Theophrastus showed "detailed knowledge" of the Philippi region "including the drainage of marshland and the development of agriculture." The influence of Theophrastus in Greco-Roman agriculture is therefore not in doubt. Nevertheless, this does not mean that his influence necessarily eclipses that of Columella as Esler and Dunn claim.

Some believe Paul deliberately reversed Theophrastus's process to make a theological point. Please indulge me for a moment to play with the allegory. What if Paul used Theophrastus's method *as it stands*? The cultivated shoots gain from the hardiness of the wild tree. This dynamic would mean that the gentile world is righteous and eschatological-Israel is lacking! Individuals or segments of eschatological-Israel would need to be added in to the gentile world to be fulfilled! One might ask, counterintuitively, whether the wild tree gains anything from the vitality of the cultivated tree through the shoot. Consequently, we might ask, does the gentile world gain anything from individuals or segments of eschatological-Israel? This reversal would be fair if Paul did use Theophrastus's method as-is. Daydream over. Many, such as Davies (1984), interpret Paul's allegory as an inversion of this practice meant to portray the gentiles negatively; they understand the cultivated plant as Israel bringing the benefit of its superior qualities to the grafted shoot as the gentile world. The problem with Davies's observation is that the strength of the wild olive tree has the potential to evoke positive ideas of hardiness since, after all, in the method dictated by Theophrastus the wild olive tree is viewed as being biologically strong and supportive. Davies elides this detail from his reading, according to the metaphysical pattern of *usure*.

Nanos (2008, 14–15) explains how "common knowledge turned upside down within a metaphor or allegory is especially suited to communicating the unexpected about the matter in hand" and finds that Paul's use of allegory is likely to fall into this category. The rationale for Paul's use is that "it communicates his concern to confront the arrogance of the Christ-believing members of the nations in Rome toward non-Christ believing Israelites" (26). The title of Nanos's article, however, which suggests that Paul's metaphor has "gone awry," introduces the pattern of *usure* into which Nanos's own interpretation falls. Nanos believes that the allegory goes astray in that Paul did not intend for the broken-off branches to represent Israelites being excluded from Israel. Instead, "the tree allegory was created with the special concern to describe the present state of the Gentile believers in Christ, and the inferences about these Israelites are (il)logical by-products of that explanation. What we have here is a Pauline metaphor gone awry" (27). However, if Paul did not mean for the broken-off or discarded branches to represent anything, then why include them in the allegory at all? Even if he did not intentionally include them, the fact that he did is significant, even if at an unconscious level. Nanos's reading therefore relies on the retention of selective aspects of the grafting practice to understand the theology but elides others according to his own theological agenda.

Esler (2003, see 109) also believes that Paul altered Theophrastus's practice deliberately to make a point. Furthermore, he is sure that Paul's audience knew of Theophrastus's method and that Paul was drawing on this. From this move Esler concludes that Paul's message is a fairly bleak indictment of the gentiles: "Moreover by situating this image within its ancient oleicultural context and attending closely to how Paul blatantly subverts the prevailing practice among olive cultivators, we are left with a rather negative picture of the non-Israelite members of the Christ movement" (123–24). Esler takes a very specific line on oleiculture, one that sees the grafting process as being about the benefit experienced by the graft rather than the tree: "They are attached to the olive tree in a way that is παρά φύσιν. Not only do they not contribute to it, since they will not produce fruit, but they are actually parasitic upon its richness" (124). Such ideological conclusions about an agricultural practice are, however, not supported by the sources we have, which indicate mutuality in the grafting process.

This accusation against the gentiles is quite strong, especially since Theophrastus's method, though stating that the grafted-in scion gains more nourishment from the tree, does not seem to go as far as Esler's assessment. In fact, Theophrastus states that the grafted scion attracts increased nourishment to the tree (see *Caus. plant.* 1.6.10.1–11), as Esler himself recognizes. Nevertheless, Esler continues that: "For the present, the original cultivated branches—meaning the part of Israel that has hitherto rejected Christ—have been cut off. Yet if they are restored to their rightful place, they will produce much more" (124).

Esler, however, elidies certain aspects of the olive grafting process and oleiculture, even those that are seemingly present in Theophrastus's text, such as the flow of fluids and substances between graft and tree and the unavoidable fact that the graft is seen as playing a role that benefits the tree, even if to a lesser extent than the tree's benefits to the graft. I therefore put forward the possibility that, despite the tendency of scholars to read the process as a one-way flow of benefit, there is a mutual flow of benefits between the tree and graft. Such biological mutuality means I can propose at this stage, even if tentatively, that there is reciprocity, synergy, exchange, and mixing between eschatological-Israel and the gentile world through the inclusion of gentile believers or communities.

Without sufficient exposition, an argument that reverses Theophrastus to condemn the gentiles can have some dangerous social and missiological outcomes. There is a potential for this horticultural paradigm developing into a reading in which the exclusion of any individual or group that does not conform to the so-called host, or where inclusion revolves around strict criteria, becomes justified as righteous. Derrida, Said, and other philosophers realized how certain metaphors associate disease and infection with the underdog or dissenter (see Mitchell 2007 and Borradori 2003, see also Anderson 2017), implying that cleanliness and healthiness aligns to the superior or orthodox—an example of this tendency is the use of metaphors for immigration in Western media, where immigrants are described as invasive insects or viruses (Anderson 2017).[6] Other metaphors of immigration have been seen as much more helpful, including that of grafting (Anderson 2017). This suggests hope for my interpretation of Romans, where I wish to reclaim this metaphor for a progressive agenda.

Reading the Text alongside Columella

We make a second graft of an ancient text on the same branch where we grafted the first. My argument develops by showing how Columella takes us further toward the truth of this text. The idea that Paul is deliberately reversing the process of grafting to show preference for Israel or Jews is challenged by other Roman evidence for the practice of grafting wild olive shoots onto cultivated plants. Grafting from wild to cultivated plants was evidently present in Western Mediterranean culture (as shown by texts such as Columella and Palladius); thus, the likelihood of the Roman audience understanding grafting in this way would be high, and, due to the Roman dimension of his identity, Paul may even have been aware of this. What is important for our argument is that Paul at least might have been unconsciously influenced by this method or able to imagine it as possible and that his followers and hearers might also have been.

Previous readings of Columella give preference to the ability of grafts to reinvigorate their hosts, which makes Israel seem existentially dependent on the gentiles. Elided from these readings is how the grafts would have no ability to produce fruit without the superstructure the tree provides or that the tree, even if it produces very little fruit, is biologically self-sufficient and can survive, whereas a graft would wither and die on its own. These readings of Columella, as detailed below, acknowledge only a limited reciprocity and mutuality, with one party providing fundamental benefit to the less useful one. They disavow the more equivalent, albeit asymmetrical, reciprocity and mutuality present in this exchange.

In their important article on Romans, Baxter and Ziesler (1985) resurrect an old essay by Sir William Ramsay (1906) in which he refers to an "elaborate" study of the olive tree and olive culture of the Mediterranean

---

6. Immigration and ethnicity is relevant because opposition to it is often used to persecute other ethnic groups, and, furthermore, the questions of Jewish ethnicity in the ancient world are not only religious, cultural, or ethnic but encompass all in different contexts.

lands by a botanist, Professor Theobald Fischer (1904). Ramsay paraphrases Fischer's German, explaining that

> it is customary to re-invigorate an olive tree [by which he means a cultivated tree] which is ceasing to bear fruit, by grafting it with a shoot of the Wild Olive, so that the sap of the tree ennobles this wild shoot and the tree now again begins to bear fruit.

Ramsay continues by explaining the "well-established fact" that both the new shoot and the old stock are affected by the grafting: "The grafted shoot affects the stock below the graft, and in its turn is affected by the character of the stock from which it derives its nourishment" (223). This means that, while the older "cultivated" olive tree has "lost vigour and ceased to produce fruit," it could regain "strength and productive power" from the influence of the "vigorous wild shoot" that is grafted onto it (223). The fruit that then grows on the new engrafted shoot will be "more fleshy and richer in oil" than the natural fruit of the wild olive from which it was cut (224). Baxter and Ziesler (1985, 27), along with Ramsay, see the wild olive (the gentiles) bringing advantage to the cultivated olive (Israelites).

Esler's (2003a) argument on the subject is worth noting here, although it may place too much weight on the ages of the trees in this allegory since it relies on a tight connection between youth and the wild olive graft: it could be argued that the shoot of the wild olive can represent something older because, in terms of existence as a quasi- or subspecies, the wild olive tree is undoubtedly older than the cultivated olive tree, which was developed by humans and is thus later. So, the idea of the gentiles invigorating Israel with a youthful freshness is undermined by the fact the wild-olive as a species antiquates the cultivated one. At the same time, the fact the cultivated tree in this description is considered to be tired and aged undermines the idea that Israel is self-sufficient and does not need the gentiles. Reading this allegory with this ageism in mind, neither tree can be seen as singularly rejuvenating the other, so we can no longer interpret Paul as affirming a universal superiority of freshness in either Jews or gentiles.

It is important to return to Ramsay in more detail than Esler, Baxter, and Ziesler have done and also to reexamine the source they use from Columella. By doing so, we will notice features that both of these camps have missed. Columella, a Roman writer, confirms the practice of grafting wild shoots onto cultivated trees in his *De Re Rustica*, which is an agricultural handbook:

It happens also frequently that, though the trees are thriving well, they fail to bear fruit. It is a good plan to bore them with a Gallic auger and to put tightly into the hole a green slip taken from a wild olive-tree ; the result is that the tree, being as it were impregnated with fruitful offspring, becomes more productive (Columella, *Rust.* 5.9.16.1–4a [trans. Rogers 2010, 220]).

Fig. 2. Bore-grafting according to Columella: Boring the hole.
Fig. 3. Bore-grafting according to Columella: Slip inserted into the bored hole.

Columella records that well-established trees that are failing to produce proper crops can be rejuvenated and made more productive if they are engrafted with shoots from wild olives. Ramsay (1906, 224) observes that Columella "does not say whether the engrafted shoot" of the wild olive plant was affected by "the character of the root" and claims that Columella meant the grafting in of the wild olive shoot was to "invigorate the whole tree by the introduction of the fresh wild life" rather than to "direct the growth entirely to the graft alone." Through this source we find fairly steady evidence that wild-olive parts were grafted onto cultivated olive trees. Although there are no adjectives to qualify the cultivation of the tree described in the opening sentence, the specification of the graft being from a "wild olive" makes it highly likely that the tree is maintained artificially.

The tree is described as "thriving well," but despite this, it is not fruitful. This opens up the possibility that Roman society of Paul's time did not consider fruitfulness to be the only indication of health and well-being in a plant. In short, a wild olive tree, though unfruitful, can still be considered a successful tree. This process involves a different act, of boring and inserting a green slip, rather than grafting a shoot. But since Paul talks about branches broken off and grafted in, we can dispense of this specificity. Our Romans textual allegory relies not on slips, grafts, or branches to make sense but on more generic parts being inserted from one tree to another.

The consequence of this in terms of the allegory is that the gentiles as a wild olive tree can be seen in a positive light through Paul's words—the possibility of this reading challenges the reading of those who posit a strict polarity in which Israel is positive and gentiles are negative, despite the work such interpretations offer in combating Christian anti-Judaism. Instead, such a reading of Columella's text adds to an argument that both ethnicities have something to offer each other through the metaphor of grafting.

Despite Paul's Roman citizenship in a cosmopolitan empire, some will argue that Paul would not have been aware of the method Columella describes, for this grafting procedure was primarily Roman rather than Greek. Even so, since my theory overturns the notion of proper meaning and denies the privilege of conscious intention, it does not matter whether Paul was specifically aware of Columella's method or not at the moment that he composed this pericope; he may have been aware of it secondarily through common knowledge or be open to it through a logical sense that all elements of a plant must contribute to its successful growth. His audience may have been consciously or unconsciously aware of this method too, influencing Paul's theology through their reaction and interactions with him. Despite the fruitless reputation of the wild olive, Columella describes how it stimulates fruitfulness in the cultivated variety. Maybe our olive tree allegory is suggesting that what the gentiles cannot do for themselves they can nonetheless help the Jews achieve, and vice versa.

A postcolonial example of this reciprocity and interconnectedness can be found in Dorothy B. E. A. Akoto-Abutiate's (2014) study of the relationship between the Bible and Ghanaian tradition. Akoto-Abutiate argues that African folk sayings must be viewed as a tree onto which biblical Proverbs are "grafted" (133). The African tree of life tradition develops this idea, as biblical texts are inserted into other traditions for missiological purposes. In doing so, the biblical texts are "taught, learned, understood, and [their] message better appropriated" (176) by African peoples—an empowering and counterimperial perspective. Converts, or those who value biblical tradition in Africa, then influence Christians of other cultures and ethnicities and by doing so transfer some of the African tree of life to them. While Christian supremacists might consider this a way to ensure Ghanaians can understand the Bible, our allegory suggests that the process also has the obverse effect, enabling biblical culture to understand other cultures, which will, ultimately, destabilize the binary between "Western Christian" and "other Christian" cultures. Instead of being a mere medium for spreading Christianity, other cultures have the crucial task of helping adherents translate biblicisms into their own traditions. Through such translation there is negotiation, and the other culture leaves its mark on the exegetical and hermeneutical outcomes, which in turn feeds back into the wider missiological project.

We should be cautious, however, when we think about mixing, which may suggest dilution. The metaphor of a cultural melting pot, for instance, suggests that uniqueness of each original culture is lost. According to George J. Tanabe (2004), a better metaphor, at least for Japanese Buddhism's integration into Americanized Hawaii, is that of grafting. Tanabe differentiates between grafting in which hybridization occurs and grafting in which the shoots appear to be part of the tree but remain separate. The latter represents Japanese Buddhism in Hawaii, he argues. This type of grafting results in some communities failing to assimilate with American culture, which leads to the dying off of the original culture when new generations choose not to identify with their Japanese heritage (77). For Tanabe, healthy integration is like a grafting where the shoot intermingles with the host tree in a way that allows a hybrid—in this case, Hawaiian Buddhism, which appeals to Americanized Hawaiian people (96). We must be careful not to make assimilation—whatever that means—a precondition that is needed in order to have the right to retain aspects of one's own cultural identity because this can play into reactionary ideologies that presuppose superiority (even though this is not Tanabe's intention). An important point Tanabe makes is how the tree of Buddhism in Hawaii has altered from what is considered Buddhism in Japan and what is considered "Japanese" in Japan has itself altered, having been somewhat influenced by Americanized and Westernized appropriations of its culture (96). While this syncretism is important, it is only possible if a difference of identity is also maintained.

The interaction between cultures should be beneficial, as long as each respects the other's identity and a social equality structures the interactions between traditions. This is why we should reject a homogenization of identity in the text of Romans, however well-intentioned, as proposed by Boyarin (1994). Boyarin sees the text integrating identity to a point in which individual identities are indistinguishable and difference does not matter. Identity, however, must be negotiated within the conditions and rules of the proposed boundaries; at the same time, we must leave space for these conditions and rules to be transgressed. To deny boundaries, for neocolonial or postcolonial reasons, is to undermine the integrity of any given identity and prevent the enrichment of exchange. To this end, my exegetical outcomes propose a radical syncretism without universalism. I see a deconstructed grafting metaphor as offering a vision of a radical syncretism founded on reciprocity and exchange across difference, not watered-down, presumed similarity.

Returning to Baxter and Ziesler, despite making progress, they too fall into a pattern of *usure*, just as Davies, Esler, and Nanos do. Along with Ramsay and others, Baxter and Ziesler believe Paul is consciously using Columella as his text of reference. They reason that "not only according to Columella, but also according to modern authorities, such grafting with scions from a wild-olive would be done only to a tree that was exhausted, unproductive or diseased, in order to invigorate it" (1985, 27). As such, they argue:

> in Paul's understanding of salvation history also, the bringing in of the Gentiles serves to restore life to Israel. Of course there is nothing wrong with the root, which is probably to be understood as the patriarchs, Abraham in particular, seen as the recipient of and responder to the promises of God. The tree as a whole, however, is not in such good condition. We know it is not, because Israel in part has responded inadequately or wrongly to Jesus Christ. (27–28)

Baxter and Ziesler's reading of Columella elides certain aspects from the allegory. We need, at this point, to briefly call out the antisemitic potential of this allegory. The allegory could be interpreted as saying that, after the advent of Christ and its developments into modernity, Judaism is insufficient or invalid. Such a reading needs to be challenged by going back to the ancient sources. Columella's recommendation does not mention disease as a reason for the grafting solution and even suggests the cultivated tree should be thriving or doing well (*laetae arbores*), despite not being fruitful—a note that has been elided when oleiculture is transferred to theology. Baxter and Ziesler (1985, 28), unlike Esler and Nanos, acknowledge a certain reciprocity, albeit one that is disproportionate: "the process not only enables the Gentiles to become fruitful, but also restores strong life to the tree as a whole.... Certainly the ingrafted branches depend on the root for their life." Nevertheless, they lean on the gentiles as being the ones who benefit Israel, saying that the gentiles, "once ingrafted and deriving sap from the root, contribute to the renovation of the tree" (28); they do not mention the other way round. The rhetorical structure of this statement gives final word to the notion of renovation, which makes Israel seem existentially dependent on the gentiles. Baxter and Ziesler have elided from their assessment the fact that the grafts would have no ability to produce fruit without the tree and that the tree, even if unproductive, is biologically self-sufficient, whereas a graft would wither and die on its own. Therefore they rely on the retention of a very limited reciprocity and mutuality, with one party providing fundamental benefit to the less useful other. They elide the more equivalent, albeit asymmetrical, reciprocity and mutuality for which I argue here.

Reading the Text alongside Palladius

A third graft is now added to the tree of our study. We do not need to cut off the first two, however. Use of Palladius takes my argument even further than Columella, moving away from the mundane implications of Theophrastus's technique to a wider, global truth. Rutilius Taurus Aemilianus Palladius was a Roman agricultural writer from the fourth century CE. This is, admittedly, some time after Paul; however, oral and practical traditions long precede written ones, so Palladius's ideas were likely influenced by preceding traditions. In his essay, Ramsay (1906) does not tell us to which part of Palladius's work he is referring, but, since he mentions that it is in verse, I determine that he is citing part of an epistle on the grafting process. This epistle appears to accompany the whole text of Palladius's *Opus agriculturae*, and, while it details the benefits of grafting, it also works as an apology to Pasiphilus (who may be someone who commissioned the work) for the lateness of the work. This is the full stanza entitled "Olives":

> The oak-strength of the Palladii olive decorates the wild.
> The berry leaves no trace of the wild kind.

The wild olive-tree makes the olive-tree fruitful.
And gifts, which it did not know it will show. (*Op. agr.* 14.51–54 [my translation[7]])

The author, Palladius, uses a pun in his opening line—a pun on his own name. The word "Palladii" denotes a subspecies of olive tree, so in this line he is referring not only to an olive tree but also to himself, inferring that he is "vigorous" or "fruitful"! Regardless, the focus of the poem is on the grafting of plants. The first two lines are not entirely clear. However, it seems likely that Palladius is referring to wild olive shoots grafted on to cultivated trees, especially if we focus primarily on the final two lines. In the penultimate line, we find the term "wild olive tree" (*oleaster*) used and are told that it makes the "olive-tree" fruitful. The final line implies that the gifts are from the wild tree but are not known by it). These gifts are shown, or taught to, the nonwild olive tree.

Palladius seems to be asserting that wild olives, although they cannot use their strength to produce their own abundance of fruit, stimulate fruitfulness in cultivated olive trees when grafted onto them. Even if this interpretation of Palladius is shown to be biologically inaccurate, it cannot be denied that this text emphasizes how the wild olive plant can convey benefits to the cultivated plant—and that is sufficient for the direction of my argument. More importantly, even if the practice were proved ineffective or even rare, it does not rule out the possibility that there were people who believed this method worked in this way and also were committed to the rationale behind it. Consequently, it implies that there could have been people who understood the allegory to mean that the included believer and eschatological-Israel benefit each other mutually.

When the wild olive is grafted into the cultivated olive tree, as Palladius illustrates here with unobtrusive poetic flourish, the former can stimulate the kind of fruit productivity that the latter cannot. This is introduced earlier in *Opus agriculturae*: "What young wood takes the tender graft I'll show / And with adopted leaves what tree will grow" (14.19–20). What follows

---

7. With thanks to Gareth Morris for help with this translation. See also the translation by Thomas Owen (Palladius 1807), 339. This is a useful yet stylistic translation that prefers retaining rhyme, which may undermine the meaning. The original Latin from Palladius's *Opus agriculturae* is: "*Robora Palladii decorant siluestria rami, / nobilitat partus baca superba feros, / fecundat sterilis pingues oleaster oliuas /et quae non nouit munera, ferre docet*" (see Palladius 1898).

this "prelude" is a poetic presentation of how grafting improves fruit-bearing plants of many different species, from olives to apples, pears, and vines. Palladius also provides these evocative lines: "The sweet juices with taste correct to blend / That with rich flavor'd fruit the tree may bend (14.17–18). The reasoning seems to be that the best parts of different plants must be mixed to increase the productivity. Both Palladius and Columella, and to a lesser extent Theophrastus, show that it was possible for olive grafting to be understood in the sense that both the flaws of the cultivated tree and the wild shoots could be turned into benefits by their union. The cultivated tree has become tired and less productive, and the flaws of the shoot's own tree do not allow its potential productivity to be realized. Once the shoot is grafted into the tree, both become fruitful and productive.

More contemporary to Paul, Plutarch in *Amatorius* uses a metaphor of grafting to explain the benefits of sex and marriage with a virtuous woman: it is like the grafting of a tree upon a proper stock. Plutarch uses this metaphor to explain that, since conception is a form of ulceration in the body and thus carries risk, it is important that a man's choice of partner is from good "stock" because "there can be no mixture of things that are not affected reciprocally one by the other" (*Amat.* 24 [Goodwin]). The implication is that, if one chooses bad stock, then the risk of physical and moral damage is higher; however, if one chooses to graft upon a proper stock of tree rather than a bad one, the trauma of the process has more chance of a positive outcome. This is because the graft and tree have a reciprocal relationship due to their mixing in the incision, just as a man and woman do in the ulceration of conception.

The graft is therefore just as important to the tree as the tree is to the graft—a principle that directs an important ethic that informs my exegesis: sometimes weaknesses in one party can be turned into strength through association or integration with another. The so-called inferior party, represented by the graft from an inferior wild tree, is in a position of usefulness and importance to the so-called superior party, represented by the cultivated olive tree. Thus, we go beyond the binaries of ethnicity, of Jew and gentile, of Israel and the nations, and are carried to a point of tension between the "normal" and the "Other," between the cultivated olive-tree as the central entity and the graft and wild olive trees as the marginal one. What results when we consider this tension is a picture of eschatological-Israel and the believer who is added to or included into it in a relationship of mutual benefit, each realizing effects that they could not realize without each other.

Palladius goes further than Columella because his grafting process does not rely on the wild shoot being ennobled by the sap of the cultivated tree. For Palladius, the insertion of the wild tree slip into the cultivated tree's bore hole allows a more general benefit to the tree as a whole, not just in the location of the insert. For our argument this shows how the identity of the people of God and the eschatological meaning of their faith is not reliant on binaries and stasis; it is ever changing. When an addition is made to the tree of eschatological Israel, the whole tree is impacted on a cosmic scale. There is no static boundary between the tree and the graft. The inclusion of gentiles, or outsiders, is not an exception or peculiarity but a process.

Taking This Further with Theory

Is our theory a graft or the insertion of a slip? We can draw out this systemic global changeability by reading the text alongside theory. In Derrida's article "Grafts, a Return to Overcasting" (*Retour au surjet*) in the appendix of *Dissemination* (1969), the intertextual nature of texts, and indeed the practice of writing itself, is compared to that of grafting. As Derrida (1988, 355) later claims, "To write means to graft. It's the same word." Referring to an earlier text of his own, which includes samples from another text, he asserts that they do not serve as "quotations," "collages," or "illustrations":

> They are not being applied upon the surface or in the interstices of a text that would already exist without them. And they themselves can only be read within the operation of their reinscription within the graft. (1969, 355)

What does this have to do with eschatological-Israel? Romans, and the New Testament more widely, is a product of both Hebraic and Greek spiritual and philosophical tradition. Belief and identity are therefore structured more around text in revelatory intervals, with space for theological and philosophical negotiation, rather than ancestral or tribal rites. That the horticultural graft is a major trope in Greek, Roman, and Hebrew literature is no accident, because it is the metaphor of metaphor itself, refreshing the seemingly original tropes of transport. Some have argued that the etymological relationship between graft and graph—grafting and writing—is significant (Spartacus 2018). The act of using other traditions and texts is not an unusual, isolated, or locally confined but instead a fundamental feature of communication within a people who are constantly negotiating an identity that, through text and tradition, requires reference to the other—the foreigner, alien, outside, intertext, intertradition.

There are two ramifications to Derrida's thesis in "Grafts." First, the main text is not fully self-sufficient in communicating its meaning without the quotation or sample of other texts that are to be inserted into it. Quotations are not merely auxiliary additions that enhance the meaning of the text; they are instead a crucial part of the meaning of that text. Second, the clipped-out samples of other texts, in isolation, are not enough to carry or prove the meaning of the main text or to prove its own meaning in relation to the main text. If we took away all the inserted samples of other texts from a main text, its meaning would not simply suffer from reduced clarity: it would not be the same. Similarly, a sample from another text that is inserted into the main text has a potentially very different meaning on its own or if transplanted into another text. As Derrida (1988, 9) states in *Limited Inc.*, "a written syntagma can always be detached from the chain in which it is inserted or given without causing it to lose all possibility of functioning," and "one can perhaps come to recognize other possibilities in it by inscribing it or grafting it onto other chains." Both the main text and the samples of other texts thus rely on each other to produce meaning and to define the meaning.

However, it is not only the main text that is affected; the other main texts from which quotations and samples are taken are too: "Each grafted text continues to radiate back toward the site of its removal, transforming that, too, as it affects the new territory" (Derrida 1969, 355). The sample thus brings with it some of the influence of the text from which it comes, changing the main text into which it is transplanted. However, its inclusion within the new text can also influence the way the text from which it is taken is read. So, a quotation or sample induces a kind of two-way portal between the texts, with both texts and the grafted piece of text itself engaged in a complex mutual exchange. The text from which tissue is taken influences the main text through being influenced by the main text!

Such a view challenges the authority and propriety of the main text of focus, and it questions its sole dominance over the inserted quotations and its subjugation of the other texts from which the quotations have been taken:

> I cull here and there out of several books such sentences as please me, not to keep them in my memory ... but to transplant them into this

work, where, to say the truth, they are no more mine than they were in the places from whence I took them. Inserted into several spots, modified each time by its exportation, the scion eventually comes to be grafted onto itself. The tree is ultimately rootless. And at the same time, in this tree of numbers and square roots, everything is a root, too, since the grafted shoots themselves compose the whole of the body proper, of the tree that is called present: the subject's career or quarry. (Derrida 1969, 356)

In the metaphor of grafting used by Derrida, the tree is the main text and the grafted-on scion is the transplanted sample of another text. The main text therefore does not dominate and own the samples transplanted into it any more than the latter's texts of origin does. It is not only the main text that reinscribes the samples: the samples also reinscribe the main text from their own force of meaning and also through the force of the text from which they come, which they carry with them. The idea of a stable *body-proper* of the text separate from the inserted sample is imploded, because arguably the whole body of the text consists of samples of other texts. There is no root-like foundation of the text that maintains a core identity, but only a main text that is akin to a tree made up from root to branch only of scions of other trees. To write is to insert a quotation—all writing is intertextual and references other texts. Such a view is not opposed to the allegory of a natural tree, because the gaze of the human spectator and their consideration of the tree is at once a grafting-in of the artificial into nature. As soon as we perceive and interpret, we alter.

Derrida's grafting allegory of writing works in a similar way to Paul's grafting allegory of eschatological-Israel, which is itself a cosmological and soteriological text. I now apply the ramifications of Derrida's deconstruction of conventional notions of intertextual reference in the next section to the olive-grafting allegory. Derrida's own grafting allegory, along with the classical sources of Columella and Palladius, show how the relationship between eschatological-Israel and the believer is one of mutual exchange of identity and meaning, which shows a relationship between God and the believer that is symbiotic and has synergy.

The Unconscious Reader against the Grain of Authorial Intention

Scholarship shows a pattern of trying to determine whether Paul was thinking about a specific form of grafting when he wrote his text and to what extent that grafting practice is aligned to the theological arguments.

Such readings, in the pattern of *usure*, elide the principles of mutuality and reciprocity, and this has an effect on their reading of the text. Such positions emphasize readings in which either eschatological Israel or the gentile believer is the sole recipient of benefit, while the other party is the sole benefactor or giver. Others, which elide much more than the reciprocity involved in the grafting process and which do not see the allegorical olive tree or grafting process as having any significant influence at all, allow for an interpretation that is bound up with prior theological presuppositions and a denial of the ability of the hearer to be influenced individually by the allegorical image. Always, the grafting process is subordinated to the theology, which must be safe from unintended consequences.

Of course, it could be the case that Paul was using a specific grafting theory or maybe even none at all, but that does not rule out the ideas of reciprocity and mutuality in Columella or Palladius exerting influence on Paul's writing or on the hearer's understanding, either indirectly or unconsciously. We carry with us the baggage of stories, motifs, and archetypes delivered through ritual, tradition, and oral culture. When I was a young boy I knew about the story of Romeo and Juliet long before I saw or read the play, because my parents used to listen to the Dire Straits song of the same title, which not only carried some of the tale but also prompted my mother to tell me it in more detail. Plenty of other plots in popular culture carry the same plot structures, including Bernstein's *West Side Story*, which I listened to on cassette tape, and Australian soap operas with their forbidden love plots. It was not crucial that I accessed the Shakespeare original to be influenced by the story. Indeed, I could have been aware of the plot without knowing this play existed at all. Ironically, *Romeo and Juliet* was not Shakespeare's intellectual property; it existed in forms of other tales and plays beforehand.

Similarly, it is not especially important to prove that Paul was aware of a precise grafting technique when he produced the text. All three grafting techniques discussed—those of Theophrastus, Columella, and Palladius—have resonance throughout Greco-Roman culture and involve mutual benefit to the tree and the scion. If one tissue is joined to another, it will exchange fluids and nutritional substances—the leaves of a developed graft will photosynthesize[8] and provide benefit for the tree, and the tree's roots will source water and other nutrients. These principles must

---

8. See note above.

exert an influence on what this allegorical olive tree and olive-grafting is representing. Without fear of accusations of anachronism or even nihilism of meaning, we can confidently move forward with a historicized view that these ancient grafting techniques were circulating in the wider matrix of first century Greco-Roman thought that Paul was plugged into.

Being open to the validity of metaphor in the text, I am unafraid of reading against the grain of some of the alleged intention of the author, appreciating how the audience may have been able to understand it, indirectly or subconsciously. Even the grafting in (*enekentristhēs*) of the wild olive (*agrielaios*) of the allegory is reminiscent of the reader putting themselves into the text. In Derrida's grafting, the very act of reading is an intertextual violence—a cutting and insertion in which the grafting in of the reader to the text is a defiance of an authorial intention held up by any authority. Any authorial intention is at the start of writing itself a product of other voices and intertexts that always already are grafted-in to them. The person of Paul has the echoes of Hebrew scripture, philosophy, and literature through which he speaks. Influences from all these other sources are grafted into Paul and Pauline theology. Many of Paul's most pertinent points rely upon catenas from scripture or the silent, unreferenced influence of Stoicism or Platonism. Thus, we move away from the need to solve the authorial intention to the everchanging tree of text, with the author's will as just another graft, and the reader's understanding as another.

Neither the Grafts Nor the Tree Are Self-Sufficient

The idea that eschatological Israel or the believer are self-sufficient and stable entities can be imploded when we read this Romans text through the ancient intertexts using a deconstruction approach. The synergy and symbiosis between graft and tree is unavoidable and cannot be elided from any theological interpretation of the allegory without dislocating the former from the latter. Even in Theophrastus's method, the cultivated graft benefits the wild olive tree by providing an outlet for its hardiness to produce fruit. If we reverse this, then we could see the hardiness of the wild olive graft benefiting the cultivated tree by giving it the ability to produce fruit under harsher conditions: both the graft or the tree would be unable to fruit without the other. In Columella's process the slip of wild olive inserted brings reviving benefits to the tired cultivated tree, thus taking this mutuality further: the slip would wither and die without its transplanting, and the tree would continue to be barren without it. In Palladius, the mutuality is much more global because the wild slip is enhanced by the sap of the cultivated tree; yet it in turn adds its robustness to the tree to help it use its sap to nourish fruit production that it formally could not. In all three processes I have focused on, there is room for reciprocity and mutual need, even in Theophrastus, who is used by many scholars to assert that self-sufficiency of the tree and the reliance of the graft means a similar pattern between eschatological Israel and the inducted gentile believer.

Derrida's use of plant grafting to explain the reciprocity of writing and the exchange between the main text, as a tree, and the grafted in quotation—or act of writing itself, as represented by the scion—is a useful guide for exploring how the theology of Rom 11 might be understood. In the context of the allegory, the tree as eschatological Israel could be seen as a text of sorts—a corpus—and the broken-off branch as the individual believer could be seen as a sample from another text, a small text in themselves, or even the instance and act of writing, which is always derivative of another text. Thus eschatological Israel as a text is *Paul and his followers' vision of what right thinking and practice are*. Meanwhile, the believer is a writing derivative of *another vision from another text, tradition, or corpus*. The other text, tradition, or corpus might be seen as such as the faiths or philosophies from where the gentiles come when they convert or from other forms of early Christianity or Judaism, which are not seen as being correct in terms of the Pauline agenda. Paul's attachment of the olive tree allegory to a system of interaction of ideas makes Derrida's own allegory of olive grafting and writing relevant and fruitful. The reciprocity and exchange inherent in the system of ideas Paul represents with his own olive grafting will also, in turn, reinforce those aspects of the olive-grafting concept itself. The two are like a hall of mirrors, continually and eternally reflecting each other. This undermines the idea that eschatological-Israel is a self-sufficient and complete entity and affirms that the believer that enters into communion with it adds to the main body of thought and tradition.

Grafting In and Breaking Off

There is, of course, something inherently political and violent about the grafting in and breaking off of parts of the olive tree representing exclusion and inclusion. At a point in religious history before the parting of the ways, when Judaism and a Christ movement were negotiating confessional views, when Paul was juggling several identities of his own (Anatolian, Greek speaking, Roman citizen, Pharisaic Jew, Christ-believer), and people found themselves in a maelstrom of influences, this allegory tempts some interpreting it to desire simplicity and regularity. Such an aim is imperial, however, and ignores the kaleidoscopic influences of cultures. I would like to consider the grafting in and breaking off maneuvers alongside marginalized texts, including those of Wendt and Jacob 5 in the Book of Mormon.

Trees as interactions between cultures rather than sites of violent extraction and adhesion carries through to postcolonial contexts. The Banyan Tree of the Mau culture in Albert Wendt's novel *The Leaves of the Banyan Tree* (1979) is a metaphor for "the Polynesian past": "Its trunk and branches [lie] in the history of Samoan-white interaction—fed by the potent sap of cultural conflict and change, *pruned by the political knife of the German authorities, forced by the strong fertiliser of democratic sentiment*" (cited in Najita 2010, 352).[9] While there is colonial suggestion that the Western powers allowed the Mau tree to "flower and fruit," Wendt adheres the metaphor of "political knife" of colonialism that tries to remove trace of the Mau through the superiority of democracy (Wendt 1979, 177; cited in Najita 2010, 352). It is also shown in *Mango's Kiss* (Wendt 2003) that the decolonizing process involves a dance between oral and written forms; the oral can accommodate imperial knowledge, but it also undoes the claims that the colonizer has civilized the indigenized church. The colonizer's traditions are not the main structure of truth into which the colonized culture's beliefs and traditions are inserted, but the latter's oral culture provides hospitality to the colonizer's worldviews as part of an exchange, not as an acceptance of the other's right to predominance. Such eventual harmony is reassuring, but what about the violence of the past? This reality cannot be forgotten. It is always there and has to be processed.

Studies in Jamaican cultural interactions show how gardens are microcosms of worlds, societies, traditions, texts, and perhaps even religions, representing the canvass of communication in which meaning is being produced (Spartacus 2018). We need to pick up on these notions of grafting text to rehabilitate the allegory for our Romans text, placing it in its wider garden of speech, as the Latter-day Saints text does. In this garden, the cultivated olive tree of any given power or ideology, while allowed priority in its context, is denied superiority and ownership of truth. Its

---

9. Wendt here is citing Keesing 1934, 177.

interactions in the ecosystem of the garden, and in turn the wider environment, affect its identity and development. The grafting process is the human writing into this matrix—the believer negotiating meaning within and outside. Being broken off or cut away may be violent, but it does not have to be disempowering. By being in the garden, as the Latter-day Saints text shows, the broken-off branch still has a presence and influence. The tree and the garden are inseparable, just as the eschatological project of God and the wider world are.

While branches may be broken off as a means to create space on trees during the grafting practice, this is not a necessary act detailed in grafting literature. That it is specified in this Romans allegory marks it as theologically significant. There is a harshness to the act of breaking or cutting off; however, at the same time, it opens the possibility of change, as well as the possibility of branches being grafted back in. Unless a broken off branch is grafted onto another tree, it is unlikely in reality that it could be regrafted later. This is where the Latter-Day Saints' holy text, the Book of Mormon, develops the allegory in a way that enhances the hermeneutics. Whatever some may think about the provenance of Latter-day Saints texts, I consider the parable of the olive tree (Jacob 5 in the Book of Mormon) to be a well-worked exposition and reimagining of Rom 11:17–24. In the parable of the olive tree (Jacob 5), the master of the vineyard instructs his servant to cut off withered branches and replace them with grafts of wild olives (as specified in Romans). However, he also orders that natural branches of the tree—not necessarily withered ones—are to be grafted onto other trees in the vineyard. Such an interpretation enlightens the allegory in Romans by including the process of grafting between different tree species.

The tree with wild olive grafts grew good fruit. The natural branches of the tree that were broken off and transplanted onto other trees also gave good fruit. A natural branch planted in good soil gave a mix of good and bad fruit. The master of the vineyard demanded that all poor fruit-bearing branches be cut off, but the servant convinced him to further care for all the trees so they might improve. However, eventually all the trees produced bad fruit. The master proposed to burn all the trees in the vineyard, but again the servant changed his mind and instead the master removed the wild olive branches that had been transplanted onto the original cultivated trees that grew the poor fruit and grafted in their place tree branches from the daughter trees that descended from the transplanted cuttings. The approach worked, and from then onwards branches of trees producing bad fruit were removed and those giving good fruit were kept and nurtured. This allegory, within a text of a religious movement reimagining Christianity, indicates a need for restoration in its own era. In the descendants of the transplanted cuttings, there is no clear division between cultivated and wild, thus indicating a blur between Israel and the gentile world. The insight from Wendt and the Book of Mormon therefore offers Romans a reinclusion and reexclusion of the grafting process. Despite the seemingly uncompromising violence of breaking and cutting off branches, we find possibility for renewal, and elements that are excluded still have influence and a potential for reintegration.

Exclusion and Reinclusion

The breaking off of branches—*kladōn exeklasthēsan*—is an act within this allegorical construct, which in 11:17 is presented as occurring before the grafting in act. Grafting literature does not tend to specify this part of the process, probably as it is either assumed or not always necessary. The breaking-off act is drawn in from the margin in our allegory and used to represent the exclusion of people from eschatological Israel who have erred from the authorized form of faith, and it also represents their disconnection from being part of eschatological Israel and being able to benefit from it.

Yet if the breaking away of branches is seen as extracting a sample of text in line with Derrida, we could say that such a clean and clear removal is not possible. For a start, their extraction leaves an absence or a gap, which nonetheless is part of the identity of the tree, or eschatological Israel. The fact that the branches have been on the tree at all, especially if they were naturally grown on the tree, means their presence can never be removed or erased from the tree, even if it is an absence-presence. If the branches have grown on the tree from the start, they have already contributed to its development and, even at the point at which they became inconsistent with it, they have exerted influence over it. Their fluids will have mingled with the other tissue of the tree, and nourishment will have passed between them. Added to this, their breaking off will leave a scar—and every scar tells a story. A space is just as meaningful as a thing filling it. The breaking off in the Book of Mormon allegory entertains this.

Since, as Derrida claims, quotations can still exert influence on the text from which they come even after being removed from it, this could mean that the broken off branches, or the believers seen as not being consistent with Pauline Christianity, could still be seen as affecting the olive-tree, or eschatological Israel. Anxiety inherent in Greco-Roman identity toward the "barbarian Other" is redeployed in Paul in terms of tensions between Israel and the gentile world in which the latter takes the role of the Other (see Marchal 2020, 171–76). Marchal shows that the Otherness of the barbarian has internal as well as external insistence on the so-called coherence of Rome because it justifies conformity and confirms righteousness (161). However, this means that the opposition forces help to shape the core— whether that is Rome or Israel. Of course, in the process of olive-grafting, removed branches would not be seen as being able to influence the olive-tree nor the other way round; presumably they would be discarded somewhere. However, Paul's allegory compares the procedure of olive-grafting with the relationship between systems of belief and believers, and I have shown that these two concepts share certain aspects such as reciprocity and mutuality, so the represented can also influence what represents it, even where there are qualities of the representing concept that are not consistent with the represented. The Latter-Day Saints text shows how hearers' may imagine where those broken off branches end up, with excluded believers able to influence eschatological Israel—even to the point of being worthy to return.

The scion that is grafted in place of a broken-off branch is also affected by the absent branch in two ways. First, by the fact it inhabits its space— either its actual spot on the tree or in that it inherits its right to be there. In some way the broken off branch is the scion's legacy: the scion has been placed there as a consequence of the branch's removal, and in some way there is a coordination or continuation between the branch and the scion. This shows how the branch, as a believer or group of believers seen as erroneous, still affects the development of the belief system of Pauline Christianity. The act of including a believer or group thus becomes a response to exclusion, with the excluded people's beliefs, thoughts, and behaviors becoming active on the inclusion of others. The included become identified against the identity of the excluded.

Politically this exclusion and reinclusion is evident in how revolution is a response to imperialism, and counterrevolution is defined through opposition to the terms of the revolutionary movement. In Western Christian history, reformation is defined against the Roman Catholic church and counterreformation in opposition to reformation theology. In eschatological Israel, the excluded affect the newly included believers because they show that the new believers are faithful and righteous and consistent with eschatological Israel. Second, the branch produces meaning from its exclusion, in that it still exists somewhere in some kind of coordination with the tree. While it has been removed from the tree, a trace of its connection still remains, and in line with what Derrida says about how samples of texts still exert influence on their text of origin when placed into new contexts, it is still relevant to the tree by what remains of it in the tree, as well as its space or absence. Thus, a believer excluded for beliefs not consistent with Pauline Christianity still exerts power over eschatological Israel, and those beliefs still affect and help shape it, even as a kind of photographic negative. The brutality of inclusion and exclusion can be seen through the dialogic qualities of the epistles and through the redaction history of biblical texts, where theological argument is not an independent ideology, but where identity is forged through negotiation, opposition, *apologia*, and condemnation in an always-already conversational relationship with other beliefs, thoughts, and ideologies. Indeed, even as we begin to write or speak, we do so in contrast and coordination with other ideas. To write or speak is a form of violence and induces conflict, but we do not need to moralize or ethicize on this but instead recognize it as part of a wider process of the negotiation of meaning and truth.

The Paradox of Grafting

Conversion to and communion with any ideological identity, be it social, political, philosophical, or religious, is paradoxical. Derrida (1969) claims that the main text into which a sample is inserted does not dominate or own the sample any more than the text from which it was extracted. The main text reinscribes the samples, yet the samples also reinscribe the main text. When someone is inducted into an organization, both they and the organization change—consequently, the terms of both are altered. In religious denominations and political parties, there is a constant negotiation for the regulation of the core identity. Look at the Church of England's debate over LGBTQ marriage, where the induction of gay and lesbian priests has influenced change. Political parties are often seen as missiological movements, and there is always tension between the left or right flanks of Conservatives, Labour, Republican, or Democrat. Some argue that the ascent of Blairism in the Labour Party has changed its identity beyond recognition. Similarly, others have argued that the rise of social-liberals in the Conservative Party has diluted its strong social values. In Christian denominations, accusations abound that the liberal wings are diminishing the morals of the faith, but evangelical and Catholic wings are equally accused of preventing the progressive agenda. Looking at the picture without judgement, we see that there are forces within organizations that influence the dynamics of their identity. Within those forces are individuals who exert their own influence of varying force and import—some more than others. An influential priest, bishop, politician, or activist can stimulate significant changes within an organization. When someone is inducted and accepted into a social structure, both they and the society change. The entrant also projects their aspirations and expectations onto the society they enter, which means it does not fulfil them fully, and they wish to change it. The individual makes an assessment as to whether they want to join, and the community decides whether to accept them. If induction occurs, then through the negotiation, both parties change, meaning their original perception of each other's consistency and constancy is undermined. Furthermore, when someone joins something, there is, from the start, friction, and disruption as both parties try to reach equilibrium, and this is not necessarily violent or impassioned, but a normal and healthy negotiation of truth and belief. Jesus emerged in Judaism and changed Judaism and Greco-Roman religion irrevocably. Paul entered the picture and changed Christ's messianic Judaism even more, reducing the focus on legalistic ritual but reaffirming the law through the spirit. After the *parting of the ways*, Judaism—in opposition to Christianity—adopted a rabbinic structure influenced by the presbytery ecclesiology of its then-nemesis. There was never a *true* Judaism, Christianity, or paganism, as each changed when individual believers and groups were inducted. Some of this change was sudden and some gradual.

The paradox here is that what is considered to be the righteous eschatological-Israel changes every time a believer is added, and the believer changes when they are added; there is no permanent and universally righteous eschatological-Israel, and no such thing as a believer who is fully consistent with a static community. When the believer is outside eschatological Israel and about to be grafted in, they might be considered righteous or not; yet when they are grafted in, or included, they change. Each grafting-in or inclusion of a believer causes change to both parties, so the idea that either is somehow consistent or that the believer is in tune with eschatological Israel is compromised. What is demonstrated by this paradox is that there is no Truth or Righteousness out there that we must attain, but instead truth and righteousness exists at the point where we interact. These are constantly negotiated terms, and the individual believer has a right and onus to push against the mainstream and institutionalization of thought and faith to affect identity. The church is not a pedagogical authority but instead a forum of believers, taking us back to the Greek word's ancient sense of "calling out" (*ekklēsia*) the members of the town into the street to agree about what needs to be done today.[10] By this direct-democratic process, each person has the opportunity to influence the structure and action of the town.

Just as a text sample removed and placed into another context will be influenced by that context, so too are believers who are excluded from eschatological-Israel and then reincluded within it. They will be different, and this undermines the whole notion of a perfect, constant, and unchanging eschatological-Israel; rather than not being reliant on believers, it is defined by them and shaped by them and the belief traditions from whence they have come or to which they have returned. The broken-off branch that is regrafted also cannot be unlinked from wherever it was exiled, as we see from the reimagining in the Latter-day Saints text. The believer, through their exclusion from eschatological-Israel, is included in another context—that of unbelief. Consequently, when the believer is reincluded in eschatological Israel, they come still linked to and affected by their former context—maybe other traditions or beliefs as well. If they were once believers, they became former believers when they were excluded, and then former-former believers when reincluded. Or to put it another way, they might have been former nonbelievers, then became former-former nonbelievers, and then former-former-former nonbelievers. So their identity is defined as much by their exclusion as their inclusion, by their being outside as much as by their being within.

Rather than being restorative, their reinclusion instead adds a further layer of complexity to the identity of the believer and thus adds more strands of identity that affect and influence the collective identity of eschatological Israel. The reincluded believer will still exert the forces of their own identity and that of where they came from (or found exile in) when they are returned to eschatological Israel. In addition, when they were banished to a new context, they brought with them the influence of eschatological Israel, too, changed that new context to a certain extent,

---

10. The most recent example of this I have in mind is the governance of Saint Kilda, a lone island off the coast of Scotland, where every day there would be a "parliament," when all the men would come out of their cottages to discuss and debate what needed to be done that day before they set to work.

and then when they are reincluded in the latter they brought with them also that altered piece of the latter's own identity as well as the identity of the new context. Meanwhile, in the perceived absence of the believer from eschatological Israel, their absent-presence was still influential, and their link to their former host from their new context continued to change all three of them.

Of course, the branch broken off and never regrafted—the person excluded from a community or assembly permanently—is never entirely removed. In his essay "Plato's Pharmacy," Derrida (1969) discusses how the scapegoat—the exile of someone or something deemed harmful for a society or city—is actually an Othering that instead transposes something from within the communal identity to the outside. Derrida examines the etymology of pharmacy—realizing that it means poison and cure at the same time. In doing so, he realizes that the word *pharmakos* (scapegoat) is excluded from Plato's texts (especially *Phaedrus*) while *pharmakon*, *pharmakeus*, and *pharmakeia*—which cover the semantics of poison and remedy—are included. From this point, Derrida challenges the boundary between inside and outside, between exclusion and inclusion, and the terms and criteria between. Furthermore, he concludes that the outside (scapegoat–pharmakos) is *always-already* present inside the accepted, healthy, and lawful domain, which is, by paradox, both poisonous and remedial. From here I take forward into Rom 11:17–24 how the scapegoated branches or grafts cut or broken off, as believers or groups, will continue to refer back to the tree, or the mainstream religious movement. Despite being removed, their absence exerts an apparitional presence in the mainstream that cannot be removed. Any concept of a tree, as a main body of eschatological-Israel, is therefore not a static whole with a definite and separate inside and outside but a moving and shifting entity in which the force of ideas and beliefs outside of its orthodoxy exert influence beyond its agreed policy.

Despite the stillness of a rock, geologists do not consider it a static mass of wholeness; rather, they analyze its layers and changes over time. Archaeologists do not see London as it looks today as its absolute being but excavate its sediments and see how each era has impacted on the next. Biologists do not see animals as a kingdom that species are either in or outside, but they make sense of how they developed new features, such as legs, and shed others, such as leaves. To look at eschatological Israel as an entity that is independent from its interactions, erosions, absorptions, and exclusions of other influences is disingenuous. The result of our reading of Romans is thus a complex system of ever-changing sediments and layers, like molten lava pumping out from a volcanic hole and making a concertina of rock folds that never seem to end, appearing distinct and permanent one moment, then merged and fluid after the next wave. This continual, and seemingly infinite, layering of identity reflects the necessity of eschatology to provide not only closure but also openness, not just certainty but also uncertainty.

Beyond the Binaries

The metaphysical binary consisting of the opposition between faith (ideas and belief seen as being consistent with mainstream Pauline Christianity) and unfaith (those that appear to depart from it) is also blurred. Both the ideologies of faith and unfaith are engaged in mutual and reciprocal exchange too, and they feed and sustain each other's identity and bring benefit to each other. It is only the ideology in this text that allows this boundary to exist between them, and this ideology is weighted in favor of what is perceived as faith—a Pauline version of Christianity dictated to us by mainstream church and academia that forgets its confessional prejudices. If we remove this priority, we find that, from a deconstruction perspective, the only difference between these two concepts is that unfaith is more distant from and less subscribed to the dominant ideology of the text whereas faith is perceivably more explicitly committed to it. Yet the boundary cannot be drawn definitively, and thus the differences between types of belief and types of believer become infinitely more varied than this polar opposition. The substance of the olive tree, or eschatological Israel, is thus defined by the variation of believers' identities and, in line with the theory of Palladius, the believer has the power to help eschatological Israel to realize fruitfulness because of the believer's variation from Pauline Christianity. The life of faith thus becomes dependent on the negotiation between it and unfaith!

An associated binary that collapses under deconstruction is the opposition between the subjective metaphysical concepts of *kindness* and *severity* in 11:22. This verse threatens that those who fall will be treated with severity, whereas those who do not will be treated with kindness. There is a kind of tautological circular logic in that to be treated with kindness you must remain in kindness, but there are no specifics about what leads one to, or maintains one in a position to, remain in a state whereby one receives God's kindness. From the point of view of our deconstruction analysis, kindness could be associated with a seemingly conventional relationship between the tree and the graft, the main text and the sample, and, therefore, eschatological Israel and the believer. This is a relationship whereby the former is seen to orient and define the terms of the latter and the latter is always viewed through the framework of the former.

Severity, on the other hand, could be seen as a result of a position that dissolves this polarity and exposes an equality between the influences of eschatological Israel and the believer—a position in which believers who have fallen are merely those who have a more distant and deferred relationship to eschatological Israel. They are not divorced from it or separate from it and indeed never can be. Indeed, all believers in some ways differ from and defer to each other and from the totality of eschatological-Israel, and all can be seen to fall within the categories of kindness and severity, as well as faith and unfaith. It is this difference that helps to shape and define the characteristics and qualities of eschatological Israel, and I see the germ of this idea in Cullmann and Lincoln in particular as I have discussed. The power and determination of the believer is thus retained even in seemingly negative categories. Severity therefore becomes normalized alongside kindness, removing the privilege of the latter and the marginalization of the former. Righteousness is not aligned with kindness, therefore, but exists between it and severity, between in and out, between faith and unfaith.

As noted above, writing itself is an act of insertion; to write is to take grafts from other texts. The tree that is the text is thus not divisible into portions such as root, branches, and grafted-on scions. There is no permanent stable foundation, for the whole tree consists of scions! In this way, the allegory of grafting is at friction with the organic way human organizations develop, because grafting involves a technological intervention into nature, whereas society and civilization is a constant intervention. However, there is precedent in Greco-Roman literature for harmonizing the physic and techne binary, whereby the intervention of humankind (*techne*) is itself a movement of nature. While some such as Lin (2016) may reject the merely biological in favor of the cyborg as a paradigm, it is my conviction that these two are inseparable: the boundaries between ecology and human intervention are not thick and fixed; they are blurred. Furthermore, the tensions between the vehicle and tenor in the allegory highlights the metaphysical presupposition of a coherent original social entity (state, religion, organization, tribe, political party, etc.) into which something different (or Othered) is inserted. Of course, the originality and stability of a said entity's identity is metaphysical. If we ask the allegory to align in truth, we do not find an original tree into which a graft is inserted and is an alien particle within, but a tree of scions into which the graft is one of countless grafts that make up the tree. Derrida's tree of grafts is thus a specter of real incorporation.

This idea resonates well with Paul's olive tree that is eschatological Israel. Rather than there being a permanent stable foundation of eschatological Israel into which scions of believers are placed and are detachable, instead the form is composed entirely of the latter. Adding in, or removing believers thus alters the very substance of what eschatological Israel is. Eventually, the myth of the olive tree allegory becomes dissolved! The contrast between the grafting process and missiological struggle of the early church is engaged in so much negotiation and feedback that they become indiscernible. Such a view does not mean we need to accept homogenization of identity, where everything is the same, as Boyarin (1994) argues. Instead, the stimulus of the process is difference and contrast, which allows exchange, friction, and negotiation.

The Analogical Consensus Revisited

The analogical consensus I discussed earlier in this chapter does not provide a stable soil from which to grow a hardy tree of exegesis. To begin with, the root of the wild olive tree was considered stronger whereas its fruit weaker, and the reverse is true for the cultivated olive tree. Some scholars have aligned the root with Abraham and the patriarchs. However, Paul claims in Romans that the weaker cultivated root supports the stronger wild graft. Roots are perceived as foundational and grafts as supported, so we have the paradox of the supposedly weaker root supporting the supposedly weaker graft—seemingly going against the rationale of both nature and cultural intervention. Despite its weakness, the cultivated tree's root is seen as foundational to the graft in Romans. Yet we see from our ancient sources that the wild graft can help transform the cultivated root, which points us toward understanding grafting as a metaphor of reciprocity. Furthermore, this intervention might, like authority, cause rhizomes to escape root structures (see Blanton 2014, 134)—a metaphor for foundational discourse being affected by the marginal one. Nature and culture is thus in flux and at paradox, as is Israel and the gentile world!

Grafting of all kinds—plant and animal—in the ancient world invokes the binary of nature versus culture. There are some ancient writers who view it as an unnatural innovation (Vergil, *Georg.* 2.69–82; Vitruvius, *Arch.* 7.5.3–4; Livy, *Ab urbe cond.* 27.37.2; m. Kil. 1:7; Pliny, *Nat.* 15.57; Varro, *Rust.* 1.40.5; Plutarch *Quaest. conv.* 2.6, and others), but most sources present it as a positive part of technology (see various texts in Virgil, Ovid, Columella Calpurnius, Pliny the Elder, Palladius, Cato, Varro and Lucretius; see Lowe 2010 for a fuller discussion on the ancient views on grafting). In our Romans text, Israel is aligned with the natural branches and the cultivated tree, whereas the gentile world is aligned with the wild tree and the grafted-in scions or slips.

While this seems tidy and stable, it is instead paradoxical. In terms of origin, we may consider Israel to be associated with wildness and the natural, and the gentile world with the cultural and cultivated (innovation adding to what is natural). We therefore have a paradox where the grafted-in part represents the gentile and culture, and the natural branch represents Israel. However, the grafted-in branch is also wild and thus closer to real nature, linking it with the naturality of Israel, and the natural branch as Israel could be seen as cultivated through innovation and thus gentilic. What does this mean? The allegory starts to fall apart at the seams because we have two parts of a binary used in contrast yet with the literal and allegorical inflections confused and tangled. Nature in the allegory means that which was chronologically prior—the literal branches that grew on the cultivated olive tree and allegorically Israelites—but culture means not posthumous in chronology—literally horticultural sophistication and allegorically the moral and religious advancement of Israel. Confusingly, other binaries are split by the literal and allegorical in contradictory ways: wildness is natural but represents gentiles; cultivation is unnatural and represents Israel. The cultivation of olive trees is more distinctive in gentilic tradition than Hebraic, with such innovation seen as mainly positive by gentiles. Israel's authority is, however, affirmed by originality and naturality that might also be aligned with wildness, and gentile culture might be seen by detractors as immoral or erroneous interference or innovation that might also be aligned with cultivation. As religious authority is based on origins, with most world religions (especially Abrahamic ones) emphasizing their original truth and purity, the natural branches seem stably aligned to Israel. They are at odds, however, with the positioning of the gentile world as the wild tree and the cultivated one as Israel, because one could align natural with wild and wildness with originality.

Perhaps the confusion is reduced when we distinguish between origins and beginning: the former is ideological and constructed, the latter chronological and consequential. For example, adoption and genealogy in the ancient world were less about lineage and historicity than a transcendent spiritual connection. An emperor's adopted son may be more original than a biological son who preceded him in time. The cultivated, in the allegory, could be viewed as Israel's improvement on the base origins of the gentile world—a development into religious sophistication from pagan barbaric past. Nature versus culture is ideological, with the culture masquerading as natural, especially in imperialist, nationalist, and fundamentalist ideologies. In this allegory, we have a cultivated tree grafted with wildness, complicating the division between the "natural" and the "cultivated." Tension between nature and culture is therefore at the forefront of grafting practice, this allegory, and its theology. On the one hand, there were misgivings about the attempt to meddle in nature and, on the other, a sense that such intervention is necessary and enhancing. Within this tension, we find interesting consequences for our allegory. Going forward, alternatively, we can raise our awareness of the instability of the nature-versus-culture, wild-versus-cultivated, binaries of the allegory. Neither Israel nor gentiles have superior origin, and both have cultural developments from their beginnings that impact on each other. Neither Israel nor gentiles are exclusively natural; neither have ultimate origin but are instead simultaneous. Neither are cultural interventions or meddling but are both equally intervened in and adapted. Oleiculture (and horticulture) is allegorical of an eschatological-Israel in which the intervention of the individual occurs, and this is neither natural or unnatural. Nature is thus an absent-presence, and any movement to affirm or deny identity is interaction between worldviews including Israel and gentiles, and this is only ever cultural. Rather than two poles, nature and culture are not so easily distinguishable, despite the tension of their contrasts, and in constant exchange.

The allegory of the olive tree and grafting does not start with stable fixtures but with unstable terms. Traditional readings that condemn one ethnicity or another through allusion are always-already undermined. However, as these readings have influence, we also have to critique their failings specifically. What we can take forward is that identity is transitional and constantly negotiated. When we pin down a definition of Israel or Judaism, itself a site of extensive debate, we find an Israel that is itself not natural but cultivated by other influences, religions, ethnicities, cultures, and identities. The Judaism of the hearers of Romans was one that was heard in the synagogues of an imperial power's main city, and its followers were part of a nation that was spread all over that Empire and beyond—perhaps even to India, Afghanistan, Arabia, and regions of the African continent. Peoples of other ethnicities have already been absorbed in to the genealogy of Judaism through migration and marriage or self-identity, such as with the God-fearers of Rome. The addition of gentiles in the scope of Paul's missiology is not a beginning but a continuation of constant exchange that is already at play, in which any who are added may carry traces of Israel's more original origins.

Eschatological Outcomes and Summary of Analysis

It might seem that Paul maintains the myth of the polar difference between the eternal olive tree as eschatological Israel and the branches and grafts as groups and individual believers respectively. Such a reading presupposes an eschatological Israel that is perfect, constant, and unchanging and not reliant on additions or development. It also grates against the "not yet complete" part of the *already/not yet* eschatological tension. There is also a presupposition here that believers can exist within their host in a way that is fully consistent with it, be excluded for changing in a way which is inconsistent with it, and then be returned and included to be consistent in an identical way to how they were before. Such a view is, however, impossible as much as it is intellectually corrupt.

This chapter, indeed this book, has demanded a major task of Cullmann's (1951) "radical application" of theology as well as Lincoln's (1981) concept of believers who "participate in the triumph of the exalted Christ over the powers" and thus "have been set free to use this world and its structures." Even the twentieth-century Cullman is placing a demand on us that transcends the rigid authoritarianism of twentieth- and twenty-first century scholarship. He demands, even if not as radically as I propose, that we not be bound to the theology prescribed to us and that we seek to interpret and apply in ways that may subvert the norm. Cullman's demands, whether intentional or not, move us away from the idea of a one-way process of transferal, in which one party, usually eschatological-Israel, benefits (but is not benefited by) the other, usually the gentile believer. It also departs from Dunn's (1988b) idea of the believer only being able to improve themselves due to being "not yet perfect" and instead raises the possibility that the progress of the believer can contribute to God and God's progress too. Furthermore, it moves away from Wright's (1991) position in which only God is seemingly active and able to accomplish glory in his people. Instead of a one-way notion of transferal from God to the believer via eschatological-Israel, in which we find the believer only able to affect their own progress and not God's, or even of a situation where only God retains the ability to accomplish anything at all in the believers, we find another possibility. This is the notion of a two-way process of exchange of benefit and identity, in which both parties influence each other mutually. The believer's role is one of power and onus.

We can support this argument by tracing a link between Derrida's concept of *always-already* and the *already-not yet* of the eschatological tension. It could be said that the *not-yet* is *always* and the *already* is *not yet*. Consequently, we open up the possibility for constant change, revision, and development. The eschatological project of God is open-ended and should hold no presuppositions of ends or absolutes. The believer is one author, among many others, of this project, inserting their utterances between the wider text. They help shape the text through their contributions as well as their responses to previous utterances. The main argument of this chapter, concerning the reciprocity, mutuality, and exchange aspects that are transferred from olive grafting to the relationship between God and the believer through eschatological-Israel, finds its foundation reassessing ancient theories of oleiculture, yet incorporates a deconstruction review of existing scholarship. Through these influences I was able to move from an alternating or stimulator-response form of reciprocity, mutuality, and exchange to a sense in which identity is never fixed, stable, or static. Instead, I uncovered an identity that is fluid, dynamic, and constantly subject to change through simultaneous and infinite mutual reflection. The believer can never be separated from the identity of eschatological Israel and thus God, because each defines and feeds into the other in limitless ways. It is not a case of God merely accomplishing things in his people, as Wright claims, or of the believer only being able to affect their own destiny as distinct to that of God's and his projects, as Dunn suggests. Therefore, not only have I affirmed the believer as having power and responsibility in their relationship with God, I have also confirmed the involuntary and necessary nature of that relationship. From here, we move to the implications of our exegetically informed analysis.

The Implications of the Power of the Believer

As summarized earlier in the chapter, the adherence of some traditional mainstream scholarship of this allegory to the one way transferal of benefit, from olive tree to wild graft and thus from eschatological Israel to gentile believer (or believer), provides theological justification for divisive and exclusionary ideology. In this section I indicate the benefits of alternative readings of mutuality and synergy.

Mutuality is favored over superiority to generate better equality.

The first implication of my reading of Rom 11 is that we can emphasize mutuality over superiority and, in doing so, open up the opportunities for a more equal society. Inequality will never be eradicated; however, its ebbs and flows can be transitioned into a mutuality in which all parties have power and onus.

Grafting and breaking off can represent a supersessionism that invites notions of superiority of one belief or view over another. There is a risk that some readings of Paul that see gentiles as falling short are destructively colonial. It is condescending that gentiles are seen as grafted-in to the superiority of Israel and can be removed if they do not meet up to those proposed standards and, even worse, replaced by the grafting back in of those who were previously excluded. Such a view descends into a cruelty reminiscent of oppressive regimes, where dissenters become obsolete and replaceable by the new agenda that takes over—overthrown monarchies, revolution, reformation, restoration, et cetera. So, grafting-in after breaking-off can become weaponized to affirm the superiority of one party and the inferiority of another. Yet we can repurpose this paradigm to make exclusion a subdivision of inclusion, with the removal of a person, group, or identity being a maneuver that actually adds to the identity of the host, through absence as much as presence.

All metaphors offer hazards because no two items in a comparison ever match up entirely. Rather than rejecting the tree for its hierarchical tendency (as per Lin 2016, 2), we have an opportunity to improve upon how we use the tree by adopting better informed theories of metaphor. The image of the garden allows a compromise between the natural and artificial in the biological arena. Any intervention, whether natural or horticultural, involves mutuality. Each culture, faith, and idea relies on the others to grow and prosper through mutuality. From this exegetical application, we find an argument for an inclusive state that gives equal status to all its cultures and faiths and helps them maintain their differences and ability to exchange. This way we can widen our mission as Paul wanted.

Appreciating the value of individual identity over the uniform corporate improves community.

Once we dispense with the autocracy of a corporate uniform identity, we begin to appreciate the value of the individual within a religious community such as the church. Individual identity is important because it distils the influence of a wide variety of sources. Each of us is unique, carrying parts of other cultures, religions, nations, traditions, philosophies, and so on. A Muslim convert to Christianity will bring with them great treasures of thought and faith from Islam. When we review our ontology of a natural item such as a tree as an integrated rather than self-contained entity, we can raise a more helpful allegory of religion. From this we can defend a paradigm that acknowledges the continuum between things in the world and their interrelation. We will be more inclined to look beyond the Western hegemony that dominates metaphor and ideology. Instead of imagining a static, impenetrable dominating power, we will be able to see that reciprocity is at the heart of how Paul has been located in the discourse of "modern Europe" (Tofighi 2017, x), which itself collapses as a self-contained entity, relying on its interactions with other cultures from "outside." Additionally, Paul, can be situated on the frontier lands between Christianity and Judaism (Tofighi 2017, xii; Blanton 2013, 1–17) and arguably other traditions too (see Tofighi 2017, 16–18; Herzfeld 2002; King 2006). Pauline Christianity is therefore wider than a limited reading of olive grafting; it is instead deeply affected by outside traditions crystalized into a person. It is sobering to remember that Paul was a Pharisee, born in Anatolia, a speaker of Greek and Hebrew, and a citizen of Rome. The Greek language was brought to the middle east by a Macedonian king who also colonized the East up to the Indus valley, mixing Hellenic with Afghan, Indic, Turkic, and other cultures. It is therefore not sufficient to limit the olive tree to Israel and the grafts to a generic gentile world in a binary way. The boundaries between cultures, religions, and identities are never absolute and rigid, and on many occasions throughout history, the sites of such exchange have been individuals bringing their unique coalescence of identity to the matrix of a community.

Dissolving the binary between inclusion and exclusion —inside and outside—highlights possibilities for exchange.

Our reading helps us to remove morality from inclusion and exclusion and see both movements as part of a process of exchange by which identity is formed. There is a danger that some readings of the olive tree allegory in Paul assist a divisive and violent agenda of those in and those out. Severity and kindness become juxtaposed in a way that is deeply prejudiced and intolerant to others. Conceptualizing the tree as having an unchanging core onto which alien branches are grafted allows for views of Israel, Christianity, or the church to be something that is absolute and uncompromising, with those inducted expected to conform with the core rather than contribute to it.

Furthermore, the removal and exclusion in cultural dominance does not end at the violence of cutting off or out. The idea that an excluded individual or group can be removed from having any impact on the dominant institution is an illusion. Even colonial or religious powers cannot prevent influence from an identity unit or group that they may exclude or refuse induction to. Those excluded impact heavily on the entity from which they are excluded.[11] Polemics of apostasy or heresy affects the apologetics, reformations, and counterreformations of religions, shaping their ideology. For instance, Christianity has been affected by resistance from the paganism that preceded and followed it. The creeds of Christianity are largely a response to ideas that threatened its orthodoxies. The idea of God is influenced strongly by what Zeus, Jupiter, or other deities are. Rabbinic Judaism after 70 CE has been influenced by Christian clericalism. The mutual exclusion of Islam and Christianity provided a space for the rejection of religious idols in worship spaces to emerge, especially during the Reformation. It is through the cracks of difference that identity emerges. The places where branches are broken off leave telling scars. The branches removed or refused exert an influence on the tree through their decomposition into the soil that feeds the tree or existence grafted elsewhere, where their chemicals interact. Similarly, where individuals or movements are excommunicated, their heresy or apostasy affects the ideology of the host religion or denomination in a way that changes it significantly. Christianity has been influenced greatly by differences between it and Judaism and Greco-Roman religion and between Catholicism and reformed tradition; Buddhism has been influenced by its differences with Hinduism, Hinduism with Jainism, and so on. The excluded or refused

---

11. It should be noted as an ethical ramification that there can still be violent consequences for some of those who are subject to any exclusion, whether expulsion, exile, banishment, or ostracism, ghettoization, or discrimination from within a community.

party exerts an influence on the main entity within the matrix of the wider cultural and social milieu.

Conclusion

The olive tree grafting allegory is entirely fit for our purposes if we read it responsibly with progressive theories of metaphor that are open and inclusive. Without this, we find a rigid and exclusionary Christian and church ontology, in which the believer must be inducted and change to conform with a corporate identity. If, however, we place this image within a context of a garden, field, or wider ecological plain, we can envisage how it affirms the values of both the social and the individual. Exclusion and inclusion do not need to be violent rejections but parts of a process of negotiation and evolution. There is no need for heresy, apostasy, or orthodoxy but instead a continued dialogue.

Prominent views on the olive tree allegory in Rom 11:16–24 are varied but exclude the notion of mutuality between eschatological Israel and gentile society. In this chapter I have used the classical sources of Theophrastus, Palladius, and Columella, alongside Jacob 5 of The Book of Mormon and deconstruction theory, to show reciprocity between the branches, grafts, and scions and the tree, and thus I have shown the same between eschatological Israel and other traditions and cultures included into it. I have examined the problems of traditional mainstream readings of the text and argued that Christianity in its inclusive spirit must be evolving as well as structured, ecological as well as economic. Such values must be translated to society to allow the gospel to proliferate there. A reciprocal and mutual understanding of this allegory and its empowerment of the believer in their relationship with God enhances the existence of the Christ-believing community affirms God's love and moves Christianity beyond the limits of tribal history into being a contributor to tolerance and peace. It is my proposal that my reading of Rom 11:16–24 can be used to achieve such aims.

IN CONCLUSION

> For I am not ashamed of the gospel, for it is the power of God for salvation to everyone who believes, to the Jew first and also to the Greek. For in it the righteousness of God is revealed from faith for faith, as it is written, "The righteous shall live by faith."
> —Romans 1:16–17

The Power Is Yours

This is not a conclusion because the power is yours. You have fresh roots feeling around for ideas and new shoots reaching for the enlightenment of the sun. You are not restricted but empowered by the debt and credit of interpretation of meaning and its ebb and flows. Economic and ecological division and delay, while limiting under certain powers, can facilitate an exchange in which every actor, even the least disposed, can realize agency and push their interpretation to the forefront.

In this spirit I have used ancient intertexts, including papyri letters and horticultural manuals, as well as other sources, under the guidance of deconstruction theory, to bring texts from Romans to ground level, away from idealism and traditional confessionalism of a one-way relationship between God and the believer. I have asked some difficult questions to realign the interpretation of the texts I have analyzed in Rom 4 and 11 away from problematic historical presuppositions, using close text-level exegesis. In doing so, I hope I have undermined the often-repeated narratives that adhere to theological convention. I have integrated deferral and delay of the economic into the charade of altruism. I have shown that *pistis* does not mean blind-acceptance but trust in an other's ability to return. I have argued that gift is never altruistic, that it is always economic, and that asserting altruism is problematic and oppressive: real grace is the reciprocal dynamism between two parties and is thus not equivalent to gift-giving but is instead always economic in the material plain, if ultimately transcendent in the heavenly realm. I have shown that olive grafting is not about the superiority of cultivated olive stock over the wild, have demonstrated that there is mutual benefit when any grafting takes place, and have argued that this translates into a theology of the individual as shaping eschatological-Israel. I have shown that the power of the believer affirms God.

In turn, I have made three main arguments. First, that *pistis* in Romans is not blind-faith but a wholesome space between interpretation and imagination, where the believer assesses and creates, rather than receives and is dictated to. Second, that gift and grace should not be conflated and that grace is not one-way altruism from God but a reciprocal dynamic. Third, that the eschatological project of God does not exclude but includes and celebrates the difference presented by the believers inducted into it. From these propositions, I have aligned important ethical movements in terms of inclusivity, respect, cooperation, cultural exchange, rehabilitation, and identity. I have indicated areas for further hermeneutical exploration that contributes not only to confessional but philosophical and political ethics. The power is yours!

Back to Ground Level

Power does not mean anything goes or "I think so it is"; it comes with accountability, respect, and accuracy. I follow in the footsteps of Oakes (2009), who explores Paul's letter to the Romans by taking his exegetical spade to the ground level of socioeconomic archaeological evidence of Pompeii, rather than relying heavily on the imperial high culture. Oakes uses the data and evidence to reconstruct likely and credible stories of the lives of ordinary people of Pompeii, which would have been consistent with those of the recipients of Paul's letter to the Roman churches. In this present study, I borrow from Oakes's approach somewhat in that I use as my touchstone the letters and documents of everyday people and the notebooks of agriculturalists, rather than the literary and philosophical texts commissioned by elites, such as Seneca or Josephus. I base my observations on these ordinary texts and construct hypotheses about their motivations and responses. In doing so, I have opened a new range of possibilities for reading Romans that I hope continues beyond the end of this present study. Ordinary sources that use words like *pistis*, *xaris*, *misthos*, and *opheiēlma*, as well as those that detail practices such as olive grafting, offer much more to our theological reading of Romans than literary or philosophical sources can under the yoke of established biblical scholarship that looks to confirm the role of the believer as totally passive.

I have shown that certain words and images in Romans have been restricted through some (not all) traditional mainstream biblical exegesis and set apart without valid reason from their uses in other influential intertexts. Too often some scholars have sought to preserve an original, absolute correct meaning—a transcendental that is the result of ideological presuppositions of interpretative authorities in the church and academy seeking to limit the plasticity and fluidity of Romans and other religious texts. I have indicated that there is no boundary between the validity of Paul's theses and those of his interpreters (see Breu 2019, 143) but instead a continuum in which those interpreting take Paul's thoughts forward and apply them to life in radical and diverse ways. Too often those who wield authority over the texts attempt to control what people think, say, and do in response. It is no coincidence that a theology of the passivity of the believer fits well with an ideology that acquiesces to the demands of dominance. Transcendental signs—those utterances that retain an absolute meaning no matter what the instance of reading—enforce political and social presuppositions. In the past these have included imperialism, nationalism, fascism, colonization, Westernization, feudalism, mercantilism, capitalism, racial supremacy, patriarchy, sexual normativity, religious supremacy, and others. Today, these include reinventions of the past that are positioned as altruistic but instead exert austerity of the material, thought, and spirit on others: neoliberalism, neocolonialism, democracy, globalization, military interventionism, fundamentalism, as well as celebrity elitism, political correctness, financial meritocracy, and technocracy, among others.

The failure to appreciate the semantic range and plasticity of words, concepts, and images in Romans (and other texts) means that the full hermeneutic potential is lost. The full richness of the play of ideas in the text is inaccessible to a reader who is under the yoke of authoritative doctrine based in an assumed authoritative exegesis. I have shown how this lack in the interpretation of these Romans texts plays out both at ground level in the past and in the hermeneutical horizon of our time. I have stayed loyal to the discipline of literary analysis of texts and intertexts, maintaining my discipline, while broadening the potential of what they have to offer through use of critical theory, thus exerting my own power as a believer in Christ and God's plan for us. While my work here is more exegetical interaction and deconstructive analysis, the hermeneutics is signposted at the end of each chapter to encourage others to develop it further into the sphere of church, politics, ethics, and life.

Consequences

My approach also owes much to deconstruction theory, particularly that of Derrida, Nietzsche, Canguilhem, and Agamben, without being slavish to it. Three examples of metaphor were analyzed here: the financial-economic imagery in Rom 4, the gift imagery in Rom 4, and the olive-tree allegory in Rom 11. I demonstrate how the reassessment of the effects of these three types of metaphor through deconstruction theory has contributed toward an understanding of the active and powerful role of the believer in their relationship to God and God's eschatological project—one that is reciprocal and enhancing.

The effect of applying critical theory in this way is that the binary of literal versus metaphorical itself allows for other binaries to dissolve, even if they are helpful to gauge the dynamics of a text. All language is metaphorical or has the potential to be metaphorical in that it can signify beyond the perceived limits of an authorial figure or an authorized reception. It is recommended here that some of the highly contentious and disputed areas of New Testament studies—and indeed other religious textual studies—might be visited with this approach in mind. Out of deconstruction of the metaphysical pattern of *usure* we can appreciate what has been perceived to have been lost from authorized interpretations and observe what might have been gained, albeit at an indirectly conscious or an unconscious level.

The consequence of my argument is that the site of relation between God and the believer is not static but constantly developing and evolving, and in it there is mutuality, reciprocity, and fellowship. I show that believers use imaginative assessment and the play of exchange to determine their place in this relationship; that rather than bending to austerity dressed as altruism believers are instead empowered by economic fairness and pride to engage with true grace; and that eschatological-Israel must interact with other cultures, traditions, and faiths, because I propose that entities are not static but dynamic. Furthermore, I show that the individual characteristics and qualities of the believer, rather than being unimportant or supplemental, are instead factors that empower the believer to progress in their relationship with God and thus enhance the existence of the Christ-believing community. God's own justice of creation is also affirmed by the very creation that is righteous and faithful, while at the same time powerful, within a matrix of grace and spirit.

As mentioned, this is a chiefly exegetical study supported by critical theory. Throughout, I have situated my readings in an multifaith perspective in which I, while not denying the difference and contentions between faiths and cultures, propose that the site of the relationship between God and the believer in Christianity or Judaism relies on the interactions with and other preceding, contemporary, and emergent traditions, including Islam, Buddhism, Hinduism, Jainism, Sikhism, Mormonism, secular philosophy, and indeed all faiths and perspectives, for its fundamental existence and continuation. Without these influences and dynamics, the relationship between God and the believer is flesh rather than spirit, death rather than eternal life. I appreciate that this is a controversial end to this book; however, I am passionately committed to it, both as an academic and as a follower of the Christ who transcends the dogma and doctrine of authorities to embrace the power of individuals and communities.

Over to You

Even if limited in power, we can raise credit, recover debt, plant roots, or reach for justice with the shoots and branches of our faith. We can respond to the environment we live in through our own experiences and values and find God in our own way, as a creeping vine emerges from a crack in the pavement. We may not be able to resist powers that try to oppress us, but Paul's Epistle to the Romans shows us that we can control how we respond through our interpretation as well as faith in God. God offers us not only discipline but space for this maneuver. The opportunities are endless and creative. God wants us to be involved, not in the passive way that so many bankrupt religious ideologies teach us, but in an active role, in partnership with him. The righteous live by faith because they take up their rights and responsibilities and create meaning and breathe further life into God's word.

So, the believer's involvement in God's eschatological project *does have* a consequence on the success or quality of it, and this is a value that should be taken into into account in both religious and secular life. The role of the believer is an active and important one: the believer, like the citizen, is a powerful agent who contributes to the vital new creation. Whatever your position is on faith, this is a value worth embracing. Given these arguments, there is no end to the role of the believer in God's eschatological project.

I provide only a reminder of the opportunity and obligation all believers bear by participating in an ever-unfolding exchange. We ebb and flow. We build debts, but we pay back. We make roots, and we grow shoots. So, from power we move to empowerment:

Over to you.

BIBLIOGRAPHY

Aaron, David H. 2001. *Biblical Ambiguities, Metaphor, Semantics and Divine Imagery*. Leiden: Brill.

Aarts, Joris. 2005. "Coins, Money and Exchange in the Roman World: A Cultural-Economic Perspective." *Archaeological Dialogues* 12:1–28.

Achtemeier, Paul J. 1985. *Romans*. Louisville: John Knox.

Agamben, Giorgio. 2005. *The Time That Remains: A Commentary on the Letter to the Romans*. Translated by Patricia Dailey. Stanford: Stanford University Press.

Akoto-Abutiate, Dorothy B. E. A. 2014. *Proverbs and the African Tree of Life: Grafting Biblical Proverbs on to Ghanaian Eve Folk Proverbs*. Leiden: Brill.

Albinus, Lars. 2000. T*he House of Hades: Studies in Ancient Greek Eschatology*. Aarhus: Aarhus University Press.

Anderson, B. J. 2017. "The Politics of Pests: Immigration and the Invasive Other." *Social Research: An International Quarterly* 84.1:7–28.

Aristotle. 1912. *The Works of Aristotle Translated into English*. Translated and edited by J. A. Smith and W. D. Ross. Oxford: Oxford University Press.

Asad, Talal. 1993. *Genealogies of Religion: Discipline and Reasons of Power in Christianity and Islam*. Baltimore: John Hopkins University Press.

Badhwar, Neera Kapur. 1993. "Altruism Versus Self-interest: Sometimes A False Dichotomy." *Social Philosophy and Policy* 10:90–117.

Barclay, John. 2015. *Paul and the Gift*. Grand Rapids: Eerdmans.

Barth, Karl. 1933. *The Epistle to the Romans*. Oxford: Oxford University Press.

Barthes, Roland. 1967. "Death of the Author." Translated by Richard Howard. *Aspen* 5–6.3: https://tinyurl.com/SBL0697a.

Baxter A. G., and J. A. Ziesler. 1985. "Paul and Arboriculture: Romans 11.17–24." *JSNT* 7.24: 25–32.

Bell, H. Idris, and C. H. Roberts. 1948. *A Descriptive Catalogue of the Greek Papyri in the Collection of Wilfred Merton, F.S.A.* London: Emery Walker Limited.

Benjamin, Walter. 1996. "Critique of Violence." Pages 236–52 in vol. 1 of *Walter Benjamin: Selected Writings*. Edited by Marcus Bullock and Michael Jennings. Cambridge, MA: Harvard University Press.

Borradori, Giovanna. 2003. *Philosophy in a Time of Terror: Dialogues with Jürgen Habermas and Jacques Derrida*. Chicago: University of Chicago Press.

Breu, Clarissa. 2019. "#John: Author-Names in Revelation and Other New Testament Texts." Pages 126–48 in *Biblical Exegesis without Authorial Intention: Interdisciplinary Approaches to Authorship and Meaning*. Edited by Clarissa Brue. BibInt 172. Leiden: Brill.

Blanton, Ward. 2007. *Displacing Christian Origins: Philosophy, Secularity, and the New Testament*. Chicago: University of Chicago Press.

———. 2013. "Paul and the Philosophers: Return to a New Archive." Pages 1–17 in *Paul and the Philosophers*. Edited by Ward Blanton and Hent de Vries. New York: Fordham University Press.

———. 2014. *A Materialism for the Masses: Saint Paul and the Philosophy of Undying Life*. New York: Columbia University Press.

Borradori, Giovanna. 2003. *Philosophy in a Time of Terror: Dialogues with Jurgen Habermas and Jacques Derrida*. Chicago: University of Chicago Press.

Boyarin, Daniel. 1994. *A Radical Jew: Paul and the Politics of Identity*. Berkeley: University of California Press.

Britton, Richard. 2017. "'Behold the Twilight Sanguine Stain': The Tension between Alliteration-Consonance and Imagery and the Theology of Ruskin's 'Mont Blanc Revisited.'" *The Ruskin Review and Bulletin* 13.1.

Bryan, Christopher. 2000. *A Preface to Romans: Notes on the Epistle in its Literary and Cultural Setting*. Cambridge: Cambridge University Press.

Bultmann, Rudolf. 1952. *Theology of the New Testament*. Vol. 1. London: SCM.

Byron, Glennis. 2000. "Gothic in the 1890s." Pages 186–96 in *A Companion to the Gothic*. Edited by David Punter. Malden: Blackwell.

Canguilhem, Georges, 1969. *La connaissance de la vie*. Paris: Vrin.

Chalmers, Patrick. 1912. *Green Days and Blue Days*. Dublin: Maunsel.

Chan, Alan T. Y., and Shu-kam Lee. 2009. "Christ and Business Culture: Another Classification of Christians in Workplaces according to an

Empirical Study in Hong Kong." *Journal of Markets and Morality* 12:91–111.
Chan, Eugene Y. 2017. "Self-Protection Promotes Altruism." *Evolution and Human Behavior* 38:667–73.
Chatterton, Thomas. 1886. "The Defence." In *The Poetical Works of Thomas Chatterton*. Edited by John Richmond: Walter Scott.
Columella, Lucius Junius Moderatus. 2010. *De Re Rustica*. Edited by R.H. Rogers. New York: Oxford University Press.
Cross, Frank Moore. 1973. *Caananite Myth and Hebrew Epic: Essays in the History of Religion in Israel*. Cambridge, MA: Harvard University Press.
Culler, Jonathan. 1983. *On Deconstruction: Theory and Criticism after Structuralism*. London: Routledge & Kegan Paul.
Cullmann, Oscar, 1951. *Christ and Time: The Primitive Christian Conception of Time and History*. Translated by Floyd V. Filson. London: SCM.
Danker, Paul F. W. 1983. "Reciprocity in the Ancient World and in Acts 15:23–9." Pages 49–58 in *Political Issues in Luke Acts*. Edited by Richard J. Cassidy and Philip J. Scharper, Maryknoll: Orbis.
———. 1988. "Bridging St. Paul and the Apostolic Fathers: A Study in Reciprocity." *CurTM* 15:84–94.
Davidson, Steed. 2015. "Building on Sand: Shifting Readings of Genesis 38 and Daniel 8." Pages 37–55 in *Islands, Islanders, and the Bible: RumInations*. Edited by Jione Havea, Margaret Aymer, and Steed Vernyl Davidson. SemeiaSt 77. Atlanta: SBL Press.
Davies, W. D. 1984. "Paul and the Gentiles: A Suggestion Concerning Romans 11:13–24." Pages 153–63 in *Jewish and Pauline Studies*. Philadelphia: Fortress.
Derrida, Jacques. 1969. *Dissemination*. Translated by Barbara Johnson. London: The Athlone Press.
———. 1976. *Of Grammatology*. Translated by Gayatri Chakravorty Spivak. Baltimore: John Hopkins.
———. 1978a. "Force and Signification (1963)." Pages 3–30 in *Writing and Difference*. Translated by Alan Bass. London: Routledge & Kegan Paul.
———. 1978b. "The Retreat of Metaphor." *Enclitic* 2.2:4–33.
———. 1982. "White Mythology." Pages 207–71 in *Margins of Philosophy*. Translated by Alan Bass. Chicago: Chicago University Press.
———. 1987. *The Truth in Painting*. Translated by Geoffrey Bennington and Ian McLeod. Chicago: University of Chicago Press.

———. 1988. "Signature Event Context." Pages 19–23 in *Limited Inc.* Evanston, IL: Northwestern University Press.

———. 1992a. *Given Time 1: Counterfeit Money.* Chicago: University of Chicago Press.

———. 1992b. "Given Time: The Time of the King." Translated by Peggy Kamuf. *Critical Enquiry* 18:161–87.

———. 2001a. 'Violence and Metaphysics (1968)." Pages 79–153 in *Writing and Difference.* Translated by Alan Bass. London: Routledge & Kegan Paul.

———. 2001b. "Violence of the Letter." Pages 101–40 in *Of Grammatology.* Translated by Gayatri Chakravorty Spivak. Baltimore: Johns Hopkins University Press.

Dinkler, Michal Beth. 2019. "Between Intention and Reception: Textual Meaning-Making in Intersubjective Perspective." Pages 72–93 in *Biblical Exegesis without Authorial Intention: Interdisciplinary Approaches to Authorship and Meaning.* Edited by Clarissa Brue. BibInt 172. Leiden: Brill.

Dionysius of Halicarnassus. 1885. *Antiquitatum Romanarum quae supersunt.* Edited by Karl Jacoby. Vol 1–4. Leipzig: Teubner.

Dixon, Paul. 2019. "'Endless Wars of Altruism'? Human Rights, Humanitarianism and the Syrian War." *The International Journal of Human Rights* 23:819–42.

Dodd, C. H. 1932. *The Epistle of Paul to the Romans.* London: Hodder & Stoughton.

Donlan, Walter. 1981–1982. "Reciprocities in Homer." *Classical World* 75:137–75.

Dunn, James D. G. 1988a. *Romans 1–8.* WBC 38A. Waco, TX: Word.

———. 1988b. *Romans 9–16.* WBC 38B. Dallas: Word Books.

———. 2006. *Theology of St. Paul The Apostle.* Cambridge: Eerdmans.

———. 2009. *Christianity in the Making: Beginning from Jerusalem.* Cambridge: Eerdmans.

Engberg-Pedersen, Troels. 2008. "Gift Giving and Friendship: Seneca and Paul in Romans 1–8 on the Logic of God's *charis* and Its Human Response." *HTR* 101:15–44.

Esler, Philip F. 2003a. "Ancient Oleiculture and Ethnic Differentiation: The Meaning of the Olive Tree Image in Romans 11." *JSNT* 26.1:103–25.

———. 2003b. "Israel and the Christ Movement (Romans 9–11)." Pages 298–305 in *Conflict and Identity in Romans: The Social Setting of Pauls Letter.* Minneapolis: Augsberg Fortress.

Fiddes, Paul S. 2000. *The Promised End: Eschatology in Theology and Literature.* Oxford: Blackwell.
Finlay, Barbara L., and Supriya Syal. 2014. "The Pain of Altruism." *Trends in Cognitive Sciences* 18:12.
Fischer, Theobald. 1904. *Der Oelbaum.* Petermanns Mitteil Ergänzungsheft 147. Gotha: Perthes.
Fredriksen, Paula. "How Jewish Is God? Divine Ethnicity in Paul's Theology." *JBL* 137 (2018): 193–212.
Gellner, Ernest, and John Waterman. 1977. *Patrons and Clients in Mediterranean Societies.* London: Duckworth.
Geertz, Clifford. 1973. *The Interpretation of Cultures.* New York: Basic Books.
Grenfell, Bernard P., and Arthur S. Hunt, trans. 1898. *Oxyrhynchus Papyri.* London: Oxford University Press.
Hands, Anthony R. 1968. *Charities and Social Aid in Greece and Rome.* London: Thames & Hudson.
Harrison, Bernard. 1999. "'White Mythology' Revisited: Derrida and His Critics on Reason and Rhetoric." *Critical Enquiry* 25:505–34.
Hardin, Russell. 2002. "Liberal Distrust." *European Review* 10:73–89.
Heidland, Hans Wolfgang. 1942. "λογίζομαι κτλ." *TWNT* 4:287–98.
Herzfeld, Michael. 2002. "The European Self: Rethinking an Attitude." Pages 139–70 in *The Idea of Europe: From Antiquity to the European Union.* Edited by Anthony Padgen. Cambridge: Cambridge University Press.
Hooke, Robert. 1665. *Micrographia.* Project Gutenberg. http://www.gutenberg.org/files/15491/15491-h/15491-h.htm.
Horrell, David. 2016. "Ethnicisation, Marriage and Early Christian Identity: Critical Reflections on 1 Corinthians 7, 1 Peter 3 and Modern New Testament Scholarship." *NTS* 62:439–60.
———. 2019. "Judaean Ethnicity and Christ-Following Voluntarism? A Reply to Steve Mason and Philip Esler." *NTS* 65:1–20.
Jewett, Robert. 2007. *Romans: A Commentary.* Minneapolis: Fortress.
Josephus, Flavius. *The Works of Flavius Josephus.* Translated by William Whiston, A.M. Auburn, and Buffalo. John E. Beardsley. London: Printed for Thomas Tegg, 1895.
Kasperson, Roger E. 1992. "The Social Amplification of Risk: Progress in Developing an Integrative Framework in Social Theories of Risk." Pages 53–178 in *Social Theories of Risk.* Edited by Sheldon Krimsky and Dominic Golding. New York: Praeger.

Keck, Leander E. 2005. *Romans*. Nashville: Abingdon.
Keesing, Felix M. 1934. *Modern Samoa: Its Government and Changing Life*. Stanford: Stanford University Press.
Keller, Catherine. 2005. *God and Power: Counter-Apocalyptic Journeys*. Augsberg Fortress: Minneapolis.
Kenney, Edward J., ed. 1982. *Latin literature*. Vol. 2 of *The Cambridge History of Classical Literature*. Cambridge: Cambridge University Press.
King, Richard. 2006. *Orientalism and Religion: Postcolonial Theory, India and "The Mystic East."* London: Routledge.
Krebs, Dennis L. 1991. "Altruism and Egoism: A False Dichotomy?" *Psychological Inquiry* 2:137–39.
Kristeva, Julia. 1980. *Desire in Language: A Semiotic Approach to Language and Art*. Edited by Leon S. Roudiez. Translated by Thomas Gora, Alice Jardine, and Leon S. Roudiez. New York: Columbia University Press.
Lakoff, George, and Mark Johnson. 1980. *Metaphors We Live By*. Chicago: University of Chicago Press.
Latour, Bruno. 2005. *Reassembling the Social: An Introduction to Actor-Network-Theory*. New York: Oxford University Press.
Leenhardt, Franz J. 1961. *Romans*. London: Lutterworth.
Leitch, Vincent B. 1983. *Deconstructive Criticism: An Advanced Introduction*. London: Hutchinson.
Lewicki, Roy J., Daniel J. McAllister, and Robert J. Bies. 1998. "Trust and Distrust: New Relationships and Realities." *The Academy of Management Review* 23:438–58.
Lewis, Theodore J. "How Far Can Texts Take Us? Evaluating Textual Sources for Reconstructing Ancient Israelite Beliefs about the Dead." Pages 169–217 in *Sacred Time, Sacred Place: Archaeology and the Religion of Israel*. Edited by B. Glitten. Winona Lake, IN: Eisenbrauns, 2002.
Lin, Yii-Jan. 2016. *The Erotic Life of Manuscripts: New Testament Textual Criticism and the Biological Sciences*. Online ed. New York: Oxford University Press.
Lincoln, Andrew. 1981. *Paradise Now and Not Yet*. Cambridge: Cambridge University Press.
Lombroso, Cesare. 2006. *Criminal Man*. Edited by Mary Gibson Nicole Hahn Rafter. Repr. Durham: Duke University Press.
Lowe, Dunstan. 2010. "The Symbolic Value of Grafting in Ancient Rome." *Transactions of the American Philological Association* 140:461–88.

Mauss, Marcel. 1969. *The Gift: Forms and Functions of Exchange in Archaic Societies*. Translated by Ian Cunnison. Introduction by E. E. Evans-Pritchard. London: Cohen & West.
Marchal, Joseph A. 2020. "Assembled Gentiles: Terrorist/Barbarian." Pages 157–98 in *Appalling Bodies: Queer Figures before and after Paul's Letters*. Oxford: Oxford University Press.
Marshall, Peter. 1987. *Enmity in Corinth: Social Conventions in Paul's Relations with the Corinthians*. Tübingen: Mohr-Siebeck.
Mason, Steve, and Philip Esler. 2017. "Judaean and Christ-Follower Identities: Grounds for a Distinction." *NTS* 63:493–95.
Mitchell, W. J. T. 2007. "Picturing Terror: Derrida's Autoimmunity." *Critical Inquiry* 33:277–90.
Moo, Douglas. 1996. *The Epistle to the Romans*. Grand Rapids: Eerdmans.
Moore, Stephen D. 1994. *Poststructuralism and the New Testament: Derrida and Foucault at the Foot of the Cross*. Minneapolis: Fortress.
———. 2019. "A Bible that Expresses Everything While Communicating Nothing: Deleuze and Guattari's Cure for Interpretosis." Pages 126–48 in *Biblical Exegesis without Authorial Intention: Interdisciplinary Approaches to Authorship and Meaning*. Edited by Clarissa Brue. BibInt 172. Leiden: Brill.
Morgan, Teresa. 2015. *Roman Faith and Christian Faith: Pistis and Fides in the Early Roman Empire and Early Churches*. Oxford: Oxford University Press.
Morgner, Christian. 2013. "Trust and Confidence: History, Theory and Socio-Political Implications." *Human Studies* 36:509–32.
Morris, Leon. 1988. *The Epistle to the Romans*. Grand Rapids: Eerdmans.
Morris, Michael. 2000. "Metaphor and Philosophy: An Encounter with Derrida." *Philosophy* 75:225–44.
Munck, Johannes. 1967. *Christ and Israel: An Interpretation of Romans 9–11*. Philadelphia: Fortress.
Najita, Susan Y. 2010. "In the Shade of the Banyan Tree." *The Contemporary Pacific* 22:349–61.
Nanos, Mark. 2008. "Broken Branches: A Pauline Metaphor Gone Awry? (Romans 11:11–24)." Paper Presented at International Symposium on "Romans 9–11 at the Interface between the 'New Perspective on Paul' and Jewish Christian Dialog." Göttingen, Germany, May 1–4.
Newman, George, and Daylian M. Cain. 2014. "Tainted Altruism: When Doing Some Good Is Evaluated as Worse Than Doing No Good at All." *Psychological Science* 25: 648–55.

Oakes, Peter. 2001. *Philippians from People To Letter.* Cambridge: Cambridge University Press.

———. 2009. *Reading Romans in Pompeii: Paul's Letter at Ground Level.* Minneapolis: Fortress.

———. 2018. "Pistis as Relational Way of Life in Galatians." *JSNT* 40:255–75.

Osborne, Grant R. 2004. *Romans.* Downers Grove: Intervarsity Press.

Palladius. 1807. *The Fourteen Books of Rutilius Taurus Aemilianus Palladius: On Agriculture.* Translated by Thomas Owen. London: White.

———. 1898. *Opus Agriculturae.* Edited by J. C. Schmitt. Corpus scriptorum latinorum. Leipzig: Teubner.

Pearson, Norman. 1911. "The Idle Poor." *Nineteenth Century and After* 70:917.

Peck, Harry Thurston, ed. 1963. "Columella, L. Iunius Moderātus." Pages 383–84 in *Harper's Dictionary of Classical Literature and Antiquities.* New York: Cooper Square.

Peterman, Gerald W. 1997. *Paul's Gift from Philippi: Conventions of Gift-Exchange and Christian Giving.* Cambridge: Cambridge University Press.

Philips, Gary A. 1990. "Exegesis as Critical Praxis: Reclaiming History and Text from a Postmodern Perspective." *Semeia* 51:7–49.

Plutarch. *Amatorius.* 1874. Corrected and revised by William W. Goodwin. Boston: Little, Brown. Cambridge: Wilson & Son.

Ramsay, Sir William. 1906. *Pauline and Other Studies in Early Christian History.* New York: Armstrong.

Reden, Sitta von. 1995. "The Piraeus: A World Apart." *Greece and Rome* 42:24–37.

Richards, E. Randolph. 2004. *Paul and First Century Letter Writing.* InterVarsity: Illinois.

Ricoeur, Paul. 1975. *La métaphore vive.* Éditions du Seuil.

Sahlins, M. 1972. *Stone Age Economics.* Chicago: Aldine.

Saussure, Ferdinand de. 1959. *Course in General Linguistics.* Edited by Wade Baskin. Columbia: Columbia University Press.

Schliesser, Benjamin. 2007. *Abraham's Faith in Romans 4.* Tübingen: Mohr Siebeck.

Schumacher, Thomas. 2009. "Der Begriff *pistis* im paulinischen Sprachgebrauch." Pages 487–501 in *The Letter to the Romans.* Edited by Udo Schnelle. Leuven: Leuven University Press.

Seneca. 1967. *Benefici*. Translated and edited by Salvatore Guglielmino. Bolognia: Zanichelli.
Seneca. *Seneca Ad Lucilium Epistulae Morales*. 1917–1943. Translated by Richard M. Gummere. Vol. 3. LCL. Cambridge MA: Harvard University Press.
Shakespeare, Steven. 2009. *Derrida and Theology*. London: T&T Clark.
Shakespeare, William. 1623. *A Winter's Tale*. Project Gutenberg. www.gutenberg.org/ebooks/2248.
Smiles, Samuel. 2014. *Self-Help: With Illustrations of Character and Conduct*. Cambridge Library Collection—British and Irish History, Nineteenth Century. Cambridge: Cambridge University Press.
Spartacus, Josette. 2018. "Graphing and Grafting in Jamaica Kincaid's Garden Memoirs." *Wagadu* 19:65–75.
Spitzer, Anais N. 2011. *Derrida, Myth and the Impossibility of Philosophy*. Continuum: London.
Strømmen, Hannah M. 2019. "Born-Again Bibles: Biblical Studies after the 'Death of the Author.'" Pages 94–107 in *Biblical Exegesis without Authorial Intention: Interdisciplinary Approaches to Authorship and Meaning*. Edited by Clarissa Brue. BibInt 172. Leiden: Brill.
Stuhlmacher, Peter. 1994. *Paul's Letter to the Romans: A Commentary*. Translated by Scott J. Hafemann. Edinburgh: T&T Clark.
Tambling, Jeremy. 2010. *Allegory*. Abingdon: Routledge.
Tanabe, George J. 2004. "Grafting Identity: The Hawaiian Branches of the Bodhi Tree." Pages 77–100 in *Buddhist Missionaries in the Era of Globalization*. Edited Linda Learman. Hawaii: University of Hawai'i Press.
Theophrastus of Eresus. 1976. *De Causis Plantarum in Three Volumes*. Translated by Benedict Einarson and George K. K. Link. Vol. 1. London: Heinemann.
Tofighi, Fatima. 2017. *Paul's Letters and the Construction of the European Self*. London: T&T Clark.
Tratner, Michael. 2003. "Derrida's Debt to Milton Friedman." *New Literary History* 34:791–806.
Vasquez, M. 2011. *More Than Belief: A Materialist Theory of Religion*. New York: Oxford University Press.
Wallace-Hadrill, Andrew, ed. 1989. *Patronage in Ancient Society*. London: Routledge.
Wendt, Albert. 1979. *The Leaves of the Banyan Tree*. Auckland: Longman Paul.
———. 2003. *The Mango's Kiss*. Auckland: Vintag.

Williams, David J. 1999. *Paul's Metaphors: Their Context and Character*. Peabody, MA: Hendrickson.

Winter, Bruce W. 1988. "The Public Honouring of Christian Benefactors: Romans 13:3–4 and 1 Peter 2:14–15." *JSNT* 11:87–103.

Witherington, Ben, and Darlene Hyatt. 2004. *Paul's Letter to the Romans: A Socio-rhetorical Commentary*. Grand Rapids: Eerdmans.

Wright, N. T. 1991. *The Climax of the Covenant*. Edinburgh: T&T Clark.

———. 1995. "Romans and the Theology of Paul." Pages 30–67 in vol. 3 of *Pauline Theology*. Edited by David M. Hay and E. Elizabeth Johnson. Minneapolis: Fortress.

Ziesler, John. 1989. *Paul's Letter to the Romans*. London: SCM.

PRIMARY SOURCES INDEX

Old Testament

Genesis
15:6	42
16:6	45

New Testament

Matthew
5:12	83
5:46	83

Mark
9:41	83

Luke
6:35	83

John
4:7–15	16

Romans
1:11	50, 95
1:12	51, 95
1:13	95
1:16–17	171
1:23	92
2:5	39
3:11–18	52
3:24	50
3:27	31
3:27–30	83
3:28	31
4	1, 7–8, 10, 21, 27, 29–30, 32–34, 37–38, 45–47, 49, 51–54, 56–58, 60, 63, 65, 67, 80, 84, 86, 171, 174
4:3	40, 45, 53
4:3–5	17, 21–22, 31, 37, 39, 42, 46–50, 56, 67, 69
4:4	43–44, 68, 82–83, 113
4:4–5	18
4:4–6	17–18, 21
4:5	40, 82–83
4:16	43
4:16–19	53
4:22–24	17, 21–22, 31
4:23	45
4:23–25	17, 21, 37, 39, 42, 44, 46, 48, 50, 55–56
4:24	45, 50, 53–54
4:24–25	31, 52
4:25	41
5	68
5:1	41
5:2	31
5:5	39
5:15–21	107
6:21	96
6:23	82
7	7
7:4	96
8:23	50
9:16–18	53
9:20–21	53, 55
11	1, 8, 19, 109, 123, 150, 166, 171, 174

11:4	51	12:11–12	79
11:12	79	12:14	79
11:16–24	116, 124, 169	13:10	79
11:17–23	19		
11:17–24	115–16, 121–22, 152, 158	Galatians	
11:22	159	1:11–17	79
11:29	67		
12:3–8	65	Philippians	
12:6–8	111	2:22	79
12:19	50		
12:20	50	1 Thessalonians	
13:6–7	48–49	2:6	79
15	102	4:2	79
15:22–23	102		
15:22–29	51, 78–79	Philemon	
15:26–27	51, 78	10	79
15:26	78		
15:27	51, 78, 102	Papyri	
16:17	39		
		P.Oxy. 3.486	40, 41, 43–45, 48, 50
1 Corinthians		7	22, 34–35, 42–43
1:22	12		
1:25	12	P.Tebt. 1.14	40, 44–45, 48, 50, 53
2:5	12	9	22, 35–36, 42–43
2:11	13		
2:12	13	P.Rein. 18	40–41, 43, 46, 48, 50, 57
3:1–3	79	10	22, 36–37, 42–43
4:17	79		
7:17	79	P.Oxy. 12.1481	19, 68, 86, 89–90, 99, 101, 104–5, 113
7:25	79		
9:1–2	79		
11:17	79	P.Oxy. 42.3057	19, 68, 74–75, 86, 89–90, 98–99, 101, 105, 113
11:23	79		
11:29	80		
11:34	79	P.Mert. 12.	19, 68, 74–75, 85–86, 89–90, 97–98, 101, 105, 113
12:4–14	65		
12:27	79		
15:8	79	P.Oxy. 12.1434.8	33
15:10	79		
		P.Flor. 2.123.7	33
2 Corinthians			
1:5	79	P.Oxy. 7.1056.5	33
1:13	79		
6:13	79	P.Mich 8.482	94
9:7–8	107		

Classical Sources

Aristotle, *De plantis*
650a.20–26   128

Astrampsychus, *Oraculum*
68.P.6H   34

Columella, *De Re Rustica*
5.9.16.1–4a   137–38

Demosthenes, *Pro Phormione*
36.57   34
32.16   34

Josephus, *Antiquitates judaicae*
1.183   81, 92

Livy, *Ab urbe condita*
27.37.2   162

Palladius, *Opus agriculturae*
14.51–54   142–43
14.19–20   143
14.17–18   144

Philo, *De Abrahamo*
46.273   42

Philo, *De cherubim*
122–123   80–81
123   81, 90

Pliny, *Naturalis historia*
15.57   162

Plutarch, *Amatorius*
24   144

Plutarch, *Quaestionum convivialum libri IX*
2.6   162

Seneca, *De beneficiis*
1.1.1   88

1.4.3   88
2.18.1   88
2.18.2   88
2.18.5   88
2.2.11   88
4.18.1   104
4.18.2   104
5.11.5   88

Seneca, *Epistulae morales*
19.11–12   88
44.7   100

Theophrastus, *Historia Plantarum*
2.2.11   128
2.6.3   128
2.7.3–4   128
6.7.6   128
7.5.1   128
8.7.7   128

Theophrastus, *De causis plantarum*
1.6.10.1–11   130, 135
3.6.1–2   128
3.9.1–5   128
3.17.5   128
5.15.2–3   128

Thucydides, *Peloponnesian War*
2.20.4   83

Vergil, *Georgica*
2.69–82   162

Vitruvius, *De architectura*
7.5.3–4   162

Varro, *De re rustica*
1.40.5   162

Rabbinic Literature

m. Kil'ayim
1:7   162

Other Religious and Literary Texts

Book of Mormon
    Jacob 5   122–23, 151–54, 157, 169

Shakespeare, *The Winter's Tale*
    4.4.88–97   115

MODERN AUTHORS INDEX

Aaron, David H	51	Danker, Paul F.	78
Aarts, Joris	78	Davidson, Steed	30
Achtemeier, Paul J	43	Davies, W. D.	116, 125–26, 132, 134, 141
Agamben, Giorgio	1, 7		
Akoto-Abutiate, Dorothy	139	Derrida, Jacques	ix, xi, 1–3, 5, 7–9, 14, 16, 20, 37, 39, 58–59, 61, 67, 73, 76–77, 79, 81, 84, 87, 93, 95, 97, 101, 103, 106–8, 112, 116, 123–24, 135, 145–47, 149–50, 153, 155, 158, 161, 165, 174
Albinus, Lars	14		
Anderson, B. J	135–36		
Asad, Talal	14		
Badhwar, Neera Kapur	109		
Barclay, John	72, 78, 82		
Barth, Karl	30, 48	Dickens, Charles	70
Barthes, Roland	9	Dinkler, Michal Beth	5
Baxter A. G.	116, 126, 136–37, 141–42	Dixon, Paul	111
Bell, H. Idris	76	Dodd, C. H.	125
Benjamin, Walter	110	Donlan, Walter	78
Bies, Robert J.	32	Dunn, James, D. G.	13, 26, 30–31, 72, 83, 116, 124, 126, 128, 133, 164–65
Blanton, Ward	3, 7, 14, 60, 91, 161, 167		
Borradori, Giovanna	135	Engberg-Pedersen, Troels	72, 96
Boyarin, Daniel	125, 141, 161	Esler, Philip F.	116, 118, 125–26, 131–35, 142
Breu, Clarissa	173		
Britton, Richard J.	30	Fiddes, Paul S.	15
Bryan, Christopher	116, 126	Finlay, Barbara L.	109
Bultmann, Rudolf	24, 32, 46	Fischer, Theobald	137
Byron, Glennis	100	Fredriksen, Paula	131–32
Cain, Daylian M.	109	Gellner, Ernest	78
Canguillhem, Georges	1, 7–9, 119, 174	Geertz, Clifford	15–16
Chalmers, Patrick	21	Grenfell, Bernard P.	xviii, 181
Chan, Alan T. Y.	23	Hands, Anthony R.	78
Chan, Eugene	110	Hardin, Russell	32
Chatterton, Thomas	1	Harrison, Bernard	9, 16
Cross, Frank Moore	51	Heidland, Hans Wolfgang	48
Culler, Jonathan	16	Herzfeld, Michael	167
Cullmann, Oscar	13–14, 31, 124, 129, 160	Heidegger, Martin	14
		Hooke, Robert	9

Horrell, David	131	Oakes, Peter	ix, 7, 11, 17, 24, 27, 133, 172
Hunt, Arthur S.	xviii, 181		
Hyatt, Darlene	43, 47, 72, 82	Osborne, Grant R.	43, 48
Jewett, Robert	45, 72, 83	Pearson, Norman	100
Johnson, Mark	10, 29	Peck, Harry Thurston	122
Kasperson, Roger E.	32	Peterman, Gerald W.	70, 76, 78–79, 87–88, 104
Keck, Leander E.	30, 42–43, 45, 47, 83		
Keesing, Felix M.	151	Philips, Gary A.	5, 7
Keller, Catherine	25	Roberts, C. H.	76
Kenney, Edward J.	122	Ramsay, Sir William	116, 126, 136–38, 141–42
King, Richard	167		
Krebs, Dennis L.	109	Reden, Sitta von	23
Kristeva, Julia	51	Ricoeur, Paul	29
Kumar, Satish	131	Saussure, Ferdinand de	16
Lakoff, George	10, 29	Schliesser, Benjamin	31–32, 43, 48, 83
Latour, Bruno	56	Schumacher, Thomas	32
Lee, Shu-kam	23	Shakespeare, Steven	107
Leenhardt, Franz J.	48	Smiles, Samuel	100
Leitch, Vincent B.	9	Spartacus, Josette	145, 151
Lewicki, Roy J.	32	Spitzer, Anais N.	77
Lewis, Theodore J.	52	Strømmen, Hannah M.	8, 30
Lin, Yii-Jan	118, 128, 130, 160, 166	Stuhlmacher, Peter	48, 126
Lincoln, Andrew	13, 31, 102, 124, 160, 164	Syal, Supriya	109
		Tambling, Jeremy	126
Lombroso, Cesare	100	Tanabe, George J.	140
Lowe, Dunstan	162	Tofighi, Fatima	78, 111, 167
Marchal, Joseph	154	Tratner, Michael	81
Marshall, Peter	80	Vasquez, M.	16–17
Mason, Steve	131	Wallace-Hadrill, Andrew	78
Mauss, Marcel	79	Waterman, John	78
McAllister, Daniel J.	32	Wendt, Albert	151, 153
Mitchell, W. J. T.	135	Williams, David J.	43, 47, 125
Moo, Douglas	125	Winter, Bruce W.	79
Moore, Stephen D.	6, 16, 82	Witherington, Ben	43, 47, 72, 82
Morgan, Teresa	11, 23–24, 27	Wright, N. T.	13, 14, 26, 31, 164, 165
Morgner, Christian	23	Ziesler, J. A.	43, 48, 116, 126, 136–37, 141–42
Morris, Michael	16		
Morris, Leon	41		
Munck, Johannes	125		
Najita, Susan Y.	151		
Nanos, Mark	116, 125–26, 132, 134, 141–42		
Newman, George	109		
Nietzsche, Friedrich	1		

SUBJECT INDEX

Abraham, 21, 35–38, 40–48, 51, 54, 57–58, 67, 80–83, 92, 108, 112, 161–63, 181
absence, 16, 76, 94, 103, 153, 155, 158, 166
absolutism, 1, 4–6, 11–14, 18–19, 26, 60, 64, 69, 94, 99, 118, 120, 132, 158, 165, 167, 173
accounting, 18, 21–22, 29, 33, 40–41, 44, 47–48, 55–56, 58, 99
agency, ix, xi, 13–14, 17, 18–19, 22, 25, 27–28, 31, 44–47, 55–57, 62–63, 68–71, 78, 80, 88–89, 91, 110–12, 171
Allah, 4
already-not yet (eschatological tension), 13, 164–65
altruism, 7–8, 18–19, 26, 28, 50–51, 59, 64, 67–68, 70–71, 73–75, 77, 79, 81, 84–85, 87, 89–91, 96–97, 99–100, 102, 105–14, 121, 171–72, 174
always-already, 5, 14, 155, 158, 163, 165
analysis, 4–8, 12, 19, 43, 55–56, 174
antisemitism, 26, 28–29
Aristotle, 23, 121, 128
assessment, 11–12, 42, 44–45, 61, 107, 117, 156, 174
Augustine of Hippo, 23
austerity, 18, 30, 68, 72, 75, 81, 90–91, 99, 108–9, 111–12, 173–74
author, 4, 7–10, 12, 15–16, 30, 38, 74, 89, 104, 119, 121–22, 129, 143, 147, 165, 174
authority, 1, 6–10, 13–17, 22, 25, 28–29, 32, 35–36, 38–39, 42, 48–49, 54, 60–

authority (cont.)
62, 65, 75–76, 78, 80, 83, 87, 90, 92–93, 98, 100, 104, 107, 109, 112–13, 119, 122, 125, 128–29, 132, 142, 147, 149, 151, 153, 157, 161–62, 164, 173–75
Baal, 51–53
believer, the
    passivity of, 1, 3, 25–26, 28, 31, 40, 45, 60–61, 70, 72, 80, 85, 89, 116, 125, 173
    power of, 4, 6, 10–16, 18–20, 22, 29, 31, 49–51, 59, 62
    reciprocity, 17, 19, 22–24, 27–28, 30–31, 35–38, 40, 42, 44–47, 53–59, 64–66, 68, 75, 80, 82, 85, 96, 98–100, 103, 106, 108, 110, 113, 117, 123, 129, 143, 147, 152, 154, 156, 158, 160, 164–65, 171–72, 174–76
Bible, 5–6, 61, 118, 140
biblical studies, 2–3, 5, 7, 13–14, 16, 22, 29, 70, 92, 104, 113
binaries, 13, 15–16, 144, 146, 159, 162–63, 174
blind-faith, 6–7, 17, 24, 27, 54, 172
Buddhism, 25–26, 89, 120, 140, 168, 175
capitalism, 11, 22, 85, 111, 173
Catholicism, 14, 25
charis, 30–31, 43–44, 50, 68, 80–83, 87, 107, 113
Christ, 4, 14, 16, 23–24, 45–47, 49–51, 55, 57, 69, 82, 102–3, 107, 111, 117–18, 127, 129, 131–35, 141, 151, 156, 164, 169, 173–75

Christianity, 2–3, 6, 14, 19, 26, 100, 117–18, 125, 131, 140, 150, 153, 155–56, 159, 167–69, 175
Christians, 3, 6, 25–26, 95, 101, 131, 140
church , 2, 10, 24, 29, 50, 60–61, 63–65, 75, 78, 80, 96, 102, 113, 119, 126, 151, 154–55, 157, 160–61, 167–69, 173–74
Church of England, 29, 155
communism, 9
cosmos, 13, 47, 97
death, 4, 13–14, 21, 45, 52, 55, 57, 59, 82, 175
debt, 8, 17–19, 21, 28–29, 35–37, 40, 42, 45, 47, 49, 51, 53–55, 57, 59, 64, 67, 69, 78, 80–81, 86, 89–91, 96, 98, 99–101, 105, 171, 175–76
deconstruction, 1–2, 6–10, 13–14, 18–19, 21–23, 32, 37, 45, 66, 73, 124, 149, 159, 169, 171, 174
dikaiō, 17, 21–22, 30–31, 33
dikaiōsis, 17, 21–22, 30–31, 33
dikaiosunē, 17, 21–22, 30–31, 33
disease allegory, 4–5, 135, 141
economic metaphor, 17–18, 22, 29, 33, 45, 54, 83
economics, 2, 7, 11–12, 18, 23–24, 26, 28–29, 32, 34, 40, 46, 51, 54, 69, 74, 77, 82, 90, 98, 104, 107, 113
enlightenment, the, 3, 18
Epictetus, 2
eschatology, 13, 58, 62, 106, 113, 124, 127, 129, 152, 175–76
essential, 18
eternity, 1, 19, 49, 55, 69, 80–83, 91, 99–100, 121, 132, 150, 164, 175
ethics, 5, 29, 60, 62, 90, 112, 129, 172, 174
etymology, 8, 23, 58, 65, 124, 158
evil, 14–15, 103
exegesis, xi, 4–5, 7–8, 22, 74, 92, 120, 144, 161, 171, 173
extremism, 2–4, 17, 19, 22–23, 25–27, 60–61, 130
faith, 2–30, 40–66, 70–73, 82–84, 90–97, 106–20, 145, 151, 153–57, 159, 166–67, 171–75

fides, 11–12, 23
freedom, 2–3, 7, 15–14, 17–18, 21, 61, 63, 108
fruit, 2, 51, 96, 122, 127, 129, 132–44, 149–50, 152–53, 159, 161
fundamentalism, 3, 17, 25–28, 173
gift-giving, 7, 18–19, 67–108, 110, 112–14
God
    authority of, 3–4, 15, 21, 25, 30, 37, 44, 46–48, 50, 53–55, 57, 59, 62, 64, 66, 84, 86, 125, 164–65
    reciprocity of, 1–2, 7, 15, 17, 19, 22, 24, 27, 29, 31–32, 35, 37–40, 44, 46–47, 50–53, 56, 61, 63 66, 68, 80–81, 85, 87, 89, 96, 103, 107–8, 110, 117, 112–14, 132, 145, 147, 152, 164–65, 169, 171–72, 174–75
grace, 3, 4, 15, 17–18, 28, 68–69, 77, 80–83, 91–92, 97, 99, 100, 103, 104, 106–8
grafting allegories, 19–20, 118, 132, 148, 169
Hinduism, 25, 168
horticulture, 1–2, 7, 17, 19–20, 116, 121–22, 126, 128–29, 135, 145, 162, 166, 171
house metaphor, 14, 39, 60–61, 90, 97, 110
infinity, 19, 26–27, 59, 67, 91, 93, 99–100, 110–11, 159, 165
intention, 8–11, 22–23, 32–33, 51, 56, 60, 73, 77, 81, 96, 108–9, 119, 124, 134, 139, 140–41, 147, 149, 164
interpretation, ix, xi, 1, 5–7, 8, 11–12, 15–16, 18, 20, 23, 37–39, 47–49, 57, 61–62, 72, 87, 91–96, 100, 104–5, 109–10, 117–18, 123–25, 128, 133–39, 141, 151–52, 164, 171–75
Islam, 25
islands as biblical context, 30
Jainism, 168
jouissance, 18
Judaism, 19, 25, 72, 118, 126, 139, 141, 150, 156, 163–64, 167–68, 175
justification by faith or works, 25–26

kenosis, 7, 39
logizomai, 17–18, 21, 22, 30–33, 35, 38, 43, 45, 47–49, 58, 65
logocentrism, 16, 30
Lutheranism, 25
Micrographia, Hooke, 9
missiology, 19, 26, 28, 96, 122–23, 164
misthos, 30, 32, 43, 68, 81, 82–84, 87, 113, 172
Mormon, Book of, 20, 116, 122–23, 151–53, 169
mosque, 2
Mot, 51–53
Naziism, 26
new perspective on Paul, 26, 83
opheilēma, 30–32, 43, 82–83, 87
pisteuō, 17, 22–23, 30–32, 34, 38, 54–55
pistis, 7, 10–12, 17, 21–24, 27, 30–32, 34–35, 37–38, 40–59, 61–66, 107, 171
Plato, 12, 24, 96, 149, 158
political correctness, 3
Primitive Christianity, 14
Protestantism, 11, 26, 29
righteousness, 1, 17, 21, 24, 40–48, 50, 56, 58, 64, 66–67, 83, 109–10, 154, 157, 161, 171
Ruskin, John, 30
sin, 3, 61, 82
Stoics, 24, 149
supplement, 8–12, 18, 37, 103–4, 106, 109, 112, 174
synagogue, 2
textualism, 16–17
thrift, 18–19, 30, 68, 75–76, 89–92, 98, 109, 112–13
tree paradigm, 1, 20, 118–19, 130–31
Ullyses, 16
unconscious, the, 8–10, 29–30, 37, 119, 147
Usure-Retrait method, the, 8, 22
violence and violation, 2–3, 5, 59, 62, 77, 110, 149, 151, 153, 155, 168
West, the, 15, 25–26, 62, 85, 118, 151, 167
wisdom, 6, 12

works, 12, 21, 25–26, 43, 72, 82, 84–85, 91
Yahweh, 51
Zeus, 14, 168

www.ingramcontent.com/pod-product-compliance
Lightning Source LLC
Chambersburg PA
CBHW022028240426
43667CB00042B/1397